Studying Lacan's Seminar VI

The second volume in the *Studying Lacan's Seminars* series, this book is the first comprehensive study of Lacan's Seminar VI: *Desire and its Interpretation*. A natural companion to Bruce Fink's recent translation of the seminar into English (2019), this book offers a genuine opportunity to delve deeply into the seminar, and a hospitable introduction to Lacan's teachings of the 1950s.

This important book brings together various aspects of Cox Cameron's teachings and systematic, careful, and critical readings of Seminar VI. Lacan's theorizing and conceptualizing of the object *a*, the fundamental fantasy, and aphanisis, as well as the ambiguous treatment of the phallus in his work at the time, are all introduced, contextualized, and explored in detail. The trajectories of his thinking are traced in terms of future developments and elaborations in the seminars that follow closely on the heels of Seminar VI – Seminars VII (*Ethics of Psychoanalysis*), VIII (*Transference*), IX (*Identification*), and X (*Anxiety*). Consideration is also given to how certain themes and motifs are recapitulated or reworked in his later teachings such as in Seminars XX (*Encore*), and XXIII (*The Sinthome*). Also included in this volume are two further essays by Cox Cameron, a most valuable critique of the concept of the phallus in Lacan's theories of the 1950s, and an overview of Seminar VI originally presented as a keynote address to the APW congress in Toronto 2014.

The book is of great interest to Lacanian scholars and students, as well as psychoanalytic therapists and analysts interested in Lacan's teachings of the 1950s and in how important concepts developed during this period are treated in his later work.

Olga Cox Cameron's first career was in literary studies, having written an MA thesis on Proust, worked as a tutor in the Department of French at University College, Dublin, and started – but not completed – a PhD on Beckett at the University of Fribourg in Switzerland. Following a decade of working with homeless people in Dublin, she trained as a psychoanalyst at St. Vincent's University Hospital and has been in private practice for the past 32 years. She lectured in Psychoanalytic Theory and in Psychoanalysis and Literature at St. Vincent's University Hospital and Trinity College from 1991 to 2013 and has published numerous articles on these topics in national and international journals. She is the founder of the annual Irish Psychoanalytic Film Festival, now in its 12th year.

Carol Owens is a psychoanalyst and Lacanian scholar in Dublin. She is the founder of the Dublin Lacan study group. She has published widely on the theory and practice of Lacanian psychoanalysis. Her most recent book is *Psychoanalysing Ambivalence with Freud and Lacan: On and Off the Couch* with Stephanie Swales. She is series editor for *Studying Lacan's Seminars* published by Routledge. The first volume in the series *Studying Lacan's Seminars IV and V: From Lack to Desire* was published in 2019.

Studying Lacan's Seminars
Series Editor: Carol Owens

Studying Lacan's Seminars brings together leading Lacanian scholars and practitioners from across the globe to participate in a contemporary examination of Lacan's seminars, many of which are newly translated into English. Featuring practical examples from case studies and packed with cultural illustrations from film, literature and beyond, these books will provide vital companions for students and readers of Lacan. The first dedicated series on Lacan's seminars, each book will cover the fundamental concepts while at the same time applying a contemporary perspective informed by the standards considered important by scholars and practising Lacanian psychoanalysts today.

For more information see https://www.routledge.com/Studying-Lacan's-Seminars/book-series/SLS

Previous and forthcoming titles in the series:

Studying Lacan's Seminar VIII: Transference
Edited by Carol Owens

Studying Lacan's Seminar VII: The Ethics of Psychoanalysis
Edited by Carol Owens

Studying Lacan's Seminar VI: Dream, Symptom, and the Collapse of Subjectivity
By Olga Cox Cameron with Carol Owens

Studying Lacan's Seminars IV and V: From Lack to Desire
Edited by Carol Owens and Nadezhda Almqvist

"What a fantastic guide this book is, I was wishing Olga Cox Cameron could lead me through all of Lacan's seminars. This is a beautifully clear and funny and insightful reading of Seminar VI, showing us that there is no one Lacan, but many, and that self-critical attention to what is of dubious value in his work is the only way to discover what is so amazingly useful. At the same time the book is conceptually dense and enjoyable. I laughed out loud at points, especially the 'Here is the News' example, and there is so much in here that I learnt and thought about."

—**Ian Parke**r, *Fellow of the British Psychological Society,
Emeritus Professor of Management at the University of Leicester,
Co-Director of the Discourse Unit, and Managing Editor of*
Annual Review of Critical Psychology

"Cox Cameron has written an elegant and clear study of Lacan's rich and complex *Seminar VI*. She skilfully walks the reader through the key tenets of one of Lacan's most important seminars and at the same time locates his teaching in the movement of his thought. A reflective and informed study that pairs beautifully with the original text."

—**Russell Grigg**

"In this book on *Lacan's Seminar VI*, Desire and Its Interpretation, Olga Cox Cameron provides extensive, lucid, and inspired commentary on some of Lacan's densest formulations, deftly elucidating such complex notions as being, the phallus, fantasy, and the object. As she contextualizes the work Lacan does here with respect to the Seminars that preceded it and the Seminars that followed it, she nicely outlines where Lacan remains Freudian and where he parts company with Freud—as regards dream interpretation and the interpretation of works of art, for example. The material is brought alive with references to mother-child experiences and myriad literary texts. The reader will thank her for providing us with such an eye-opening guide to a sometimes murky Seminar!"

—**Bruce Fink**, *Lacanian psychoanalyst, analytic supervisor,
and Professor of Psychology at Duquesne University,
Pittsburgh, Pennsylvania*

Studying Lacan's Seminar VI

Dream, Symptom, and the Collapse
of Subjectivity

Olga Cox Cameron with
Carol Owens

Routledge
Taylor & Francis Group

LONDON AND NEW YORK

First published 2021
by Routledge
2 Park Square, Milton Park, Abingdon, Oxon OX14 4RN

and by Routledge
52 Vanderbilt Avenue, New York, NY 10017

Routledge is an imprint of the Taylor & Francis Group, an informa business

British Library Cataloguing-in-Publication Data
A catalogue record for this book is available from the British Library

Library of Congress Cataloging-in-Publication Data
A catalog record has been requested for this book

ISBN: 978-0-367-75283-5 (hbk)
ISBN: 978-0-367-35344-5 (pbk)
ISBN: 978-1-003-16183-7 (ebk)

Typeset in Bembo
by Newgen Publishing UK

For Roisin, Nigel, Liam, and Olive
who have brought me back into the springtime of life

Contents

Acknowledgements

Thanks to Cormac Gallagher's indefatigable work as teacher and translator of Lacan I have had access to this and other seminars in English as well as French since 1988. The teaching inspired me, the translations opened locked doors, so in the first instance I owe a huge debt of gratitude to Dr Cormac Gallagher.

Second, this book would not have been written without the dynamism, support, and persuasive cajolery of Carol Owens, who convinced me and kept me convinced, despite overwhelming evidence to the contrary, that turning a series of lectures into a book would be "no trouble"! Without her support, her endless kindness, and her help, there would have been no book.

I worked on these lectures with a great study group whose energy, insight, and left-of-centre questioning made of every meeting a learning experience and – of all things – fun. Before then I was lucky enough to teach this seminar for many years while also working clinically as a psychoanalyst, and I would like to thank the very many students who pushed me to expand my thinking, and crucially the courageous analysands who have faced into "the pain of existence" during years of psychoanalytic work.

Carol and I take this opportunity to gratefully acknowledge Bruce Fink's excellent 2019 translation of Seminar VI.

Carol wishes to thank Elliot Morsia at Routledge for his interest in, and enthusiasm about, the *Studying Lacan's Seminars* series in its proposal phase, and Alec Selwyn, Alexis Monroe, and Saloni Singhania for their continued work on the series.

We thank Ian Parker (Series Advisor) for his excellent feedback on the series in general, and on this volume, which benefits from his keen eye for structure, and his kind encouragement.

We also thank the following publishers and people for granting permission to reproduce various elements, or quote from them in the book:

* the Irish psychoanalytic journal *Lacunae*, for allowing us to include Olga's essay "Seminar VI: Anamorphosis or Palimpsest?" first published in *Lacunae*, issue 10, May 2015, pp. 59–75.

- New Directions for allowing us to quote Stephane Mallarmé, translated by Paul Auster, from A TOMB FOR ANATOLE, copyright © 1983 and 2003 by Paul Auster. *Pour un tombeau d'Anatole* copyright © 1961 by Editions de Seuil. Reprinted by permission of New Directions Publishing Corp.
- Routledge, for allowing us to include Olga's essay "The Phallus of the Fifties – Those Years of 'Tranquil Possession'" first published in Owens, C. and Almqvist, N. (2019). *Studying Lacan's Seminars IV and V: From Lack to Desire.*
- Tate Images at The Tate Gallery London for the use of Ophelia, by Sir John Everett Millais for the book cover.
- Members of the Dublin Lacan study group whose comments (indicated with their initials) are included in the lectures with their kind permission: Nadezhda Almqvist, Andrei Berezkine, Geraldine Cuddihy, Magda Kurzawska, Ivana Milivojevic, Sarah Meehan, Liz Monahan, Kevin Murphy, Pauline O'Callaghan, and Pauline O'Connell.

About the authors

Olga Cox Cameron's first career was in literary studies, having written an MA thesis on Proust, worked as a tutor in the Department of French at University College, Dublin, and started – but not completed – a PhD on Beckett at the University of Fribourg in Switzerland. Following a decade of working with homeless people in Dublin, she trained as a psychoanalyst at St. Vincent's University Hospital, and has been in private practice for the past 32 years. She lectured in Psychoanalytic Theory and also in Psychoanalysis and Literature at St. Vincent's University Hospital and Trinity College from 1991 to 2013 and has published numerous articles on these topics in national and international journals. She is the founder of the annual Irish Psychoanalytic Film festival, now in its 12th year.

Carol Owens is a psychoanalyst and Lacanian scholar in Dublin. She is the founder of the Dublin Lacan study group. She has published widely on the theory and practice of Lacanian psychoanalysis. Her most recent book is *Psychoanalysing Ambivalence with Freud and Lacan: On and Off the Couch* with Stephanie Swales (Routledge, 2020). She is series editor for *Studying Lacan's Seminars*. The first in the series *Studying Lacan's Seminars IV and V: From Lack to Desire* (Owens and Almqvist) was published in 2019.

Preface

I remember very well the day I finally persuaded Olga Cox Cameron that her lectures on Seminar VI constituted, in fact, the makings of a book. We were en route to the June 2017 meeting of the Dublin Lacan study group – the occasion of her last lecture on the seminar – making our way across the beautifully restored TU Dublin campus on the site of the old Grangegorman psychiatric hospital, the sun was shining, and Olga, probably at this stage, exhausted and worn down by my constant urging, finally agreed to it. It was a good day! This book, however, is really much more a palimpsest than a simple writing up of a bunch of lectures. Olga had taught Seminar VI (among other seminars) to several intakes of students at TCD and UCD over a span of some 20 years or more, and for me and my fellow students, for those who came before my group, and for those who trained after us, Olga's lectures stood out as sparkling gems, providing truly inimitable and captivating teaching. We were really blessed.

So first there was the teaching. Then, in 2014, Olga was invited to give a keynote address at the APW annual conference in Toronto on the theme of desire. That paper was subsequently published in *Lacunae* in 2015 (and with their kind permission is included in this volume in Part III). The study group having worked their way through Seminars IV, and V, in the meantime were ready to begin on Seminar VI in 2016 and to our delight Olga agreed to provide a frame within which we could study the seminar – four lectures – covering the ground Lacan worked during the year 1958–1959. At the time we recorded the lectures on a variety of devices (the little *lathouses* Lacan spoke about in his seventeenth seminar!). When Routledge accepted my proposal to publish a series of volumes on Lacan's seminars, I had already worked on *Studying Lacan's Seminars IV and V: from Lack to Desire* with Nadezda Almqvist (Owens and Almqvist, 2019), and I had already decided that the next volume in the series *Studying Lacan's Seminar VI* had to be written by Olga. (Dany Nobus says I'm nothing if not tenacious!) So, the different layers of what appears in this book represent the many years of teaching, the lectures for the study group, and finally the preparation of the chapters for this volume. Sadly we somehow lost the lecture on *Hamlet*, but of course this story had to contain a lost object! I hope you will enjoy reading the lecture transcripts as much as I have when transcribing them – listening once again to Olga's voice as she made Lacan's teaching come alive for us in her own anecdotes, richly personal, shot through with excerpts from Joyce, Beckett, and Shakespeare, sometimes hilariously comical, other times poignantly tragic. The lectures are included because they also capture the essence of the study group work practice: questioning, wondering, and interacting with the seminar as much for its clinical relevance as for its theoretical value.

The reader of this volume holds in their hands a wonderful accompaniment to Lacan's Seminar VI; much more than a guide, it invites the reader to the experience of an odyssey in Lacan's thinking of the 1950s and to pass through the gateway – as Olga describes this great seminar – into his further theoretical developments and elaborations. As such, there are generous offerings of much-needed contextualization for some of Lacan's more difficult concepts – the phallus, the o-object, the cut, etc. – as well as considerations of where these concepts go to afterwards in Lacan's teaching.

It has been a tremendous honour and great privilege for me to work with Olga on this book. During a class with Cormac Gallagher one time, he explained how he had been utterly blown away by an essay he had received from one of the early students he had taught on the "Rome Discourse"; entitled "Bedazzled, Bejaysus"! The essay found things in Lacan, that were there all along, just waiting to be discovered, like the proverbial hidden treasure. You can guess who the student was.

I imagine that you too will be bedazzled, bejaysus, with this terrific book.

Carol Owens
Series editor

Editor's note

This book is arranged in three parts.

Part I consists of six chapters: these are the written up and expanded lectures Olga Cox Cameron delivered in various formats over the course of her teachings on Seminar VI, most recently to the Dublin Lacan study group.

Part II contains three chapters which consist of the transcripts of three out of the original four lectures Olga gave to the study group between 2016 and 2017; lecture 3 on *Hamlet* being lost.

Part III (Chapters 10 and 11) reprints two essays previously published by Olga in other publications (*Lacunae*, 2015, and Routledge, 2019).

Together, all three parts assemble almost 25 years of teaching, essays, and other addresses on the theme of Lacan's *Seminar VI: Desire and its Interpretation*.

Carol Owens

Part I

The chapters

Chapter 1

Introduction to the seminar[1]

This, hopefully, is the book I would like to have had in hand myself when I first began to read Lacan's seminars more than 30 years ago. Many of the early seminars – between IV and X say – are hugely wordy, and the initial experience of reading is like standing under an avalanche, a hail of brilliant ideas, stunning one into either admiration or indignant befuddlement. It takes a while to see that these huge unwieldy masses are actually carefully structured, and that working through each lesson with this overall structure in mind permits one to step out from under the avalanche and engage critically with what is being said. Hence the rather plodding approach adopted here. Many of the previous books published on different seminars turn out to be a series of highly engaging riffs by different authors on topics germane to the seminar in question, rather than a step by step commentary. My own approach stems from a youthful attempt to read *Finnegans Wake*, and the useful footholds provided by writers such as Anthony Burgess and Roland McHugh who by shadowing Joyce's great work, illuminated it, releasing the baffled reader into the enjoyment of "laughters low".

As with all the other seminars Lacan's sixth seminar on desire confronts the reader with levels of complexity that are both exhilarating and daunting. What one must try to hold onto in this vertiginous venture is some exercise of one's own intelligence. There is a fine line to be drawn between close reading and swamping one's brain to the point of mere glazed iteration. In his delightful series of essays entitled *The Consolations of Philosophy*, Alain de Botton invokes Montaigne in the section on "Consolations for Intellectual Inadequacy" in order to put forward the view that boredom can sometimes be an indication of robustness of mind: "Though it can never be a sufficient judge (and in its more degenerate forms, slips into willful indifference and impatience), taking our levels of boredom into account can temper an otherwise excessive tolerance of balderdash" (2000, p. 158). As de Botton goes on to say, every difficult work presents us with the choice of judging the author inept for not being clearer, or ourselves stupid for not grasping what is being said. The challenge is to remain open to both possibilities.

One more warning before we start. Reading Lacanian theory as a series of successive stages in his thinking, elaborated over the course of 26 seminars, is on the one hand, standard teaching practice, and on the other, a fraught and foolish undertaking. Not that the stages aren't there, but inceptions, reversals, foreshadowings, and retrospective inclusions blur the outlines of definitive departure. In his tenth seminar *L'Angoisse*, Lacan describes an insect creeping along a *Moëbius* strip. Starting on the inside, the insect, simply by crawling cussedly on, will pass without perceptible transition to the outer surface and back again, the apparently radical distinction between inside and outside having been effaced by the loop which creates one continuous surface. A novice reader of the seminars will empathize with this insect. So for example, "the cut", a major feature of the topological seminars will appear without warning towards the end of this seminar on desire and without anything like the lengthy elaboration it will later receive in the ninth seminar *Identification*.

That said, in certain respects Seminar VI, *Desire and its Interpretation*, stands clear of this *Moëbian* structure. Gateway to the great middle seminars, it explicitly signals new directions. Unusually right from the start Lacan announces these departures. They are several, and they are significant. The earlier seminars had consistently relied on Freud's sexed distribution of "being" and "having" as specifying the outcome of the Oedipus complex. From Seminar VI onward, this fulcrum will be increasingly tipped by a new emphasis on "being" heralded by the recognition in lesson two that he may have irked his listeners with too much juggling between being and having (Lacan, 2019, p. 35). A number of other earlier accents are also explicitly re-calibrated. Speaking of a stage in the specular experience he tells his listeners that "[W]e shall use all of this in a context that will give it a very different resonance" (ibid., p. 19). And towards the end of the year he punctures the tranquil possessiveness of the successfully assumed paternal metaphor by pointing out its status as fiction, the fact that this metaphor is just a mask for the metonymy of castration (cf. Cox Cameron, 2019; also Part III of this volume). The entire seminar will also be a rewriting of "the object", now no longer metonymical (without quite ceasing to be so) but which by the end of Seminar VI is no longer an object at all in the strict sense of the word, but an index of impossibility. In lesson twenty-three he signals this re-write of the object which is he says "no longer simply a question of the function of the object as I tried to formulate it two years ago" (Lacan, ibid., p. 412). It is also in this seminar on desire that we can locate the inception of a new definition of the subject, a progressive re-write which will culminate in the gnomic statement three years later that it is the signifier which represents the subject for another signifier. The "big Other" too is rewritten. Without explicitly referring to his admirably clear definition of this big Other in his third seminar *The Psychoses* he effectively demolishes the status accorded it in the earlier seminar where the Other "is that before which you make yourself recognized. But you can make yourself recognized by it only because it is recognized first […] It is through recognizing it that you institute it […] as an irreducible absolute […]" (Lacan, 1993, p. 51). By the end of Seminar VI this necessary reciprocity has been bankrupted. On the 8th April 1959 he clarifies that; "I have absolutely no guarantee that this Other, owing to what he has in his system, can give me back […] what I gave him- namely his being and his essence as truth" (Lacan, 2019, p. 299).

Well aware that his critics decried Lacanian psychoanalysis as overly intellectualist, Lacan in the opening lessons of this seminar, mocks the poverty of so-called theories of affect and then goes on to situate this seminar right at its coalface.

The Lacanian vocabulary that has been the armature of his teaching, will continue to be used, but freighted now with these new meanings. The stated purpose of the five earlier seminars – a return to Freud – continues to be the banner under which Lacan advances, and one of the most remarkable features of the seminar on desire is a reading of Freud that is seemingly exact and faithful but also angled to reveal an altogether new dimension to psychoanalytic theory.

This dimension is tragedy. Over the next two years and to a lesser extent in Seminar VIII this dimension will be deepened and made explicit to the point that the final section of Seminar VII will bear the title "The Tragic Dimension of Psychoanalytic Experience". In Seminar VI the opening up of this new dimension will be tightly, even impressively, corralled within the coordinates of Freudian doctrine. But by the end of Seminar VII when in the manner of all effective anamorphoses the hidden otherness begins to impose itself more insistently on the viewer, Lacan although still referencing this foregrounding of tragedy to Freud's appropriation of *Oedipus Rex* via the Oedipus complex, acknowledges its inadequacy. He in fact then radically modifies the classic Freudian position, suggesting that if tragedy is at the root of our experience this is so "[I]n an even more fundamental way than through the connection to the Oedipus complex" (Lacan, 1992, pp. 243–244).

Rather extraordinarily the harbingers of this new topic had appeared for the first time in lesson thirteen of Seminar V right after a kind of rock hard installation of certainty and confidence supposedly attendant on the successful outcome of the Oedipus complex, where the subject, with the title deeds to the penis stuffed tranquilly in his pocket goes on his merry way into grown-up life (Lacan, 2017, p. 189). Following on the heels of this inspiring pen-picture, the phrase "the pain of being" a pivotal concept in Seminar VI appears for the first time; "this pain of being that, for Freud, seems to be linked to the very existence of living beings" (ibid., p. 229). In point of fact, this is a very Lacanian reading of Freud's rather dry discussion of the interweave of Eros and Thanatos in "The Economic Problem of Masochism" (Freud, 1924c, pp. 159–173). Annihilation is spelt out in this lesson similarly to later in Seminar VI as "reducing his existence as desiring to nothing and reducing him to a state that aims to abolish him as a subject" (Lacan, 2017, p. 221), and the phrase "*me phunai*" "better not to be", taken from Sophocles' *Oedipus at Colonus*, attributed correctly in earlier seminars to the chorus now for the first time is (wrongly) cited as the final curse on existence of Oedipus himself, a misquote which will be hugely expanded on in Seminars VI, VII, and VIII. Also in this lesson, the Saint Augustine story which had featured in Lacan's work since the 1940s reappears with a new tragic resonance. From the seminar on desire to that on anxiety it will be invoked as the specimen story for the founding catastrophe which marks the birth of the Imaginary. When one reads lesson thirteen of Seminar V from the vantage point of Seminar VI, it sounds like an overture. But as mentioned above, this is typical of the forward momentum of the seminars. Brush-strokes appear very briefly, vanish for extended periods, then reappear fully elaborated. While Lacan in Seminar VII can insist that as analysts, tragedy is at the forefront of our experience, this bias was much less visible in the early years of his seminar. It is true that already in Seminar II he quotes Oedipus, blind and crushed at Colonus: "Am I made man in the hour I cease to be?" (Lacan, 1988, p. 230), highlighting the bleakness of this essential drama of destiny. And already in Seminar II, for Lacan this ultimate suffering is captured in the phrase "*me phunai*", translated as "better not to be". But by Seminar VIII, *Transference*, this phrase will have undergone a number of metamorphoses and will now designate the true place of the subject as subject of the unconscious. By Seminar IX tragedy will have abruptly vanished from the seminar, giving way to topology.

While presenting as one of the longest, most unwieldy of Lacan's seminars, the seminar on desire is in fact quite tightly organized, falling as it does into four sections: the dream of the dead father, the Ella Sharpe dream, Hamlet, and lastly, summarizing these three sections, Lacan indicates how they might usefully illuminate the everyday symptomatology of the psychoanalytic clinic. So in three different configurations, as he points out himself in lesson three, Lacan presents a father, a son, death, and the relation to desire. While the sections echo each other thematically they also each represent, and in entirely different ways, unheralded points of entry into a more expanded exploration of Lacan's mantra "The unconscious is structured like a language" than the two rhetorical tropes, metaphor and metonymy, already well established in previous seminars.

Note

1   I first encountered this seminar in 1989 via Cormac Gallagher's translation. Cormac used the term "o-object" as a straight translation of Lacan's *objet a*. Other translators, including Bruce Fink whose more recent translation is the one used here have chosen differently. Having worked with Cormac's term for so many years, I like it best, and use it here, so as the reader will see, "o-object" is the term which appears in my own text, while remaining faithful to Fink's translation in the quotations from the seminar itself.

References

De Botton, A. (2000). *The Consolations of Philosophy*. London: Penguin.

Cox Cameron, O. (2019). "The Phallus of the Fifties: Those Years of 'Tranquil Possession'", in, Owens, C. and Almqvist, N. (Eds.). *Studying Lacan's Seminars IV and V: From Lack to Desire*. London: Routledge.

Freud, S. (1924c). "The Economic Problem of Masochism". *S.E., XIX*, pp. 155–172.

Lacan, J.:

The seminars:

——. (1988). *The Ego in Freud's Theory and in The Technique of Psychoanalysis, The Seminar of Jacques Lacan, Book II, 1954–1955*. (Ed.) Miller, J.-A. (Trans.) Tomaselli, S. Cambridge: Cambridge University Press.

——. (1992). *The Ethics of Psychoanalysis. The Seminar of Jacques Lacan. Book VII. 1959–1960*. (Ed.) Miller, J.-A. (Trans.). Porter, D. London: Routledge.

——. (1993). *The Psychoses. The Seminar of Jacques Lacan, Book III. 1955–1956*. (Ed.) Miller, J.-A. (Trans.) Grigg, R. London: Routledge.

——. (2017). *Formations of the Unconscious, The Seminar of Jacques Lacan, Book V.* (Ed.) Miller, J.-A. (Trans.) Grigg. R. Cambridge: Polity Press.

——. (2019). *Desire and its Interpretation, The Seminar of Jacques Lacan, Book VI.* (Ed.) Miller, J.-A. (Trans.) Fink B. Cambridge: Polity Press. Also (Trans.). Gallagher, C. Unpublished. www.lacaninireland.com

Chapter 2

"He did not know that he was dead"

Seminar VI begins with an extremely dense and difficult discussion of the relations between repression, representation, and the primary process. Vintage Lacan one might say – dense clouds of abstraction shot through with rays of poetry that pierce his listeners with sudden recognition – but right from the start he introduces his listeners to what will be the kernel, the pith of this year's teaching, the non-opposition of subject and object in the fantasy. The first seven lessons comprise what I will isolate as Section 1.

Central to these lessons is an initial sketching out of the structure of fantasy which is also now a version of the structure of the subject. This section also provides a first outline of what will become the o-object, at this stage specifically linked to narcissistic passion.

He sets out his stall in the first lesson of the year. "we will ask ourselves, 'What is desire?'" (Lacan, 2019, p. 5) and further on "[I]t will be our goal this year to try to define what fantasy is" (ibid., p. 10). However in typically Moëbian fashion, since he has not altogether abandoned this mode of advance, the first two lessons pick up on and expand the graph of desire, covering material he had been presenting to his audience for most of the second half of the previous year's seminar (Lacan, 2017, pp. 313, 321, 371, 400, 444–445, 486–490) while now inserting into it the central new tenet of this year's teaching, the installation of fantasy as essential defence. It is heartening to hear in lesson two that what Lacan considers to be the repetition of a learned lesson has been greeted with moans and groans from his audience! To those who enjoy visual aids, the graph is inspired; to those who don't, its ever-increasing complexification represents brain demolition. For those interested in Lacan's teaching style, lesson two offers a fairly typical example of Lacan recognizing that clarification is called for, and having compliantly announced that: "I do not wish to discuss things in a way that goes over your heads" (Lacan, 2019, p. 25) then going on wittingly or not, to do just that, and to offer something even more obscure than the previous exposition, although in fairness, not devoid of some valuable addenda.

One of the great advantages of the graph is that it presents the beginning of psychic life as a kind of mesh of simultaneity and anteriority, rather than a series of successive stages. As Derrida points out in *Freud and the Scene of Writing*, the beginning is itself a fictional construct (Derrida, 1978, p. 203). It is easy to see the concrete instantiation of Derrida's dense argument for the "crossing out of primariness", his insistence on "a non-origin which is originary" (ibid., p. 203) when one looks at how life begins. Recognitions which are not yet recognitions happen in the womb – voices that calm the mother, voices that frighten, music that soothes, moods that jangle. The baby who encounters the mesh of events traced on Lacan's graph is already someone with a dim, fleeting, and unowned pre-history. While discussing this with the study group, we were keen to recognize this uterine pre-history as a background inevitably inflecting the events traced in the graph. In other words we wanted to wrestle the graph off the page into a real-life conjunction with babyhood.

Lacan starts with a point he had been making for years – the fact of the code that pre-exists the subject – not just a given language but a whole world of assumptions and pre-suppositions, differently accented in different cultures and at different historical moments. The most obvious and immediately relevant perhaps to the small sexed pre-subject, being the masculinist bias of certain cultures. This insistence on the predominant reality of the code is of course not specific to psychoanalysis. A central tenet in linguistics, it had been brilliantly demonstrated in the domain of history in Lucien Febvre's *The Problem of Unbelief in the Sixteenth Century,* and its inexorable constraints memorably railed against in the domain of literature by Beckett's protagonist in *The Unnamable*: "I am walled round with their vociferations, none will ever know what I am, none will ever hear me say it. I won't say it, I can't say it, having no language but theirs […]" (Beckett, 1959, p. 328). Already in Seminar IV Lacan himself had emphasized its ineluctability: "It is in a human world organized by this symbolic order that the child appears, and this is what he must confront" (Lacan, 1956–1957, p. 472). Certain conditions exist in this world which as he says

> allow the subject to preserve a sufficient presence, not only in the real world but also in the symbolic world, that is to say so that he can tolerate himself in the real world organized as it is with its weft of the symbolic
>
> (ibid., p. 429)

These conditions pre-date the subject: "For as long as there have been signifiers that function, the psychic system of subjects has been organized by the very play of these signifiers" (ibid., p. 47). Furthermore if as he persuasively insists, the symbolic order is what literally gives us our world, it will be very difficult to think outside of this frame. Here in Seminar VI he inserts a small but telling caveat just prior to making this point again: remarking that while man's capture in the signifying chain is linked to the reality of man, "it is *not* coextensive with it" (Lacan, 2019, p. 10, my emphasis). An important caveat, even though it remains true that there is no way of escaping this capture. So the reality of the code is the first point to be made.

The next point is riveting despite its dry formulation. This is what Lacan calls the point of encounter with the code: the message. What happens here? Several things at once. The baby's cry is heard by the other, most likely the mother as:

Welcome.
This baby needs me and I love that.
A pain in the ass – impossible to satisfy, really annoying.
Terrifying. What on earth is wrong? I can't cope with this.
A real pleasure. I enjoy not feeding this baby, letting him suffer.

This list is infinite and not trivial since Lacan will return with great frequency to this earliest of encounters.

As he goes on to say here, the baby's cry which initially can be pure need must pass through the defiles of the signifier which will re-shape its meaning, and form "the first stamp [*seing*] or *signum* of its relationship with the Other" (ibid., p. 13). This Lacan describes as the first primary identification. The implications of this process, what Lacan calls "the mark or seal placed on need by demand" (ibid., p. 14) can hardly be overstated, and the questions raised by it utterly crucial. What has this railroading of need through the defiles of the signifier, a few of which possibilities are listed above, made the baby become? Lacan recognizes that this is much more than an affair of language. Something goes beyond the capture of language and this is the presence of the other. Punning on the near homophony of *sein/seing* (breast/sign), Lacan insists on the baby's need for and awareness of what this presence purveys. In particular this other has her own desires which will be brought to bear on the baby and which the baby will sense, in however dim and enigmatic a fashion. What does this all-powerful other want? The study group rightly insisted that in pretty much every encounter with a new-born baby this question, "What do you want?", Lacan's *che vuoi* cuts both ways. As indeed does the experience of helplessness attendant on it. In a clever move the term "helplessness" is here given a potent psychoanalytic lineage by soldering it to Freud's usage in "Inhibitions, Symptoms and Anxiety" (Freud, 1926d).

But a few words first about the *che vuoi* which will be an important element in Lacan's teaching in the coming years, and which appears for the first time in this seminar. To start with, Lacan's reference here is somewhat unexpected. As he tells us, it is taken from a late eighteenth-century gothic novel, *Le Diable Amoureux* by Jacques Cazotte. The phrase appears twice in the text, and certainly the scene in which it first appears can hardly be described as one that leaves the addressee without recourse. Like a number of other gothic tales of the era, the protagonist, Alvare, has begged for and been promised an encounter with the devil. He has furthermore bragged of his bravery, even announcing himself ready to pull the ears of the biggest devil in hell (Cazotte, 1772, p. 113). He is brought (at night of course) to a dark and cavernous ruin, with the usual bats and owls in attendance, and instructed that on no account must he show fear. On the contrary he must establish himself in a commanding position vis-à-vis the evil spirit. He must summon this devil by calling him by name three times. Having uttered the name "Beelzebub" three times, a horrendous apparition with huge ears surges up at the window bellowing the question "*Che vuoi?*" in a voice that echoes in the vaulted roof of the ruin (ibid., p. 120). But Alvare, though terrified, is not without recourse. Notwithstanding the cold sweat in which he is bathed, he takes command of the situation, roaring back at the apparition: what do you mean, brazen one, showing yourself to me in this hideous form? This response cows the devil. While the scene that follows seems a little ludicrous, it is worth recounting here just to show the gap that exists between Lacan's annihilatory *che vuoi* and that of Cazotte. Answering Alvare's angry question, the devil, lowering his tone, and sounding like a rebuked servant says, "you called for me?", a drop into humility that does little to mollify Alvare. "Does the slave seek to frighten his master? If you want to receive my orders, show yourself in a more agreeable form" (ibid., p. 121). And this terrifying apparition, who has roared the menacing *che vuoi*, ends up turning itself into … a white spaniel (ibid., p. 121)!

As is the way with this type of narrative (think Faust, think Peter Schlemihl), ascendancy over the devil is always illusory, always temporary, and when at the end of the novel, the devil repeats the question *che vuoi?* it is simply to mock the hapless and destroyed Alvare who goes on to be rescued by – of all things – submitting to his mammy and letting her choose a good wife for him (ibid., p. 285)!

As English speaking readers are unlikely to be familiar with the source of Lacan's *che vuoi*, this digression may be useful. In Lacan's version of this scene, fright is the dominant note. He presents it as "the bellowing of the terrifying form that represents the appearance of the super-ego, in response to he who invoked it in a Neapolitan cave; the response is '*Che vuoi?*' or what do you want?" (Lacan, 2019, p. 15). Lacan's reading of this scene is unambiguous, and of course it is Lacan's reading that concerns us here: "Finding himself in the primitive presence of the Other's desire as obscure and opaque, the subject has no recourse, he is *hilflos. Hilflosigheit*, to use Freud's term, is known in French as the subject's 'distress'" (ibid., p. 17).

A second point to be made here is the following. While the demand of the Other has been an essential factor in Lacan's theorization of the coming into being of the subject, as shown on the graph of desire, this demand has not appeared before now in an interrogative form. As we will see further on in this seminar the fact that this demand is now in the form of a question is so central, so essential that its occurrence is conflated with *being* itself. In lesson twenty-one Lacan puns on the verb to be *esse*, reading it as the interrogative *Est-ce?* Not at all an ordinary question, but one that is described as "the first stage of the actual constitution of the subject" (ibid., p. 375), what Lacan calls the subject in abeyance (ibid., p. 376). Lacan spells this out very explicitly: "This S is the id [*Ça*], and in an interrogative form. If you add a question mark, S is in fact articulated as *Est-ce?* ['Is it?' or 'Is this?']" (ibid.).

The question, situated as a radical *calling into question* of the subject is a very powerful trope. It reappears a year later in "The Subversion of the Subject and the Dialectic of Desire in the Unconscious", an essay in his *Écrits* published in 1966. In this reference what one might call its boomerang effect, operating between the subject and the Other is more immediately graspable:

> That is why the Other's question [...] – that comes back to the subject from the place from which he expects an oracular reply – which takes some such form as "*Che vuoi?*" "What do you want?", is the question that best leads the subject to the path of his own desire [...]
>
> (Lacan, 2006, p. 690)

Its centrality is further highlighted in the seminar *Anxiety* where it is "the key to what Freudian doctrine introduced as subjectivity" (Lacan, 2014, p. 6). Here too Lacan emphasizes the fact that it is multi-directional in its reach:

> *Che vuoi?, Que veux-tu?, What wouldst thou?* Push the functioning, the insertion of the key, a little further and you have, *Que me veut-Il?* [...] It's not simply, *What does the Other want with me?* but also a suspended questioning that directly concerns the ego, not *How does He want me?*, but, *What does He want concerning this place of the ego?*
>
> (Ibid., p. 6)

Third – and lastly for the moment before we return to the lesson in hand – in the seminar on transference the *che vuoi* is that which reveals the fact that there is a missing signifier (Lacan, 2015). This is an interesting if bizarre moment in Lacan's teaching. Referencing Jakobson, he begins by acknowledging the obvious fact that there can be no missing signifier in language *per se*, thus tacitly moving the discussion onto the terrain of discourse, and not language. Given this obvious fact Lacan asks: "At what moment can a lack of a signifier possibly begin to appear?" And goes on to respond: "In the dimension that is subjective and that is called questioning" (ibid., p. 238). What he is referring to he tells us is "the enigma of questioning itself" (ibid., p. 240) as we see it in children. The fact of questioning, and the fact that there is a question, or questions to which there is no adequate response, is crystallized in the child's question to herself "What am I?" to which there is essentially no answer that is articulable, although of course she may rush headlong into various pacificatory identifications, such as "I am a child". Lacan rather wonderfully describes the impossibility of adequately answering this question as "my signifying inchoation" (ibid., p. 241), and makes it clear that what is in question is indeed the *che vuoi*:

> What is at stake in every question formulated is not situated at the level of "What am I?" but at that of the Other, in the form that analytic practice

allows us to unveil – namely, "What do you want?" What is involved at this precise point is to figure out what we desire by raising the question.

(ibid.)

Bizarrely the phallus manages to step in at this point as a substitute for the lost object/o-object although this latter is in fact the only possible non-answer to this question. Since what concerns us here is the incidence and centrality of the *che vuoi* in Lacan's teaching, we need do no more than raise an eyebrow at this particular phallus which has taken on the trappings of the Catholic Eucharist and is here referred to as "real presence" (ibid., p. 243).

Interestingly, the writer Marguerite Duras, who had no knowledge of Lacan's work has a very remarkable passage about the missing signifier in her novel *Le Ravissement de Lol V. Stein*, published a few years after this seminar on desire. What Lol reaches for is "a single entity but unnameable for lack of a word" (Duras, 1964, p. 38). For a second Lol had believed that this word might exist:

> It would have been an absence-word, a hole word, whose center would have been hollowed out into a hole, the kind of hole in which all other words would have been buried. It would have been impossible to utter it, but it would have been made to reverberate.

(ibid.)

It was Lacan's very great achievement to have theorized this unnameable entity over the very many years during which he explored what he called the o-object and its ex-centric position with respect to representation.

Returning to the lesson in hand, the reader can see that these elements – a question to which there is no answer, the terror of "signifying inchoation" to which the little pre-subject must respond – are present in the very first appearance of the *che vuoi*, and it is indeed these elements that are underlined in Lacan's invocation of the Freudian concept of *Hilflosigheit*.

Picking up on this Freudian concept then, Lacan describes the entry into subjecthood as constituting a necessary confrontation by this small pre-subject with the unanswerable question of the Other's desire, a terrifying moment since the small subject finds herself utterly without recourse faced with this question. It is important to note that, for Lacan, this moment is to be aligned with originary trauma: "It is the foundation of what, in psychoanalysis, has been explored, experienced, and qualified as 'trauma'" (Lacan, 2019, p. 17). At this crisis point, represented as a third moment on the graph, only the Imaginary can provide a bulwark against annihilation by permitting the subject to guard against this helplessness in relation to the desire of the other with the help of – rather surprisingly – the ego: "[t]he subject defends himself with his ego" (ibid., p. 19). Here we have the very first avatar of the o-object which will evolve in directions very far removed from the Imaginary in the years to come. For now, it is specular, albeit giving to the specular what he describes here as a "very different resonance" (ibid., p. 19). Throughout this seminar, as we will see, Lacan repeatedly reminds his listeners that this o-object has the closest possible relation with narcissistic passion. A year later, via *das Ding*, he will begin his search for a non-narcissistic entity, unamenable to the laws of representation, a search that will radically alter the contours of the o-object. And a year later again, in the eighth seminar *Transference*, basing himself on Freud's 1914 paper "On Narcissism", he perhaps for the first time, clearly distinguishes two different levels of object:

> although the field of narcissistic cathexis is central and essential – and it is around this field that the entire fate of human desire is played out – it is not the only field. The proof thereof is that, at the very moment Freud introduces this field [...] he distinguishes it from another field: that of the relationship to the archaic object, the nourishing field of the maternal object.
>
> (Lacan, 2015, pp. 375–376)

This, Lacan insists, is "of an altogether different order" (ibid.). These modifications noted, it would nevertheless be a real impoverishment to fail to appreciate the electric urgency in these first outlines and the immediacy of their relevance in our lives of love and mourning as Lacan goes on to reveal them in his reading of Freud's dream of the dead father.

For now this very first outline, inscribed on the graph of desire allows Lacan to launch the major theme of this seminar by installing the fantasy as central, and to foreground the very new insistence that human desire is predicated not on an object but on this fantasy.

Lesson one actually provides a relatively clear reading of the graph while adding in this new element. Lesson two purporting to be a clarification of lesson one for his disgruntled audience is hard to describe as an exercise in illumination. In particular in the way that it introduces not just any old phallus but the phallus of the previous year's seminar – the signifier which designates the relationship of the subject with the signifier – into the encounter with the "*Che vuoi?*". In this second exposition, the *Hilflosigheit* of lesson one has morphed into "a threat directly targeting the phallus" (Lacan, 2019, p. 35), an assertion open to multiple interrogations. Once again the presentation of the phallus as a signifier and not an organ, will be difficult to subscribe to when in lesson six he injects the fragment of a case history about male impotence as a lead-in to the suggestion that the major question for the subject is: have I a big enough phallus? Do I possess the absolute weapon? From "real presence" to "pearl of living plenitude" to pre-eminence by virtue of its "imposing form", the conflation of masculinism, "empiricism", and a rather touching fondness for this phallus creates an ongoing problem in Lacan's writing. Mercifully, it is not much expanded on in this first section of the seminar which at this point, in lesson three, introduces Freud's dream of the dead father (Freud, 1911b).

While it is mentioned here, Lacan's reading of this dream initially segues into two difficult explorations of the relation of the subject to the signifier and the distinction between "the enunciation" and "the enunciating", both topics presented in dauntingly abstract terms but hugely interesting when set in motion in everyday exchanges. Lacan seems to be aware of the difficulties of following him here, describing this section as an altogether inevitable preamble and in typical fashion, throwing a highly provocative, and for the moment, unelaborated sentence into this turgid mix: "To tell someone, 'I desire you,' is to tell him, 'I include you in my fundamental fantasy'" (ibid., p. 39).

It is helpful I think to read lessons two to four alongside *Problems in General Linguistics* by the eminent linguist Émile Benveniste (1971). We know from Roudinesco that since 1951 Lacan had been working with Benveniste, who during these years wrote a collection of essays published in 1966 under the above-mentioned title (Roudinesco, 1990, p. 560). In these essays, Benveniste repeatedly insists on the deceptive ease with which habit obscures the profound difference between language as a system of signs and language assumed into use by the individual. Accordingly a number of the chapters focus on the tiny but essential grammatical ties by which man lays hold of language, and in doing so constitutes himself as subject. Lacan had been quoting Benveniste since his third seminar *The Psychoses*, in this context which he calls "the relations between the I and the signifier" (Lacan, 1993, p. 281). In that seminar, while discussing Benveniste's article on the middle voice in the verb, Lacan is explicit in stating the near identity of their respective fields, saying of Benveniste's article that what is in question is "the entire register at work precisely in analytic experience" (Lacan, ibid.). In Chapter 21, under the title, "Subjectivity in Language", Benveniste isolates the pronoun "I" as the means by which the individual takes hold of or appropriates language to herself. He is at pains to emphasize the highly peculiar status of this "I" which unlike other lexical entities, for example "chair", has no existence outside of its moment of utterance. Benveniste calls it "an instance of discourse that only has momentary reference" (Benveniste, ibid., p. 226). Not necessarily the fleeting, fading, evanescent subject which Lacan will go on to discuss in this seminar, but certainly something not unrelated to it in that it "does not denote any lexical entity" (ibid.) and its existence, sustained only by the moment of utterance could reasonably be described as punctiform. Benveniste goes on to demonstrate that personal pronouns are only the first instances of subjective mooring. Other pronouns which share the same status are the indicators of deixis, "this", "that", "here", "now", and all their correlatives, "yesterday", "last year" etc., which of necessity are defined only in relation to this speaking I, as are also verbal tenses. "Linguistic time is self referential", as Benveniste writes, "determined for each speaker by the instances of discourse related to it" (ibid., p. 227).

Again, a small glance in the direction of Beckett's work will allow us to see that linguistics and psychoanalysis were not alone in these years in highlighting the problematic and fragile status of the "I" and its attendant linguistic correlatives. It is the fault of the pronouns says the Unnamable. "I will not say I again […] enough of this cursed first person it really is too red a herring" (Beckett, 1959, p. 345). The impossibility of this "I" recurs like a leitmotif in this great novel: "Do they believe I believe it is I who am speaking?" (ibid., p. 348). As well as the first-person singular all the other small grammatical ties which knot the speaker to his utterance visibly come undone in Beckett's late prose: "How long have I been here, what a question, I've often wondered. And often I could answer. An hour, a month, a year, a century, depending on what I meant by here and me, and being, and there" (Beckett, 1974, p. 8).

These small grammatical ties can distinguish the enunciating subject from the enunciation. As well as personal pronouns and indicators of deixis, Benveniste lists a number of verbal forms by which an enunciation can be turned into an enunciating such as "I believe" or "I am afraid that …". The question is, basically: is the speaking subject discernible in the statement? Many statements, including almost all of academic discourse, are devised to eliminate the speaking subject. The Nine O'clock News is a good example. "Here is the news", not "You're never going to believe what happened today …". In the study group, we supplemented these "instances of discourse" with other elements which effect this transformation, such as tone: "SORRYEE" as roared by a defiant teenager where the enunciating subject clearly inflects the enunciation; or certain types of phraseology; "the fucking transport minister" as uttered by a newsreader. This distinction between the enunciating subject and the enunciation is of course extremely important clinically and a knowledge of some of these papers by Benveniste would be a useful adjunct on training courses.

Lacan supplements Benveniste's instances of enunciating with an old favourite of his – the discordant "*ne*" explicated by Damourette and Pichon in an article which he had been quoting and would continue to quote for very many years. This pleonastic "*ne*" demonstrable only in French, seems to introduce the trace of an unacknowledged wish into a sentence such as: *Je crains qu'il ne vienne*, which looks as if it is to be read as "I am afraid he will not come", but actually means "I am afraid he *will* come", an ambiguity allowing one to discern in it velleities proper to unconscious desire. This reference brings into focus "the dimension of the unsaid", and opens the whole explication to the subject of the unconscious as revealed in the enunciating. The discordant "*ne*" is one of the places Lacan locates the work of repression, suggesting that a whole part of grammar – the essential part – the taxemes, are designed to maintain a necessary distance between these two lines (Lacan, 2019, p. 75). It also allows Lacan to point to the elision of the enunciating subject as the defining characteristic of repression: "Repression, when it arises, is essentially linked to something that appears to be absolutely necessary – namely – that the subject be effaced and disappear at the level of the enunciation process" (ibid 74). It is interesting to see this difficult statement being buttressed by a surprising number of references to grammatical structure:

the relationship between these two lines that represent the enunciation process and the statement process is quite simple: it is the whole of grammar. If you like, I can tell you where and how, in what terms and in which tables, this has been articulated within the framework of a rational grammar.

(ibid., p. 74)

This view is one from which he will radically distance himself in his last spoken seminar, where he announces that "in the structure of the unconscious it is necessary to eliminate grammar" (Lacan, 2013, p. 20).

Here on the contrary, grammar is where it's at and while it is at this point that Lacan introduces the relation between subject and object which distinguishes the desiring subject of psychoanalysis from the philosophical subject of knowledge, there are discernible echoes here of the article mentioned above, to which he had alluded in his third seminar *The Psychoses*. In this article Benveniste charted the manner in which the very ancient interweave of subject and object was gradually rebraided into oppositional entities. Benveniste draws the attention of his readers to earlier grammatical forms where voice in the verb was not either active or passive as in modern usage, but active and middle. The point here and it is one that Lacan picks up in the seminar on the psychoses is that whereas the active and passive voices position one as either subject or object, the older middle voice blurred this distinction. Certain verbs existed only in the middle voice, among them the verbs to be born, to enjoy, to suffer, suggesting that one could be grammatically both subject and object at these times. These are the positions which are in question for Benveniste, and of course this is also what is in question in the Lacanian formula for the fundamental fantasy which supports the desiring subject. So the o-object could be said to have had its beginnings not just in language but specifically in grammar.

The great middle seminars of Lacan's teaching allow us to see ideas and events in the making. Certainly as Lacan develops the concept of the evanescent fading subject of desire specified in the structure of the fantasy, he will be impelled to seriously upend normal modes of thinking in order to create the contours of the o-object, as something absolutely not aligned with the normal rules of representation. Three years later when he returns to the problematic status of the enunciating subject in the seminar on identification, he reminds his listeners of this section of Seminar VI, repeating that

this subject of ours, this subject that I would like today to interrogate for you in connection with the Cartesian way forward is the same one that I told you we could not approach any closer than is done in this exemplary dream which is entirely articulated around "He did not know that he had died".

(Lacan, 1961–1962, lesson of 22 November 1961, p. 11)

An extraordinary instance as he continues, where the enunciating subject is actually to be designated in the third person (ibid.). And before the end of this year's seminar, using a term he rarely employs, he will forge a very explicit link between the pronoun "I" and the o-object when he suggests that "on the plane of the unconscious" the o-object functions in such a way as to make it the analogue of this "I":

> We can find an analogue of what happens next in the function of certain symbols that linguists distinguish in the lexical system, which go by the name "shifter symbols". I have already mentioned the personal pronoun "I", which designates the person who is speaking. At the unconscious level, the same is true for little *a*. This *a*, which is not a symbol but rather one of the subject's real elements, is what intervenes to support the moment, in the synchronic sense, at which the subject falters in attempting to designate himself […] at the level of the instance of desire.
>
> (Lacan, 2019, pp. 367–368)

For me this "analogue" represents an early step in the progressive de-substantiation visible in a number of Lacanian concepts over the years, the most obvious of these being of course the phallus, which having presented itself sturdily as noun over 1,500 times in the first ten years of the seminars, gradually morphs and subsides into the rather less forceful adjectival "phallic function" as time goes on. What we are witnessing here is the inception of a search for an entity outside the normal possibilities of representation. In subsequent seminars, Lacan will call on zero, "the figure that stands for no number" as it was described in the twelfth century, to take this process a step further than his use of the pronoun here had done. A sign for "nothing", having no locatable existence outside of the act of counting, and therefore of which it can reasonably be said that it designates not an object but the counting subject itself. A year after his twelfth seminar *Crucial Problems in Psychoanalysis* which focusses on this zero and its problematic relation to representation, Lacan finds another – and ingenious – way to make this point again, this time via the vanishing point, the function of which in perspectivist painting is not to designate the object but to indicate the place from which the spectator looks, and by extension this look itself (Lacan, 1965–1966).

Lacan's departure from grammar, language, and literature into topology, mathematics, logic, perspectivism, and eventually knot theory, in order to engage with the questions which preoccupied him, interests me greatly, especially as that which makes numeration possible, in lesson nine of *Crucial Problems*, reveals this manoeuvre to be entirely a matter of grammatical trickery (ibid., lesson of 24 February 1965, pp. 6–18). In this lesson Lacan invites Jacques-Alain Miller to take the floor in order to show how zero functions to underpin numeration. Miller's account of the historical manoeuvres necessary to bring this about is brilliant. In it he explicitly calls on his audience to recognize "how absolutely astonishing this conjuring trick is" (ibid., p. 12). Since zero cannot be done without, it will be generated by sleight of hand: as Miller goes on to explain, the one is generated from the fact that the zero as number is able to become concept and object. It is essentially these grammatical shifts which rather astonishingly generate a nothing that henceforth exists while the act of nomination discreetly calls attention to the shadowy presence of the subject who does the naming. The fact that it is grammar and not computation that has achieved this astounding hat-trick – the passage from zero to one which is the fulcrum of Lacan's teaching in these years, falls below the radar in this seminar, notwithstanding Miller's brilliant if dizzying exposition (ibid.). The fact that it falls below the radar is itself interesting. While Miller bases his exposition on Frege, he is at pains to highlight the fictional element in the transformation achieved: "in this gift of the name to which the function of the subject can let itself be reduced, there originates its definition as creator of the fiction" (ibid., p. 7). What is in question is representation and the attendant sleight of hand that brings it about, what Miller calls "the transgression by which the zero comes to be represented by one, a representation necessary to produce as an effect of sense, the name of a number as successor" (ibid., p. 13). But the fictional gesture itself is not as such queried.

Similarly, with respect to Lacan's examination of the role of the vanishing point, the link between representational forms as they evolved via the roughly contemporaneous popularization of perspectivist painting and the rise of both autobiography and the novel does not feature in his teaching. At one point, welcoming Michel Foucault to his seminar, Lacan alerts his listeners to a particularly relevant point of intersection between his own field of research and that of Foucault, and brings a copy of Velasquez's *Las Meniñas* to the auditorium in order to illustrate what is involved in the division of the subject by the presence of Velasquez himself in this painting at the place where in Foucault's famous phrase, representation undertakes to represent itself (Foucault, 1966, p. 31). But where Michel Foucault in his discussion of perspectivist painting in *Les Mots et les Choses*, indicates a kind of literary equivalent in the extraordinarily complexified doublings and inversions of Don Quixote's relation to language in Cervantes' sophisticated narrative, Lacan remains more focussed on the inside-out structure of the gaze.

The status of this seminar as gateway renders necessary this rather lengthy parenthesis, reaching out from Seminar VI over developments throughout the following six years. It is also crucial to highlight the centrifugal direction taken by Lacan's thought with respect to grammar. In his deeply interesting book *L'objet a: approches à l'invention de Lacan*, Guy le Gaufey charts these directions in Lacan's thought in the context of similar work by other thinkers, and seems to suggest that the direction taken by some of these thinkers with respect to grammar was by contrast centripetal (le Gaufey, 2012, p. 163). The American philosopher Willard Quine wrote about variables in mathematics as "pro-numbers", replicating some of the functions of pronouns in the field of grammar: "Variables are essentially pronouns", he opines, and goes further, citing an unfindable statement from Charles Sanders Pierce that reverses the usual prioritizing relationship between pronouns and names, these latter in Pierce's view, being more aptly called "pro-pronouns" (ibid., p. 167). It is this reversal, emphasizing the absence of a stable entity supporting this lexical feature that vaults us back to the new "evanescence" of Lacan's desiring "I" and its problematic relation to being in Seminar VI.

Here in the first part of this seminar it is immediately after the long dry disquisition on the distinction between the enunciating and the enunciation that he refocuses his listeners on this crucial point he is setting out to make, which is the non-opposition of subject and object in the fantasy. Here in lesson five he begins to expand this statement, and as often happens in the seminar dry abstraction gives way to something akin to poetry. The relationship of the subject to the object is "complex" since the object is found to be:

> something that props the subject up at the precise moment at which the subject has to face, as it were, his existence [...] at the very moment at which he, as a subject, must be effaced, vanish, or disappear behind a signifier. At that moment, which is a moment of panic, so to speak, the subject must grab hold of something, and he grabs hold of the object qua object of desire.
>
> (Lacan, 2019, p. 84)

This is an enormous statement, shifting the entire disquisition from abstraction to immediacy. A panic point suggests existential crisis, with the object interposed as solution, something that for the moment Lacan leaves in abeyance. At this point his focus is on the necessity for this object of desire to function as hidden underlay and he offers three vivid examples of what happens if it threatens to surge into visibility. In order to maintain one's self-presence in the world this hidden underlay must not be exposed; consequently its unmasking undoes the contours of both the self and the world as we know it since what inadvertently appears is something too close to the subject for him to be able to bear reference to it. Lacan describes it as the most important, most intimate part of oneself: "[w]hat is propped up by this object is precisely what the subject cannot reveal even to himself. It is something that is at the cusp of the greatest secret" (ibid., p. 85). The artist Bracha Ettinger offers a striking metaphor to describe this structure:

> Subject and o–object are as inseparable as the front and back of the same fabric, the recto and verso of the same sheet of paper. When the subject appears (as in everyday life) the o–object disappears, and when the o–object finds a way to penetrate to the other side (as in art), or to reappear as hallucinations in the Real, signifying meaning symbolic and imaginary, exchangeable through discourse, disappears and goes into hiding.
>
> (Ettinger, 2006, pp. 41–42)

Some years later, in his ninth seminar on identification, Lacan says much the same thing, when he observes that the emergence of the o-object in the fantasy is correlative to a fading or vanishing of the Symbolic, of the normal supports which maintain self and world in position: "It is at the point where every significance is missing, is abolished, at the nodal point called that of the desire of the Other […] that the object, little o […] comes to take its place" (Lacan, 1961–1962, lesson of 27 June 1962).

Here in lesson five, Lacan offers three examples of the inability of the "I" to sustain itself at these moments. First the response of the miser when confronted with the loss of his money box – a response he says we can only ridicule, since it is far too close to the unconscious for us to be able actually to take on board. Second, in the film *La Regle du Jeu*, the moment when Delio the collector, in front of an audience, blushes, overcome with emotion at the sight of a particularly beautiful music box. As Lacan says of this blush, he effaces himself, he disappears. Readers of *Ulysses* will be reminded of Stephen Dedalus' blush in the newspaper office when unexpectedly "wooed by grace of language and gesture" (Joyce, 1993, p. 177).

The third example of the subject's disappearance, or aphanisis as Lacan will go on to call it, is a verse from a poem where what the poet desires is too intimate to be expressed in the first-person singular and therefore solicits the infinitive form of the verb in order to say itself in a manner denuded of person: *Être une belle fille*. This third example raises two crucial issues for Lacan: the fact that this object is somehow unamenable to first-person ownership, and the question: how to communicate to others something which is constituted as secret? The reply – "through some sort of lie" will allow him to move directly into what is the centrepiece of this section, the dream of the dead father, a version of the fundamental fantasy which functions as exactly this kind of essential veil (Lacan, 2019, p. 87).

This long lead-in is of interest to Lacanian scholars as an example of the intrication of highly abstract grammatical elucubrations shot through with the immediacy of what the heart knows of grief and pain. *Le coeur a ses raisons* as Pascal so memorably mused but Lacan's intrication of these domains is altogether his own. Relying mainly on the three grammatical indications discussed in the opening lessons, the function of negation, the potential slippages of the personal pronoun, and the collapse of the distinction between subject and object, Lacan introduces his listeners to the founding catastrophe which marks the inception of human subjectivity, and marks this inception as irremediably tragic. So here, for the first time we see profiled what Lacan will later go on to call "the tragic dimension of psychoanalytic experience" (Lacan, 1992, lessons twenty-two to twenty-four).

He does this via the reading of a dream which appears twice in Freud's writings, first in *Formulations Regarding The Two Principles of Mental Functioning*, and second as a late addition to the text of *The Interpretation of Dreams* (Freud, 1911b, 1900a [1930]). Lacan notes the point at which Freud adds it in – under the heading "Absurd Dreams" – dreams to which Freud attributes a particular intensity, particular levels of passionate repudiation, and of which he remarks: "Dreams are often most profound when they seem most crazy" (Freud, 1900a, p. 444). Freud's wording is slightly different in each of his two published accounts. Lacan uses that of *The Interpretation of Dreams*, and, citing Freud, focusses what he has to say around three separate phrases: "he did not know", "that he was dead", "as he wished" (Lacan, 2019, p. 88). As read by Freud this is an Oedipal dream. Here it becomes a stark iconography, an austere etching of the pain of existence.

How does this difference in function of the two readings come about? For Freud, the son's wish that the father's suffering might be cut short by death adumbrates and stirs into life the earlier, now unconscious, death wish of Oedipal rivalry, so as such it is a near-perfect example of repression functioning as omission, subtraction, more of its weight carried in the suppressed phrase "as he wished" than in the preceding two "he did not know" "that he was dead". Lacan's anamorphic feat is to preserve this Oedipal frame while angling it to reveal the lineaments of the fundamental fantasy. For Lacan, the phrase "he did not know" represents the authentic signature of the subject of the unconscious. As he says, this phrase does not concern anything factual and is "an essentially subjective reference [...] going to the core" of the structure of the subject(ibid., p. 113). Here in this dream the "he did not know" can be seen in action, so to speak, as an utterance of the unconscious, since to paraphrase Lacan, the ignorance imposed on the other is nothing other than the ignorance of the subject himself who does not know, because to know would be intolerable (ibid., p. 115). Nonetheless in the manner of repression, this not knowing is of course also a knowing: "what is certain, in any case, is that the dreamer knew about this pain" since in the second phrase "that he was dead" is hidden the dangerous proximity of the pain of existence leached of all desire (ibid., p. 91). In both phrases, this existential weight is carried and concealed by one of the three grammatical elements listed earlier which is the slippage of the personal pronoun, effectively permitting the unsustainable loss of that which supports this subject in his existence to find expression. If the fundamental fantasy is itself a brink phenomenon, Lacan situates the dream of the dead father on the knife-edge of this brink.

In Lacan's reading the son's rivalry had functioned effectively as a mask for the pain of existence giving him a focus, a distracting dissatisfaction, and an immediately engaging obstacle hiding the truth of the *me phunai* which is the hopelessness of the human condition. But now with the father's death Lacan suggests the son is from now on,

> confronted with death, having been protected from it hitherto by the father's presence. "Confronted with death" – what does that mean? Confronted with an *x* that is linked to the father's function, that is present

here in the pain of existing, and that is the pivotal point around which what Freud discovered in the Oedipus complex revolves – namely, the signification of castration.

(ibid., p. 96)

So the wish for this father to be castrated turns back on the son since it is now his turn to be castrated and this "he must not see at any cost" (ibid., p. 92).

Castration here is something very different to the Symbolic necessity so brilliantly theorized in his seminar on formations of the unconscious from the previous year. Here, for the first time, developing the remarks made in lesson thirteen of the previous year, he allows us to glimpse the levels of devastation it entails. This "wish for the father to be castrated" aims at keeping the dreamer in an ignorance which consists in not knowing that it is better not to have been born. "[I]f there is nothing at the end of existence but the pain of existing, it would be so much better to take that pain as though it were the other's" (ibid., p. 92).

Lacan very explicitly links this drama to the Imaginary, describing the relationship of the subject to the imaginary functions as encapsulated in the algorithm for fantasy, $\$ \lozenge a$, in the sense that "desire as such raises for man the question of his subjective elision, $\$$, with regard to any and every possible object" (ibid., p. 116). To be or not to be, to be able to go on being: these are questions posed at the level of the Imaginary. At several points in the seminar, Lacan makes the point that as human beings we don't just "be" – we question ourselves about being. We are aware that we might not be. Similarly with desire. We don't just desire, but we count on ourselves as desiring. We are aware that it is possible to lose the *élan vital*. Ernest Jones had written of this in his 1927 paper "The Early Development of Female Sexuality" using the Greek word aphanisis to designate the disappearance of desiringness: "the total and of course permanent extinction of the capacity (including opportunity) for sexual enjoyment" (Jones, 1927, p. 461). Jones sees the male dread of castration as simply a particular instance of aphanisis; aphanisis itself as dread of this extinction of desire being a phenomenon that is common to both sexes. Lacan borrows this word, slightly altering its meaning so that it now designates, not the disappearance of desire, but the elision of the subject attendant on too direct a confrontation with the object of desire. Because this peril is real, the subject dreads the satisfaction of his desire, and generally speaking makes of his life a series of obstacle courses, ensuring by successive avoidance that this minatory confrontation does not take place (Lacan, 2019, p. 102). In Lacan's reading of this dream, Oedipal rivalry can provide one such obstacle.

That what for Freud is an Oedipal drama is an instantiation of something more fundamental is made quite explicit by Lacan. While Lacan does not pause here, he has in fact made quite a large statement, to be expanded on in the coming months. Freud had described the Oedipus complex as the central phenomenon of childhood and pretty much the lynchpin of psychoanalytic theory (Freud, 1900a, p. 226). Here Lacan seems to be minimizing its outcome, defining the identification to the image of the father as being "but a specific case of what we must now broach as being the most general solution of the subject/object relationship, the most general solution of the confrontation between the barred subject and object *a*" (Lacan, ibid., pp. 108–109). In the previous lesson he states: "This wish here is but the mask of what is most profound in the structure of desire as it is revealed in the dream […]" (ibid., p. 93). Overwhelming as the suffering of the dreamer may be he is not altogether annihilated. In the precarious and senseless space of the other's not knowing, he the dreamer can maintain his existence, or as Lacan puts it, can maintain the veil which ensures that he continues to be a subject who speaks (ibid., p. 94). For Lacan, the dream of the dead father encapsulates the all but unbearable pain of mourning. The switch of pronouns and the negation in the phrase "he did not know" are both a last-ditch attempt at not foundering entirely, and an indication that this foundering has in fact occurred. The pain of existing, the impossibility of knowing, belong to the dreamer and necessitate some form of repudiation and as Lacan puts it: "The whole nature of fantasy is to transfer this fear to the object" (ibid., p. 109). Since this "he did not know" is an essentially subjective reference which goes to the foundation of the structure of the subject, not only does he not know but crucially he must not be told, because if he knew it he would be it. To demonstrate this, Lacan gestures to a dream of Trotsky in which Trotsky meets Lenin long after the death of the latter. Trotsky cannot let Lenin know that he has died and in the dream refers only to "the moment at which you were very, very ill" (ibid., p. 115). As if, Lacan remarks, a precise formulation of what was in question would by its very breath dissipate the shade before whom at this decisive moment of his existence Trotsky maintains himself. Had this seminar taken place two years later Lacan would have had a much more powerful dream at his disposal. In 1961, the literary critic Jean Pierre Richard published 202 newly discovered poetic fragments by one of France's greatest poets Stephane Mallarmé. These fragments, translated by Paul Auster are collected under the title *A Tomb for Anatole*, and like the dream of the dead father concern a father, a son, and death except that this time it is a father trying to address the death of a beloved child. Mallarmé's son Anatole died in 1879 aged 8. The fragments, notes for a possible work, are as Auster says a kind of *ur*-text, the shards of a poem that simply could not be written. Their very fragmentariness and piercing immediacy are an indication of what Lacan was beginning to track down in this seminar – the fragment having been singled out by Freud as privileged carrier of unconscious desire (Freud, 1900a, p. 312). Very many of Mallarmé's fragments describe a recurrent dream in which the beloved child returns because he does not know that he is dead. Several could be cited but one in particular captures the precipice visited each night by the distraught dreamer:

what do you want, sweet
adored vision –
who often come
towards me and lean
over – as if
to listen to secret (of
My tears) –
to know that you are
dead
– what you do not know
– no I will not
tell it
to you – for then you
would disappear –
and I would be alone
weeping …
       (Mallarmé, 2005,
        pp. 149–150)

Over and over throughout the book, this dilemma is powerfully and poignantly evoked in fragments that cannot complete themselves and which read almost like sobs in the work of this austere and abstract poet.

Freud introduced this dream as a recurrent one. In my experience it is a dream which does not recur in all mourning but only in those mournings which involve the loss of the o-object. While the formula for the fundamental fantasy is a writing of the subject as such, in lived experience its components are transferred onto the indispensable loves of ongoing life. Unsurprisingly the death or disappearance of the one who occupies that indispensable place menaces the entire structure. The everyday ups and downs and the routine securities of relationship can conceal the degree to which one's existence is sustained by this other. Death rips away this oblivion, laying bare what cannot be borne, since what is supported by this now lost object – the most important, most intimate part of oneself is precisely what the subject cannot unveil even to herself; hence, the absolute necessity of the fantasy. It is here "that the subject maintains his existence, maintains the veil that is such that he can continue to be a subject who speaks" (ibid., p. 94). Negation, the switch of pronouns, and the vanishing of the I, represent some of the grammatical sleights of hand available to the dreamer of Freud's dream at this crisis point.

It is of course true that the conjunction of a negatory narrative and the impossibility of the "I" was one of Freud's earliest discoveries about the unconscious insofar as it speaks. In *Studies on Hysteria* he recognizes that the memories encapsulating unconscious desire can only emerge as radically disowned. The subject will not approach this nexus with a widening sense of recognition, but will narrate and negate it in the same breath: "The deeper we go the more difficult it becomes for the emerging memories to be recognized, till near the nucleus we come upon memories which the patient disavows even in reproducing them" (Freud, 1895d, p. 289). A level of negatory insistence that even prompts Freud to query the representational status of this nucleus: "Are we to disregard this withholding of recognition on the part of patients [...] or are we to suppose that we really are dealing with thoughts that never came about, which merely had a possibility of existing [...]?" (ibid., p. 300). Here in Seminar VI a new existential weight tilts these insights towards a much starker vision freighted with the intensities of the Imaginary and shot through with flashes of poetry. The reader cannot but notice a very different vocabulary to that of Freud in the seminar. "The pain of existence", "intolerable concatenation", "fundamental anguish", "an evanescent pallid vanishing subject"; these phrases are repeated almost as in poetry with a cumulative force which insists that for every subject Hamlet's question "to be or not to be" may well be answered in the affirmative but is always marked by the same fragile equipoise as the question itself. And in the same space as this poetry, we the readers, are also repeatedly nailed down by graphs and algorithms, in particular the new algorithm $\$ \lozenge a$, the formula for fantasy, in which each of its elements keeps the others in balance.

An important new feature of Lacan's teaching, appearing briefly in lesson seventeen of the previous year's seminar on the formations of the unconscious and expanded on in this seminar is the situating of Freud's *Hilflosigheit* not just on the side of the subject, but also and irremediably, on the side of the big Other.

Lacan returns to this topic many times in the course of the seminar, but there are two places, one at the beginning in the course of the very first lesson in November 1958 and one towards the end of lesson twenty in May 1959 where he comes close to spelling it out in palpably existential terms. The first as mentioned above, is at the point of the "*Che vuoi?*" the absolute helplessness of the pre-subject vis-à-vis the demand/desire of the Other. The second addresses the moment when this little pre-subject encounters not so much her own helplessness, but the helplessness, or at least the radical impotence, of this big Other, which does not have at its disposal the necessary signifier which would guarantee or authenticate this little pre-subject in her existence. The big Other at this point, Lacan says, can only respond in the name of a common tragedy since there *is* no possible signifier which can guarantee the authenticity of the sequence of signifiers, and in fact it is at this impasse, this panic point as Lacan calls it that "that the subject brings in from elsewhere – namely from the imaginary register – a part of himself that is involved in the imaginary relationship to the other. This is little *a*" (ibid., p. 377). What might this object be? As mentioned above, at this early stage of its theorization, Lacan repeatedly reminds his listeners that it has the closest possible relation with narcissistic passion, and indeed he often vacillates in naming this essential support of the subject so that sometimes it is clearly o-object, and sometimes narcissistic eros, on occasion making one the core of the other. As Guy le Gaufey points out it is not for nothing that these two notations o and o-object are so similar, the second bearing witness to its origins in the first (le Gaufey, 2009, p. 27). In his ninth seminar *Identification* one will be the mask of the other, in his tenth seminar *Anxiety* one will be the lining of the other, and by then will be obliged to propose another form of imaginarization adequate to a seriously complexified theorization.

Here, however, it remains soldered to narcissistic passion so the outline of Freud's description of a crisis averted by "narcissistic interest" is not breached but has become electric and urgent, since as Lacan goes on to say here " object *a* is defined first of all as the prop that the subject gives himself [...] *inasmuch as he falters in his certainty as a subject*" (ibid., p. 366.). There is a very palpable sense of brink here. One cannot but note the crucial, one might almost say last-ditch, juncture at which this o-object intervenes and the manner in which it serves as both the point of stoppage and its index. "Any and all possibility of naming himself ends here" says Lacan (ibid., p. 378). "But at this terminus we also find the index [of desire] [...] this object is also what stops the subject from blacking out, from having his pure and simple existence wiped out" (ibid.). This, Lacan continues "is what constitutes the structure of what I call fantasy" (ibid). Two of its grammatical features are visible in this formulation. First a pronominal impasse: here the object is that which supports the subject in his very existence at the point where the "I" cannot say itself. Second, speaking of how desire sustains itself by means of this fundamental fantasy, Lacan says it is "no longer simply a question of the function of the object [...] nor is it the function of the subject [...]" but "the correlation between the two" (ibid., pp. 412–413).

So the subject of the unconscious is not to be found at either of the end terms, but is to be located in the interval, the between-space, and this inextricable interdependency is what will maintain what Lacan calls the fragile equilibrium of one's desire. Lacan's commentary on the dream of the dead father allows him to point to what one might expect to encounter when this equilibrium is disturbed and the essential fantasy is threatened with collapse. The pain of existence when desire is no longer there. There is nothing more intolerable, he insists, than existence reduced to itself, existence sustained in the abolition of desire (ibid., p. 96).

Thus we need a phantasmatic structure to shield us from the unbearable pain of existence when this existence subsists "beyond anything that can sustain it" (ibid., p. 96). Freud had of course described fantasy as "a protective structure" in his letters to Fliess (Freud, 1950a, p. 247). What is new here is the level of devastation which must not be known so that the speaking subject can perdure. In this first section of the seminar on desire, Lacan demonstrates how the dream manages to keep this minatory devastation at bay by way of the pronominal substitution that characterizes the fundamental fantasy since the whole nature of the fantasy to transfer it on to the object, this object being most often the human object (ibid., p. 107). In this way Lacan shows how the fantasy as a protective structure operates in a dream dreamed at the point where the subject is menaced by the real-life disappearance of the vital support of his subjective structure.

References

Beckett, S. (1959). *Trilogy*. London: Calder and Boyars.

Beckett, S. (1974). *Stories and Texts for Nothing*. London: Calder and Boyars.

Benveniste. E. (1971). *Problems in General Linguistics*. Miami: University of Miami Press.

Cazotte, J. (1772). *Le Diable Amoureux*. Project Gutenberg: eBook.

Derrida, J. (1978). *Writing and Difference*. (Trans.) Bass, A. Chicago: University of Chicago Press.

Duras, M. (1964). *Le Ravissement de Lol V. Stein*. (Trans.) Seaver, R. New York: Grove Press. (1986).

Ettinger, B. (2006). *The Matrixial Borderspace*. London and Minneapolis: University of Minneapolis Press.

Freud, S. (1895d). *Studies on Hysteria. S.E., II*.

Freud, S. (1900a). *The Interpretation of Dreams. S.E., V*.

Freud, S. (1911b). "Formulations on the Two Principles of Mental Functioning". *S.E., XII*. pp. 213–226.

Freud, S. (1926d). "Inhibitions, Symptoms and Anxiety". *S.E., XX*. pp. 75–176.

Freud, S. (1950a). "Extracts from the Fliess Papers". *S.E., I*. pp. 173–280.

Foucault, M. (1966). *Les Mots et les Choses*. Paris: Gallimard.

Jones, E. (1927). "The Early Development of Sexuality". *International Journal of Psychoanalysis*. Vol. 8, pp. 459–472.

Joyce, J. (1993). *Ulysses*. London. Penguin.

le Gaufey, G. (2009). *C'est a quel sujet?* Paris: Epel.

le Gaufey, G. (2012). *L'objet a: approches à l'invention de Lacan*. Paris: Epel.

Mallarmé, S. (2005). *A Tomb for Anatole*. (Trans.). Auster, P. New York: New Directions.

Roudinesco, E. (1900). *Jacques Lacan*. Chicago: Chicago University Press.

Lacan, J.:

Lacan, J. (2006). *Écrits. The First Complete Edition in English*. (Trans.) Fink, B. New York and London: W.W. Norton & Co.

The seminars:

——. (1956–1957), *The Seminar of Jacques Lacan Book IV: The Object Relation, 1956–1957*. (Trans.). Roche, L.V.A. Unpublished.

——. (1961–1962). *The Seminar of Jacques Lacan, Book IX, Identification*. (Trans.) Gallagher, C. Unpublished. www.lacaninireland.com

——. (1965–1966). *The Seminar of Jacques Lacan, Book XIII: The Object in Psychoanalysis*. (Trans.) Gallagher, C. Unpublished. www.lacaninireland.com

——. (1992). *The Ethics of Psychoanalysis. The Seminar of Jacques Lacan. Book VII. 1959–1960*. (Ed.) Miller, J.-A. (Trans.) Porter, D. London: Routledge.

——. (1993). *The Psychoses. The Seminar of Jacques Lacan. Book III. 1955–1956.* (Ed.) Miller, J.-A. (Trans.) Grigg, R. London: Routledge.

——. (2013) *Le Séminaire de Jacques Lacan, Livre XXIV.* L'insu qui sait de l'une-bevue, s'aile a mourre (1976–1977). (Trans.) Collins. D. Unpublished.

——. (2014). *Anxiety, The Seminar of Jacques Lacan, Book X. (Ed.).* Miller, J.-A. (Trans.) Price, A. Cambridge: Polity Press.

——. (2015). *Transference, The Seminar of Jacques Lacan, Book VIII.* (Ed.). Miller, J.-A. (Trans.) Fink B. Cambridge: Polity Press.

——. (2017). *Formations of the Unconscious, The Seminar of Jacques Lacan, Book V. (Ed.).* Miller, J.-A. (Trans.) Grigg. R. Cambridge: Polity Press.

——. (2019). *Desire and its Interpretation, The Seminar of Jacques Lacan, Book VI.* Miller, J.-A. (Trans.). Fink B. Cambridge. Polity Press. Also (Trans.) Gallagher, C. Unpublished. www.lacaninireland.com

Chapter 3

A master class in dream interpretation

Over the many years during which I have been teaching this seminar, most students found this section, the analysis of a dream already analyzed by Ella Freeman Sharpe, to be the easiest, while finding the section on *Hamlet* to be the most captivating. From the very beginning in lesson eight of what we are calling Section 2, the overall title of the seminar, *Desire and its Interpretation* is recalled, with the focus now on interpretation. "Since we spoke about desire quite a lot in the last few classes, we are now going to begin to broach the topic of interpretation" (Lacan, 2019, p. 133). In order to do this, Lacan presents a different version of the same coordinates in lessons eight to twelve from that of the earlier lessons, namely a father, a son, death, and desire. As we have seen, the early lessons offered an analysis of a dream as inserting a protective structure, dreamed at a moment when this protective edifice was under threat. Section 2 also focusses on the analysis of a dream, this time a dream illuminating the dreamer's subjective structure, what Lacan calls his "positional affects related to being" (ibid., p. 141). To do this, he makes use of a dream already analyzed by Ella Sharpe in her writings (Sharpe, 1937). Thus the reader will encounter the same dream analyzed in exhaustive detail by both Sharpe and Lacan, each making use of a different theoretical paradigm. This amounts to a master class in clinical psychoanalysis. Obviously, we will pay close attention to this master class, while recognizing that the real importance of this section is in its last lesson. Lesson twelve is altogether pivotal to the theoretical edifice being erected by Lacan throughout this seminar and will be subjected to a close and detailed reading. While once again deploying something of a snow-storm around the concept of the phallus, this lesson marks a new emphasis on being rather than having, repeating more than once that the subject both is and is not it (the phallus). Referring to a slippage in the verb to be this lesson picks up on and expands ideas first mooted in lesson thirteen of Seminar V, gesturing towards something much wider in scope than the classic understanding of the Oedipus complex (Lacan, 2017, p. 226), now described as resulting in "a subjective assumption that is inflected between being and having" (Lacan, 2019, p. 214).

Furthermore, "having" is no longer the tranquil possession envisaged in Seminar V (for a development of this critique, see Cox Cameron, 2019, also Part III in this volume). The subject now is "not without having it" a double negative instead of a positive attribution. The complexities adumbrated in this lesson will eventually be developed as the formulae for sexuation in his later work. In this lesson too the Saint Augustine story will be evoked with the new tragic resonance first seen in lesson thirteen of Seminar V (Lacan, 2017, p. 230). Over the next few years, more and more it will be seen to offer a kind of narrative equivalent of the algorithm for the fundamental fantasy $\$ \lozenge a$.

But first, the master class. While Lacan is famously scathing about much of the other psychoanalytic writing of his era, it has to be acknowledged that he was strikingly well versed in these writings, and his criticisms, while not always justified, are never superficial. The British school is very well represented in his work, and not just the big hitters like Klein, Anna Freud, and Winnicott, but also several interesting women analysts, among them Margaret Mahler, Barbara Low, and here in this seminar Ella Freeman Sharpe. A prolific writer and highly regarded training analyst, Ella Sharpe's interest in language and literature, evident in her many published papers on Shakespeare's plays as well as her work on metaphor would have brought her to Lacan's attention in what appears to be his constant scanning of newly published psychoanalytic works. And indeed he references her emphasis on metaphor here as being not discordant with his own thinking (Lacan, 2019, p. 203). Certainly, his admiration for her in this seminar is unusually unguarded, unusually unreserved. She is "one of the best analysts, one of the most intuitive and penetrating who ever lived" he tells his audience (ibid., p. 145). Her book, *Dream Analysis A Practical Handbook for Psychoanalysis*, first published in 1937 and still in print, was hailed as a sequel to Freud's *The Interpretation of Dreams*, no mean accolade, and it is the fifth chapter from this book that Lacan selects for his focus on interpretation. This focus ties in well with Sharpe's own purposes, since as she says at the outset of this chapter entitled "Analysis of a Single Dream", its aim is to test "whether one's interpretations are helping to bring the repressed and suppressed emotional attitudes, phantasies or affective memories to conscious understanding" (Sharpe, 1937, p. 125).

To a very large extent, Lacan will be entirely in agreement with Ella Sharpe in her interpretation of this dream. As he says, she has accurately identified all its essential elements, but has not quite understood how best to use them. Her occasional lapses, which are few, stem from sometimes relying on preformed theory, and sometimes extrapolating meanings which are not present at all in either the text or the associations to the dream. Reading these comments in the study group, we allowed ourselves to raise an eyebrow, and to murmur to each other about the kettle calling the pot black! Just as Sharpe's "boring and biting penis" does not appear anywhere in the analysand's discourse, Lacan's "prolapsed vagina", repeated four times, also seems something of an interloper. But back to the matter in hand.

Lacan begins this master class with some remarks about *The Interpretation of Dreams* that solder Freud's project to his own. The first point to be made is Freud's emphasis on those elements in the narrative of the dream that reveal the enunciating subject, in particular, the dreamer's vagueness or her propensity to distance herself from bits of the dream. So doubt, indirect reportage of someone else's words, and riddles, enigmas all herald the enunciating subject. Doubt in fact is to read as the colophon of certainty: "I insist that the whole scale of estimates of certainty shall be abandoned, and that the faintest possibility that something of this or that sort may have occurred shall be treated as complete certainty" (Freud, 1900a, p. 516). Straight Freud then, and a point made repeatedly in *The Interpretation of Dreams*, but also clearly in line with Lacan's importation of contemporary linguistics into psychoanalytic theory. Benveniste makes exactly the same point when he isolates phrases like "I think", "I feel", "I believe" as the indices of enunciating – the phrases by which the enunciation is appropriated, owned by the speaker. Hard not to glance fleetingly at *Finnegans Wake* in this context, awash as this great book of the dream is with riddles and uncertainty, where the narrator vanishes continually into "plurible numbers" (Joyce, 1975, p. 290) and one of the recurrent dilemmas of the book is "to me or not to me. Satis thy quest on" (ibid., 269). So the enunciating subject can be traced directly to Freud himself. As can the fragmented signifying chain that specifies unconscious discourse which is the second point Lacan makes in these introductory remarks. Lacan speaks of the signifying chain as having two aspects, holophrastic and fragmented, meaning presumably that our ordinary discourse is relatively coherent, keeping repressed knowledge at bay, but free association tries to access its fragmented underlay, in which resides what is "beyond the subject – that is to say, the Freudian unconscious" (Lacan, 2019, p. 139). Freud is at pains to show that the often reasonably coherent "story" of the dream is generally speaking, a façade, which while sometimes in itself significant, is mostly a jumble of fragments, "jammed together almost like pack-ice" (Freud, ibid., p. 312). What he calls "this conglomerate", must "for purposes of investigation, be broken up once more into fragments" therefore free association and interpretation are to be brought to bear on each of these fragments (Freud, ibid., p. 449). As readers of *The Interpretation of Dreams* cannot help noticing, Freud is frequently caught between his nineteenth-century drive towards complete elucidation and the solving of all mystery, and his Copernican realization that hints of truth are more likely to reside in meaningless fragments that refuse to add up, and that the pursuit of meaning in the dream eventually runs underground into an indecipherable and impregnable tangle like the mycelium under the mushroom. When contemporary psychoanalysts speak of the Real unconscious, associated with *lalangue*, one cannot but wonder if it is all that different to Freud's meaningless heap of fragments; "*lalangue* appears as the vast reserve from which deciphering extracts only fragments […] the *lalangue*-unconscious remains as an impregnable knowledge whose effects exceed us" (Soler, 2014,

p. 23). Here in this lesson Lacan impressively solders what he has been saying about the fragmented signifying chain to classic Freud.

Third, in a very important footnote in Chapter 7 Freud warns his readers of the complexity that interpretation will entail. While initially it was hard to get people to recognize the distinction between the manifest and latent content of dreams, many analysts have now fallen into another confusion "by seeking to find the essence of dreams in their latent content" (Freud, ibid., p. 506). The dream work, that which turns one into the other, and as such a truly mysterious process, is, Freud insists, "the essence of dreaming" (ibid., p. 507). This footnote is more momentous than perhaps Freud himself realized since it changes the question "*What* does it mean?" into the much more sophisticated "*How* does it mean?" with its focus on the intermediate space in which one layer is transformed into the other. And for Lacan too, it is the between-space that solicits his attention.

> The restoring of the meaning of the fantasy – that is, of something that is imaginary – is inscribed on the graph between the two lines: between the statement of the subject's intention, on the one hand, and the enunciation in which the subject reads his intention in a profoundly decomposed, fragmented, and refracted form through spoken language [*langue*], on the other. Fantasy – in which the subject usually suspends his relationship to being – is always enigmatic, more enigmatic than anything else.
>
> (Lacan, 2019, p. 140)

As referenced above, the "between" will be a major preoccupation in Lacan's work, and a major player in the process of "desubstantiation" also referenced above. In his ninth seminar *Identification* he will describe the subject "who is only of course the subject of discourse" as

> in some way torn away from its vital immanence, condemned to fly on high, to live in this sort of mirage which flows from this redoubling, which ensures that he not only speaks everything that he lives, but that he experiences living being by speaking it and that already what he is living is inscribed in an Epos, a Saga woven right throughout his act.
>
> (Lacan, 1961–1962, lesson of 20 December 1961, p. 2)

Here in this seminar the between is the location of the fantasy; "[F]antasy finds its place on the graph of desire halfway between the signifier of the barred Other, S($\bar{A}$), and the signified of the Other s(A)" (Lacan, 2019, p. 181). At several different moments in this seminar Lacan makes a number of remarks which may throw light on the above rather enigmatic definition. Perhaps the most concrete example occurs when he speaks of need passing through the demands of the signifier, and emphasizes not demand itself but what the baby will become by virtue of this demand, a much more thought-provoking observation. Need will pass through signifiers such as "bold", "good", "tired", "impossible", and what Lacan repeatedly says is that

> There is a gap between the purely and simply *interrogative* language of demand, on the one hand, and the language with which the subject answers the question of what he wants and constitutes himself in relation to what he is, on the other. It is in this gap that what is known as desire arises.
>
> (Lacan, ibid., p. 172)

Difficult and abstract statements, but the real-life picture profiled behind them of the intense emotional space created between a given (m)other and a given baby, is much more nuanced than a lot of other attachment theories.

The last point Lacan makes in his introductory remarks to the Ella Sharpe dream concerns the importance of the points of rupture in the dreamer's account of her dream. A few years earlier in Seminar II Lacan had produced a brilliant commentary on Freud's dream of Irma's injection, relying largely on the places in Freud's own narrative where the story either breaks off or fades out. As he says here in this preamble, it is in the points of rupture that there lies the thing psychoanalysis is tracking down; the essential thing that has happened to the subject that keeps certain signifiers in repression (ibid., p. 140). This preamble to the dream in hand is a brilliant endorsement of Lacan's description of himself as a reader of Freud, a description which will fit less snugly as the years go by and his departures become more clear-cut. Early indications of these departures will be discussed in the final section of this commentary.

And so to the dream. For us as readers it is important to realize that we are just playing here. We will be looking at the dream with the help of two different theoretical paradigms, and we will be throwing in our own observations, maybe even insights, but it is all just play. We are not in the presence of the dreamer and are not caught in the same transferential vortices that would then occur. However this is how a masterclass works. We are learning to listen, to become more alert to where and how the unconscious speaks. The dream selected by Lacan is particularly useful in this respect as it is not simply the analysis of a given dream but one that Sharpe has very cogently situated at a particular moment in an analysis, even pinpointing the exact place it surfaces in the dreamer's associations in the session. Since we will now be working with two texts in hand – Sharpe's analysis and Lacan's commentary – it seems best to specifically reference each in what follows except when glaringly obvious.

Both theorists set out their stall from the start. Sharpe announces her extremely nuanced exposition as explicitly Kleinian in its goal;

> the task of analysis is to reduce the fear of the aggressive wishes experienced in his first three years. The terror of the aggressive wish and its phantastic

consequences will be modified only by bringing this wish to consciousness, and only so will the libidinal wishes not continue to mean death.

(Sharpe, 1937, p. 128)

Lacan, keeping his earlier promise to engage with affect sees the analytic project
as that of interpreting desire, defined as follows; "To interpret desire is to restore
something to which the subject cannot gain access by himself – namely, the
affect [...]" (Lacan, ibid., p. 140) which he goes on to specify as the positional
affects related to being (ibid., p. 141). A definition worth pausing over. What
are the core feelings that dictate the basic stances of my being? How do they
mark my work, my love-life, all my relationships with the other? Since a very
usual criticism of Lacan is that he is too intellectualist and ignores affect, this
definition is worth highlighting in its forthrightness and its clarity. Affect "is not
something that is purely and simply opaque and closed off, not something that
is somehow beyond discourse or a nucleus of lived experience that comes to us
out of the blue", he says bluntly, but rather it is "something that is always and
very precisely connoted by a certain stance the subject adopts with respect to
being" (ibid., p. 141). These positional affects are tangled in repressed signifiers,
the restoration of which will lead not to the primordial demand of the subject
but to a discovery of who he has become in the function of that demand. This
will be very brilliantly demonstrated in the commentary which follows.

Once again we are confronted with a father, a son, death, and desire. The
dreamer in question has been in analysis for three years and the first thing
Sharpe tells us is that his father had died when he was three years old, and that
in all his remarks about this father, it is always and only his deadness that is
referenced. So much so that the patient is startled one day when he realizes that
this father must also have been alive, and even that he, the patient, must have
heard him speak. The patient replicates this deadness in his symptoms, and also
to a notable degree in his demeanour in the analytic session. Sharpe paints a
vivid picture. Unlike other patients who stumble or thunder up the stairs to her
room, and when there, cautiously or carelessly approach the couch, she never
hears this patient on the stairs. His behaviour on arrival never varies.

He always gets on the couch one way. He always gives a conventional
greeting with the same smile, a pleasant smile, not forced or manifestly
covering hostile impulses. There is never anything as revealing as that
would be. There is no sign of hurry, nothing haphazard, no clothes awry;
no marks of a quick toilet; no hair out of place. The maid at home may
have been late, his breakfast delayed, but these facts if I am lucky I may hear
before the hour is over, and often I may hear them only the next day. He
lies down and makes himself easy. He puts one hand over the other across
his chest. He lies like that until the hour is over.

(Sharpe, ibid., p. 130)

Sharpe and Lacan are in agreement in seeing this dead perfection as obsessional. They also agree that what has been rendered problematic for this patient has to do with potency, and this point of agreement also marks where they will diverge. For Sharpe, this patient has become dead, and has no access to his own potency in function of his father's dying words: "Robert must take my place", entailing a repression of unconscious aggressive fantasy towards this father. For Lacan this has to do with the role of the phallus, and the perceived necessity of protecting it by keeping it safely out of the game.

Like a good novel Sharpe's narrative begins at the point where a tiny infraction occurs in this deadly sameness. The patient coughs on the stairs. Even Jane Austen might have chosen a more impactful event with which to cut into a continuum with the start of a story, but as the patient's chain of associations goes on to demonstrate, this is indeed a significant happening, a harbinger as Lacan calls it, announcing that somewhere behind all that dead perfection, feelings are still alive.

As analysts know, it is all but impossible to replicate what actually happens in an analytic session, so we are fortunate in the almost word for word transcription leading up to this dream. A striking feature in this session is the insistence with which the analysand draws the analyst's attention to certain phenomena that occur both in the associations to the dream and in the session. Given Freud's recognition that the unconscious tends to mask itself in doubt, negation, and enigma, this repeated insistence is interesting, and aroused a certain amount of suspicion in our study group. Why would this man whose *modus operandi* seems always to involve a not being there, insistently signal certain given elements? Doesn't Nietzsche ask somewhere: what is it we hide when we set out to show?

The first thing that happens in this session is that the patient draws attention to the little cough he has given lately just before entering the room, and to how much the fact that it is involuntary annoys him. Sharpe proceeds with caution to elicit his associations, and what follows is a whole series of memories in which the cough functioned as a way of announcing his presence, and also more bizarrely, his absence.

> when, for example, I was a lad of fifteen and my brother was with his girl in the drawing-room I would cough before I went in so that if they were embracing they could stop before I got in. They would not then feel as embarrassed as if I had caught them doing it.
>
> (Lacan, ibid., p. 157; Sharpe, ibid., p. 131)

Ella Sharpe is cautious:

ANALYST. And why cough before coming in here?
PATIENT. That is absurd because naturally I should not be asked to come up if someone were here, and I do not think of you in that way at all. There

is no need for a cough at all that I can see. It has however reminded me of a phantasy I had of being in a room where I ought not to be, and thinking someone might think I was there, and then I thought to prevent anyone from coming in and finding me there I would bark like a dog. That would disguise my presence. The someone would say; Oh it's only a dog in there.

ANALYST. A dog?

PATIENT. That reminds me of a dog rubbing himself against my leg, really masturbating himself. I'm ashamed to tell you because I did not stop him. I let him go on and someone might have come in. The patient then coughed.

(Sharpe, ibid., p. 131)

Clearly something must not be there – either the sexual activity in the room or himself in so far as either his presence is transgressive (he shouldn't be in that room) or what he is up to is transgressive – letting the dog masturbate against his leg. Lacan recognizes the message in these fantasies as "there is nobody here" but immediately hones it analytically to – in what sense and how is he *not* a person – and with whom? The ludicrousness of barking like a dog to announce "there is nobody here" allows Lacan to make a useful observation. Just as Freud had signalled absurdity in dreams as significant, Lacan recognizes here that where the feelings are sufficiently strong, something completely absurd, including a fantasy, can be asserted with absolute conviction. Were he alive today Lacan might gesture towards the imperialist posturing of high Tory Brexiteers as a good example of a discourse which is not in "the realm of the comprehensible, but of imaginary structure", the apparent continuity of which is "a law; the less affects have an explainable cause [*sont motivés*], the more understandable they appear to the subject" (Lacan, ibid., p. 162). It is immediately after this run of associations culminating in the fantasy of himself barking like a dog in order to signify his absence, and the sexual memory the bark sets out to conceal, that the patient again coughs, and announces himself as surprised at this point to remember last night's dream. "I do not know why I should now think of my dream last night" (Sharpe, ibid., p. 132). Again as readers we note the curious fact that he draws the analyst's attention to this timing, to the moment in the sequence of associations that the dream comes to mind.

Lacan does not make much of this. Having read the dream to his audience, he is still much taken by the associative lead-in, the memories and fantasies which brought it to mind, and the patient's question to himself and to his analyst about the involuntary cough. This question signals a recognition in the analysand of unconscious activity, translated by Lacan as: "But what does this Other want?" (Lacan, ibid., p. 159). A second degree message Lacan says, since the patient is signalling this question to the analyst and not just putting it to himself. To a very great extent it is in this associative lead-in that Lacan will find much of the material for his own analysis of the positional affects of this subject with respect to being (ibid., p. 141). Indeed while Lacan's ostensible focus in this section of the seminar is on the dream analyzed by Sharpe, he in fact devotes a very considerable part of his commentary to both the conscious and unconscious fantasies of the patient that usher in this dream. So although he reads out the dream to his audience in the very first lesson of this section of the seminar (Lacan, 2019, lesson eight), he then goes on to devote most of the next two hours to the introductory fantasy and to the patient's cough, and does not return to the dream until a fortnight later. But when he does begin to seriously engage with the dream in lesson ten, we realize why the cough has been such a repeated reference in his commentary up to now. That cough is where it's at, in that it offers an instance of the fundamental fantasy, with the barred subject in some kind of confrontation with the object. The barred subject is the dreamer who can only appear in the guise of absence or as other than who he is (a dog barking). The insistence with which this patient situates himself as not there in these fantasies does indeed open on to this new conception of the fundamental fantasy, defined here as "the subject insofar as he vanishes in a certain relationship to his elective object" (ibid., p. 173). The fantasy, he goes on to say, always has this structure; it is never simply a relation between subject and object. In the first section of the seminar, Lacan had underlined the role of this object in supporting the subject at certain crucial points where he encounters desire since as he put it then: "desire as such, raises for man the question of his subjective elision, $, with regard to any and every possible object" (ibid., p. 116). Commenting on this patient's non-presence in the fantasies he recounts, Lacan amplifies this earlier statement: "It is something that cuts. It implies a certain vanishing or signifying blacking out [*syncope*] of the subject in the presence of an object" (ibid., p. 173).

The object turns out to be who Ella Sharpe is in the transference, or as Lacan specifies, more accurately, his relationship with "what is found in the room" (ibid., p. 176). This assertion stands up to scrutiny given the patient's denegation: "I do not think of you in that way at all" followed immediately by the account of his fear of discovery in the room with the masturbating dog (Sharpe, ibid., p. 131). "What is veiled is the right hand side of the formula for fantasy, the object, x. This object is not, I would say, his analyst, but what is found in the room" (Lacan, ibid., p. 176). It is the dream that will reveal more fully who Ella Sharpe is in the transference. The transference is imaginary, specular, and the analyst insofar as she is the image of him is in the process of doing what? Dreaming of masturbating, just as he had been doing. The analysand's comment on the intransitivity of the verb Lacan now says, is enough to put us on the track of the signifying phantasy that is in question; the belief that potency as such will be on the side of the other. Ella Sharpe is potent, she can do it, and is masturbating in her room while the subject's own only access to potency brings about his disappearance.

Not a lot has been written psychoanalytically about conscious fantasy, so it is interesting to see Lacan finding in this dreamer's remembered fantasies the lineaments of what he is in the process of developing this year, which he will call the fundamental fantasy. In Lacan's view, the non-presence of this subject in the fantasy, is in fact a prelude to the dream.

So in Ella Sharpe's account, having drawn the analyst's attention to the moment in the session when this dream came to mind, the dreamer recounts it, splicing it from the start with his fluent and prolific associations. Ella Sharpe reproduces this dual text, varying the typeface so that the associations are clearly discernible:

> *I dreamt I was taking a journey with my wife around the world, and we arrived in Czechoslovakia where all kinds of things were happening. I met a woman on a road, a road that now reminds me of the road I described to you in the two other dreams lately in which I was having sexual play with a woman in front of another woman.* So it happened in this dream. *This time my wife was there while the sexual event occurred. The woman I met was very passionate looking* and I am reminded of a woman I saw in a restaurant yesterday. She was dark and had very full lips, very red and passionate looking, and it was obvious that had I given her any encouragement she would have responded. She must have stimulated the dream, I expect. In the dream the *woman wanted intercourse with me and she took the initiative which as you know is a course which helps me a great deal.* If the woman will do this I am greatly helped. In the dream *the woman actually lay on top of me; that has only just come to my mind. She was evidently intending to put my penis in her body. I could tell that by the manoeuvres she was making. I disagreed with this but she was so disappointed I thought I would masturbate her.*
>
> It sounds quite wrong to use that verb transitively. One can say "I masturbated" and that is correct but it is all wrong to use the word transitively.
>
> (Lacan, ibid., pp. 143–144; Sharpe, ibid., p. 132)

ANALYST. To use the verb transitively is all wrong?
PATIENT. I see what you mean. It is true that I have only masturbated myself.
ANALYST. Only?
PATIENT. I only remember masturbating another boy once and I forget all the details and I feel shy about mentioning it. That is the only time I can remember. The dream is in my mind vividly. There was no orgasm. I remember her vagina gripped my finger. I see the front of her genitals, the end of the vulva. Something large and projecting hung downwards like a fold on a hood. Hoodlike it was, and it was this that the woman made use of in manoeuvring to get my penis, The vagina seemed to close around my finger. The hood seemed strange.

> (Sharpe, ibid., p. 133; latter fragment from
> patient in Lacan, ibid., p. 177)

So here we have the narrative of the dream.

As Oscar Wilde famously remarked of Wordsworth, he found under stones the sermons he had already hidden there, a remark that should be framed on the wall of every psychoanalyst's consulting room, alerting us to the ever-present danger of doing just that. Lacan commences his commentary on the dream with precisely this warning, asking:

> [S]hould we immediately reduce it to a series of time-tested, preformed significations? Should we place behind this image everything we are used to finding there, having put it there ourselves, as if we were pulling it out of a magician's hat?
>
> (Lacan, ibid., p. 179)

Or should we rather attend to the specificities of what is being said? Neither analyst entirely avoids these pitfalls, something that should alert us to our own proclivities.

Both analysts immediately focus on the dreamer's grammatical gloss on the non-transitivity of the verb "to masturbate" and are in agreement on interpreting the dream as a masturbation phantasy. Both also recognize it to be a dream about potency. For Sharpe, working within the Kleinian paradigm potency is lodged in the fantasied omnipotence of the baby, for Lacan in the equally fantasied omnipotence of the mother. Also for Klein the life-drives function in dangerous proximity to aggression. Sharpe's interpretation then will read the hidden desire in this dream in the sense of aggressive conflict. This patient's dread of his own aggression means that he has to play dead. Lacan is interested in the "positional affects" of this client's being, his need to keep what is most precious to him safely out of the game. He had made a very similar observation in the first section of the seminar, when giving an example of how the miser relates to the o-object by hiding it, never putting it at risk. As Lacan develops his commentary, it is difficult not to find his reading to be the more persuasive of the two, but we should not lose sight of the extraordinary effect of Sharpe's interpretation on the patient, ultimately more impressive perhaps than our purely theoretical musings.

Sharpe's skill is obvious to the reader. She tells us that she is as monosyllabic and minimalist as possible in her interventions, because just as in the dream the woman took the initiative, in real life this is what the patient tries to recreate in the transference. Both analysts are greatly taken by the dreamer's highlighting of one element in the dream – the hood-like vulva and its attendant associations. Indeed a most striking feature of the narrative of the dream is the persistence with which the dreamer draws the analyst's attention to this hood. Not only does he mention it a total of eight times, but three of these mentions are direct pointers making sure the analyst is alerted to its reappearance. So after referring to a joke about labia, lips, and Chinese writing, he states: "I'm still thinking about the hood" (Sharpe, ibid., p. 134). A little further on, talking about a car hood, he gestures to what he has just said: "that's motor hood again you see" (ibid., p. 135), and a few sentences later, now remembering urinating into a paper bag as a child, he again reminds the analyst: "Still I think of the hood" (ibid., p. 135).

The associations to this hood take him to the childhood memory of another compulsive act (like the cough) when he used to cut up the straps of his sister's sandals, and again he registers displeasure at having been at the mercy of a compulsion, but goes on to think of the straps in a pram and his temptation to say they had no pram, when of course they must have had, leading him to his recent omission to send out letters, and this undone thing reminding him in turn of his undone fly. As mentioned above, while both analysts pick up on the theme of potency, this is also where they begin to diverge. Sharpe sees the fantasy of omnipotence in the enormity of the dream, "the longest he has ever had", full of excitement and interest (ibid., p. 132). Omnipotence too in its scope. He is travelling around the world, in Sharpe's words "dreaming of encompassing mother earth, of being adequate to the huge cave beneath the protruding lips" (ibid., p. 139). Lacan sees this as a leap, a step taken too quickly, not warranted in what is said, too mired in psychoanalytic cliché. Where Sharpe sees the dreamer inflating his world with gestures of omnipotence, Lacan sees the exact opposite process. The dreamer announces the dream as immense, long, exciting, "full of incident", and then shrinks it down to a small remembered fragment having forgotten the rest (Lacan, 2019, p. 183). And where he could have exercised his potency, he only puts his finger. In Lacan's view this subject is concerned always with making himself small, and far from feeling omnipotent he locates omnipotence always on the side of the other (Lacan, ibid., p. 185).

Sharpe is explicit about directing her interpretation of this dream in light of what she sees as the patient's need, "namely his fear of aggressive bodily movements", and at a certain point in this process she lets us see how she streamlined this interpretation:

> After this I correlated the associations made to aggression and deduced that he had wished to prevent any more children being born; because there had been no more children born after him his aggressive phantasy of omnipotence had been reinforced by this fact, and thus further enhanced his dread of his mother, as a revenging person. I then affirmed my conviction of his actual sight of his mother's genitals and the projection onto them of revenge phantasies which were to be correlated with the phantasies of aggression associated with his own penis as a biting and boring thing and with the power of his water. All this I said was the significance of the masturbation which the dream represented.
>
> (Sharpe, ibid., pp. 145–146)

For Lacan, despite his admiration, this is a tunnel within which the thinking of the analyst is engaged. These interpretations, he remarks, are extremely active, even brutal, suggesting that the root of the question is the aggressive character of his own penis (Lacan, 2019, p. 187). Lacan's focus on the contrary is locked to the theme of this seminar: "where does the question arise in what one might call the patient's fundamental fantasy, inasmuch as it is rendered present in the transference?" (ibid., p. 188).

While it is hard not to be dismayed by Sharpe's summary which certainly looks as if an interesting and complex run of associations has been shepherded into a turgid clump of Kleinian cliché, it is worth trying to distinguish the plausible elements from the riskier inferences. She actually does this herself though perhaps without quite realizing it, in the very notable number of times she uses the verbs "deduce", "infer", "justified", in introducing certain classic psychoanalytic conclusions. At her best, her literary background guides her. She is well aware of the significance of sequence, so her recognition that behind the dream is a masturbation phantasy is largely based on the exact moment in the session in which it is remembered (immediately after the phantasy of the dog masturbating).

Also interestingly she doesn't pluck the theme of aggression out of nowhere but in doing so, is guided by the sequence of the dreamer's associations; namely the straps of his sister's sandals that he compulsively cut up, the straps of a pram, and his refusal to think there was a pram, then that there had been two other children before him, and finally at that point he remembered that he had forgotten to send tickets to two new members of the Club (Sharpe, ibid., p. 142). The word "undone" leads to the memory of leaving his fly undone, allowing Sharpe to include the penis here: "taken in its setting in the sequence of references first to aggressiveness by the cutting, then to not sending tickets, the penis is unconsciously associated with phantasies of aggression" (ibid., p. 143).

Sharpe's attention to the sequencing of associations is indeed interesting and instructive, even if read to some extent in the light of pre-existing theory. She is at her best here, and it is worth noting that in all the instances where Lacan accuses her of unwarranted leaps, she prefaces them with verbs denoting some small degree of reservation, and as Benveniste would say, indicating the presence of the enunciating subject. To give a brief example of the frequency of this occurrence:

> I *should deduce* that the memory of the actual cave which he visited with his mother also acts as a cover memory. *I would deduce* that there is projected onto the motor with its scarlet lined hood this same forgotten memory and that the peak of speed has the same significance as the projection in the genitals in the dream – it is the peak of the hood. *I infer* there is an actual repressed memory of seeing the genitals of someone much older than himself; of seeing them when he was very tiny and *I infer* this from both the car and the cave and going round the world in conjunction with the immense potency required. The peak, the hood, *I interpret* as the clitoris.
>
> (Sharpe, ibid., p. 140, italics mine)

While it is easy to demonstrate the omnipresence of these verbs in the case Sharpe is building, and to assume that by their presence there is a tacit recognition that what they point to does not actually feature in the patient's discourse, it is a lot less easy to explain away the galvanizing effect of these interpretations on the patient. Two days later, this highly inhibited "dead" man for the first time ever, expresses desire: he doesn't need his car as such but he wants it, he likes it. Sharpe knows exactly what she is hearing: "Here at last libidinal desire was expressed" (ibid. p. 147). The following night and rather astonishingly, the patient wets his bed, bringing the penis into play certainly, but how? And a week later, on the tennis court, being teased by an opponent for playing badly, this rigidly controlled man grabs his opponent around the neck in a playful stranglehold and warns him never to tease him again. So as we turn to Lacan's rectifications of Sharpe's analysis, we need to keep before us this result, sturdily standing in the way of complete dismissal.

Endorsing Sharpe's interpretation of this dream as a masturbation fantasy, and her recognition that the theme of potency is a central one, Lacan almost immediately inserts a discriminatory knife into the Kleinian paradigm, pointing out the inadvisability of suggesting to this patient who has structured every subjective affirmation along the lines of not being present, that what he wants is to kill his counterpart (Lacan, ibid., pp. 161–162). He then very cautiously sifts through Sharpe's observations, repeatedly drawing attention to his own caution. He sets aside her (momentary) equation of the projecting hood with a penis, "possible but why be in a rush?" he says (ibid., p. 179). His own guess that the hood looks more like a prolapse is also set aside: "that's not it", although this is an image he nonetheless continues to invoke as the commentary goes on. Similarly, the phallic mother is "not in the dream", nor is there any hint of the mother's genitals seen from below, "we are not at that point just yet" (ibid., p. 180). In eliminating all of these possibilities Lacan nonetheless suggests that it is "not invalid" to consider the imaginary associations to the mother's womb entrenched in ethology, folklore, and psychology. And then he carefully homes in on the dreamer's image of inserting his finger in the woman's vagina, adding in elements of dread and fright, which it must be said, are not present in the dream text. "It is something that already has a certain structure, that covers, that crowns, and that is also feared. The finger introduced into this sexual, vaginal element, which seems to "close round" it, gives us a very precise image" (ibid., p. 178). One is reminded here again of Lacan's stellar reading of Freud's Irma dream in Seminar II where the horror evoked appears to be very much Lacan's and is not to be found in Freud's dry phraseology. Lacan describes Freud examining Irma's throat as the first break in the dream leading to

> the apparition of the terrifying anxiety-provoking image, to this real Medusa's head, to the revelation of this something which is properly speaking unnameable [...] the primitive object par excellence, the abyss of the female sexual organ from which all life emerges.
>
> (Lacan, 1988b, p. 164)

Here for Lacan, the image of the dreamer putting his finger in the woman's vagina is enough to put us on the track of one of the keys to the meaning of the dream, the signifying phantasy that is in question which is the close link between a male and a female element expressed in a sort of enveloping. For Lacan this is who this subject is: "It is in relation to this image that he situates his desire. It is there that his desire is in some sense stuck" (Lacan, 2019, p. 189). This central image is in the first instance a sheath, a glove, in fact a vagina. Lacan underlines this point by stating that etymologically both words are identical: "[t]he fundamental image presented in the dream is that of a sort of glove or sheath turned inside out. Sheath and vagina are, moreover, the same words: *gaine* [sheath] is the same word as *vagin* [vagina]" (ibid., p. 188).

The textual progress of Lacan's argument is worth noting. Having carefully sifted through and set aside other possibilities, this then, this relationship of enveloping, is what he surprises his listeners by marking as the element we should look to in order to engage with the dream work, rather cleverly adding status to this statement by making use of Freud's term *Traumarbeit* (Freud, 1900a, p. 506).

At first glance this does not seem all that convincing although the evidence Lacan will eventually adduce in its favour will be impressive. For now he feels the need to do a little more to justify it, and he reminds his listeners of the dreamer's dread of his car breaking down on a road along which the King and Queen were due to travel, thus blocking them. While Sharpe had seen this as further evidence of the omnipotence dreaded by the subject for himself, Lacan focuses on the shelter afforded him by his car where he is protected "having the same characteristic as the cave's cover" (ibid., p. 189). The link between this and feminization is forged with a considerable degree of opaqueness at the end of lesson ten. When the dreamer early on in his associations, talks of the motor hood he recalls that it was strapped back and further on is reminded of the straps which harness a child in the pram. This allowed Sharpe to deduce some restriction to prevent masturbation, and now, after all Lacan's caveats about readymade theories, here he launches into just such a similarly clichéd supposition, that of the enjoyment of the child "urinating" in proximity to parental coitus (ibid., p. 190). That this should feminize him, however, does not appear self-evident. At that moment he becomes what, Lacan asks, and answers by describing what he calls a game of hide and seek. He becomes

> the female partner about whom he tells us that she has such a need for him that he must show her [how to do] everything, and that he must do everything, becoming feminised in the process. Insofar as he is impotent, as it were, he is male. And it is clear that this brings him some compensation at the level of his ambition to garner power. But inasmuch as he is liberated, he is feminized.
>
> (ibid., p. 190)

For Lacan, this is where the analysand's problem lies, in this non-separation of the two aspects in him of masculinity and femininity. We shall see.

Much more immediately convincing, even brilliantly so, is the manner in which he reads in the dream and its associations, evidence of the exact same subject position he had discerned in the phantasies of this patient. Ernest Jones' word "aphanisis" introduced earlier in the seminar is now invoked again, but in a sense that differs from that of Jones. As we will see too it also differs somewhat from its earlier meaning in the first section in its focus on "making disappear".

> what we see at every moment and what constantly returns as a theme or leitmotif in the patient's remarks brings to mind the term "aphanisis" – except that its meaning here seems more like "to make disappear" than "to disappear". There is a perpetual game here in which we sense that, in various forms, something that I will call, if you will, the interesting object is never there.
>
> (Lacan, ibid., p. 195)

The elusiveness and non-presence which had characterized the subject has now migrated to the object. In his associations to this dream, the dreamer, Lacan points out, "never puts anything out there without immediately, in some way, taking the essential part of it back" (ibid., pp. 195–196). One assumes that this was what Lacan meant at the end of lesson nine when he suggested that what the dream put forward runs counter to the patient's fantasy (ibid., p. 170). Lacan lists the quite numerous instances of this in the dreamer's associations. In the dream we are in the presence of three characters because it must not be forgotten that his wife is there. Once the subject has said it he does not speak about it anymore. Then the hood which Lacan sees as the feminine sexual organ (and is not driven like Sharpe, to make of it a penis), leads the dreamer to remember a clever friend and to immediately berate himself for swanking because this friend is well known, just as he might swank by boasting about his great wireless. As Lacan says he uses these details to feel guilty about swanking: "In sum, he does not want to take up too much space" (ibid., p. 195). Same thing a little further on with the pram. He thinks there was no pram in his family, though obviously there must have been one since there were two children older than him. "The same style dominates all of the patient's associations: one thing appears in the form of something else that is missing" (ibid., p. 200). One cannot but be impressed by the astuteness and attentiveness of Lacan's reading here. Sharpe had highlighted the importance for the analyst of noting the sequence in which associations occur. Straight after the unremembered pram, there is another unremembered image, that of his father in his invalid chair, something neither analyst pursues and this is followed by a sequence, Lacan's reading of which brilliantly endorses what he has just said about aphanisis.

> I've suddenly remembered I meant to send off letters admitting two members to the Club. I boasted of being a better secretary than the last and yet here I am forgetting to give people permission to enter the club.

> Ah well. We have undone those things we ought to have done and there is no good thing in us.
>
> (Sharpe, ibid., pp. 135–136)

This is the exact same sequencing from which Sharpe deduced the dreamer's aggressive phantasy, so here we have the juxtaposition of two entirely different readings of what is the same text, the collision of two very different psychoanalytic interpretations. It is hard not to lean in Lacan's direction, particularly as he actually goes to the trouble of tracking down the dreamer's citation from *The Book of Common Prayer* and demonstrates how the dreamer's misquote is a further instance of the aphanisis which Lacan sees as central here. A truly impressive piece of sleuthing! The correct citation is "we have left undone the things we ought to have done" and not the dreamer's "we have undone the things [...]". Also Lacan suggests, the rest of that confession in *The Book of Common Prayer* – "and we have done those things we ought not to have done" is omitted by the dreamer, since for him: "[D]oing things" Lacan observes, "is not his thing" (Lacan, ibid., p. 201). As Ella Sharpe had pointed out, the patient's symptomatic incapacity with respect to action stemmed from his fear of being too successful. The misquoted version of the end of this citation – "and there is no good thing in us" instead of the correct "and there is no health in us", permits Lacan to make a rather touching though not entirely implausible little leap of his own; "the good object is not there. This is truly what is involved. He confirms once again for us that what is at stake is the phallus" (Lacan, ibid., p. 201).

But the evidence accumulated about something not being there is very convincing. "Never there", "never where you might expect it", "never quite what presents itself", as Lacan repeatedly points out. Even the golf bag will be a covering made out of another covering which is the motor hood. As Lacan says we find ourselves faced with a sort of slipping away: "Another one will follow [...]" (ibid., p. 200). And of course instead of a penis in the dream, there is a finger. Throughout lesson eleven, examples of this non-presence pile up, counterpointed by the repeated questions; "where is the penis?", "where is the phallus?", all converging on a wonderful Hercule Poirot moment. (We are after all in 1959). It turns out that the dreamer's potency, the phallus "is, in the dream, represented quite simply by the person who would seem least likely to represent it – namely his wife" (ibid., p. 205). And just as when Poirot zeroed in on the least likely suspect, the reader here cannot but be impressed. Lacan makes a very good case though it is fair to suggest a margin for those who will not be convinced by it.

In keeping with the generalized position in psychoanalytic theory, female power, a very notable element in human life, cannot be conceived of except under the masculine rubric of the phallus. Lacan having made this startling statement, comments on the clinically observable fact that it is very frequently seen that patients locate what is "most taboo in their potency" in their feminine partner, a phenomenon that translates as "his wife is his phallus" (ibid., p. 205). We will come back to this. For now, indubitably, looking at the dream, it is obvious that the woman is the active potent player. And in the transference phantasy that occasioned the patient's cough, the person who is up to something sexual is also the woman, the analyst. It is therefore hard not to agree with Lacan when he points out that it is not the subject who is omnipotent, but the other; it is on the side of the woman that omnipotence lies (ibid., p. 225) and the locus of omnipotence must be kept safely out of the game. Although the dream shows the dreamer to be not entirely at the mercy of this omnipotent desire.

In order to maintain the belief in the omnipotence of the other it is vital that the subject not come up against the fact that this other does not in fact possess the signifier phallus, that the woman is castrated. As a result, his wife in the dream must be kept out of the game, and the patient must warn Sharpe, with his cough, but more importantly he must protect himself from the possible discovery on entering unannounced, that; there is nothing but a bag (Lacan's phrase!) "because were he to see that, were he to see that there is nothing but a bag, he might lose everything" (ibid., p. 206).

Lacan may well be correct in stating that the signifier phallus is identical for this subject with everything that transpired in his relationship with his mother (ibid., p. 205), but this is certainly not elaborated in what Sharpe reports. (It does, however, chime exactly with what he will say about the fundamental fantasy in lesson twelve). He also suggests that this subject found support in a feminine identification with his sister who was eight years older. This may well be an inspired guess but is a lot less conclusively established than the dramas of aphanisis described above. As we will see further on, however, Lacan makes of the subject's reference to cutting up his sister's sandal straps a version of the fundamental fantasy. The slippage between penis and phallus, which is a recurrent feature in Lacan's writing in these years is operative here. The supposition that the other possesses the signifier that contains all the values seems an accurate description of this patient's stance. For Lacan, this signifier which presumably could have any number of names is called the phallus: "the phallic signifier takes on all values and especially the drive-related values and aggressive tendencies that the subject has been able to develop" (ibid., p. 226). At one level this statement could be read as a bridge between Sharpe and Lacan with Sharpe focusing on the aggression located in the penis, while Lacan's focus is the phallus occupying a position equivalent to that of the object in the phantasy. By way of supporting the privileging of this signifier Lacan embarks on a highly idiosyncratic appropriation of Kleinian theory (ibid., p 212). This will be spliced with some classic Freud, and in the final lesson of this second section of the seminar, he will elaborate on and enrich the central theoretical insights which dominated the earlier section.

And so we come to lesson twelve which is announced with opaque panache. Invoking Lewis Carroll at the end of lesson eleven Lacan speaks of a mysterious gate that could be opened by the double rule of three, and this is what is now promised: "Next time, I will show you what this "rule of three" is" (ibid., p. 209). In his notes to the seminar, Jacques-Alain Miller is kind enough to supply the quote in full from Lewis Carroll – a nice little touch since it encapsulates what the reader often feels after one of Lacan's "clarifications".

> He thought he saw a Garden-Door
> That opened with a key:
> He looked again, and saw it was
> A double rule of Three:
> "And all its Mystery", he said,
> "Is clear as day to me!"
> (Miller, in Lacan, 2019, p. 500)

Indeed yes.

The real highlight of this lesson will be his setting forth what years later he will call "the founding revelatory image of desire" (Lacan, 1961–1962, lesson of 14 March 1962, p. 9) and the manner in which this puts in place the fundamental fantasy. But first he hopes to specify this character of signifier "without which one cannot give the function of the phallus its true position" (Lacan, 2019, p. 211). As we saw earlier if in fact there exists a signifier in which all values inhere – a supposition to be subjected to serious questioning – for Lacan this would be the phallus. Here in lesson twelve he has some new and interesting things to say about this rather extraordinary privileging, things that radically modulate previous stances. As his readers know, theoretical stances are often established in mantric fashion, with no immediate back-up. On occasion Lacan even points this out to his audience, asking them to use what he is saying as a guiding handrail without understanding it. What follows will be different and given this proclivity in his own teaching it is amusing to see him now invoke Melanie Klein with comments on her dazzlingly forceful approach and her statements that "are so categorical that I would almost say they are not open for discussion" (ibid., p. 212).

Already in Seminar I, five years previously, Lacan had made use of a celebrated paper by Klein, "Symbol Formation in the Development of the Ego" in order to propose an answer to the question: what constitutes a human world? He was much interested in Klein's suggestion that this happens by way of "the interest brought to bear on objects as distinct entities or as equivalent ones" (Lacan, 1988a, p. 68). For Klein, this process is anxiety-driven. The first objects, breast, faeces, penis, are fraught with all kinds of intensities, and as such are too hot to handle, so the child finds substitutes on which to vent her love, need and hatred; the blankie, the teddy, the piece of cloth, can be conduits, channelling and diluting these early intensities, and in their turn provoking ever new fields of interest. As Klein describes it:

This anxiety contributes to make him equate the organs in question with other things; owing to this equation these in turn become objects of anxiety and so he is impelled constantly to make other and new equations, which form the basis of his interest in the new objects and of symbolism.

(Klein, 1988 p. 220)

What Klein introduces here is the possibility, indeed the necessity, of substitution, an idea Lacan will pursue two years later in his third seminar *The Psychoses* when he elaborates the metaphor of the Name-of-the-Father, and interestingly will somewhat undercut a year after this sixth seminar, *Desire*, in his celebration of Antigone's stance on the refusal of all possibility of substitution (Lacan, 1992, p. 255). For the moment, however, it is a question of the necessary substitutions that dilute the impossible intensities accruing to the first "object(s)", and as such, permit the subject to enter into and "possess the infinity of objects that characterize the human world" (Lacan, 2019, p. 214). In "Symbol Formation", Klein speaks of objects in the plural and not of "the good object" as quoted by Lacan. Also these objects, breast, faeces, penis are not as such good, but tend to oscillate in a continual good/bad interchange, fuelled by the anxiety of the paranoid-schizoid position. In other papers, however, Klein does speak of the little girl's tendency, because of her oral receptivity, to turn to the father's penis as a good object in preference to the disappointing breast. All this by way of showing that while Lacan's appropriation of Klein here is not invalid, it is also not straightforward. Furthermore, there is a world of difference between the penis in Klein and the penis/phallus in Lacan. This topic would necessitate an essay in itself but to make one simple distinction, for Klein the mother has everything already in her body, so the father's penis is there among other enviable possessions, while for Lacan, the penis/phallus is precisely what the mother doesn't have, what she lacks and what initially the child would like to become in order to fill that lack. When Lacan first made reference to Klein's paper on "Symbol Formation" in 1954 he was more interested in the necessary anxiety which impelled the subject out into the "allness" of the world. Here the focus is on the phallus as first substitute and Lacan segues very skilfully from Klein's seeing this as the outcome of an altogether primordial fantasy involving aggressive conflict to his own placing of the phallus as having a crucial relationship "with the subject's *being*" (Lacan, ibid., p. 213). A segue that will take us on to very new territory.

Initially this new territory looks like old territory in that the statement about the phallus having a relationship with the being of the subject marks a shift from a Kleinian to a Freudian-Lacanian paradigm and is grounded in the early stages of the Oedipus complex as elaborated in Seminars IV and V. In these earlier seminars the child recognizes that the mother is highly interested in the phallus and therefore competes, wants to be this for her. The new approach here encompasses but modulates the classic Freudian outcome of the Oedipus complex when it refers to a renunciation of being as a precondition not to solid possession of the phallus, but to something much more tentative – "under certain conditions" managing to have it (ibid., p. 213). This new relationship with being is highly specific and has not been elaborated before now. Once again Lacan reminds his audience as he does throughout this seminar that he is not talking about the subject of classic philosophy "the subject of knowledge who is a noetic prop for all objects", but rather the speaking subject by which he means the subject, not just insofar as he exists but insofar as he takes on his identity in the field of language (ibid., p. 213). Lacan's repetition of this point is important since this is the subject we encounter in the new algorithm, which is the fundamental fantasy. Lacan spells it out here: it is "a barred subject - namely, a desiring subject [...] – insofar as, in his relationship to the object, he himself is profoundly called into question" (ibid., p. 214). By definition, this subject is never going to be all that stolid, since the whole point of this algorithm is to show that "in his relationship to the object, he himself is profoundly called into question" (ibid.). This subject it turns out is not to be located on one side or other of the classic "being or having" opposition, since he "both is and is not the phallus (ibid.). Very strikingly within an interval of five minutes, this oxymoron is put before his audience three times in succession: "The subject both is and is not the phallus", "[H]e *is* it [...] and he *is not* it [...]", "[..]the subject is the phallus, but the subject, of course, is not the phallus" (ibid.).

Is this by any chance the double rule of three that we were promised in the previous lesson?! For Irish readers, these statements are not so very momentous since the conjunction of yes and no (it is and it isn't) is not unfamiliar to us. But something momentous is in fact afoot here. Following those three repetitions Lacan devises a way of managing this new insight which devolves, he tells us from a slippage that concerns the use of the verb to be (ibid., p. 214). He does this by calling on the resources of grammar: "one can say that the subject both is and is not the phallus, but he is [also] not without having it" (ibid.). Readers of the previous year's seminar will note how the sturdy positivity of Seminar V wavers into the muted tentativity of this double negative. Being able "in all tranquillity" to bask in "the fact of having a penis", in fact having the title deeds securely in one's pocket appears to have been upended and its serene assurance shafted by the wariness of this grammatical formula, as well as by the repeated cautious phrasing that "one can say that it is possible, under certain conditions, to designate him with the phallic signifier" (ibid.). Something very significant has just happened. The result is that the earlier opposition between being and having which had rather bizarrely defined the male and female positions respectively in previous theoretical statements has now been modulated as follows:

> The man is not without having it.
> The woman is without having it.

What is in question in castration now is "the subjective assumption that is inflected between being and having" (ibid.), which, in fact, describes the

situation of every human being. We all confront being, we all have to ask ourselves on occasion if we have what it takes. And as Lacan will say further on in
this lesson, we all face into these questions with something missing – "human
beings cannot help but consider themselves to be nothing more than beings
who are, in the end, missing something" (ibid., p. 218).

There is a sense that the "having" bestowed on the male by the Oedipus
complex is beginning to raise questions for Lacan here. The Oedipal law he
says, both takes the phallus away and restores it; "the penis is restored to a man
by a certain action that one can almost say deprives him of it" (ibid., p. 215). By
the time he is teaching the seminar on identification (1961–1962), he is of the
view that this event would be impossible if the Symbolic was not already there,
"if the Other and the discourse in which the subject has to place himself were
not always waiting for him before his birth […]" (Lacan, 1961–1962, lesson
thirteen, 14 March 1962, p. 9). But it is this drama that, like Klein's centripetal
flight from anxiogenic objects, will deliver to the subject the fullness of the
world: "it is to the degree to which he gives up his relationship to the phallus
that the subject can possess the infinity of objects that characterize the human
world" (Lacan, 2019, p. 214). Just before this remark is an interesting observation about this penis/phallus. The reason it can do all this, that is, deliver the
entire world to the subject, is, Lacan states obscurely, that this penis (sic) finds
itself in "a certain experience" to have been "weighed in the balance against
the object", and "has taken on a certain function as an equivalent or standard in
the relationship with the object" (ibid.). Does Lacan mean the o-object here?
This is by no means clear, and yet in reading this phrase, one is reminded of the
end of the seminar on identification where he refers so poetically to "the identification of the object of desire to what must be renounced in order that the
world as world should be delivered to us" (Lacan, 1961–1962, lesson twenty-six,
27 June 1962, p. 8).

And now we come to the great centrepiece of this lesson, which is a re-
telling of the Saint Augustine story, present in his work from the 1940s but here
weighted with a new and tragic resonance.

> *Vidi ego et expertus sum zelantem parvulum: nondum loquebatur et intuebatur*
> *pallidus amaro aspectu conlactaneum suum,* I have seen with my own eyes
> and known very well an infant in the grip of jealousy: he could not
> yet speak, and already he observed his foster-brother, pale and with an
> envenomed stare.
>
> (Lacan, 1977, p. 20)

This story, which featured in his seminars of earlier years, will now encapsulate
"the first correspondences between the subject and his own identity" (Lacan,
2019, p. 217). It is prefaced by a point already made about the unavoidable
alienation that occurs for the baby in his first coming in contact with the
mother's world, the mother's signifiers (Lacan, 2019, p. 217). Fitting in to "the
world of insignias that are represented by all his mother's behaviors" means

that from the very start the baby may be in a more or less faulty, more or less deflected relation with his own drives (Lacan, 2019, p. 218). But the Saint Augustine story is of an altogether different order. Before the little child saw his brother at the breast, the breast was simply a part of his ongoingness, part of the rhythms of his being, not something he might or might not have; but this vision of his brother rocks him to the foundations of his existence, at a level which has nothing to do with either need or satisfaction. The mortal pallor of the onlooking child tellingly marks his virtual eclipse as he takes in the fact that he is not there. The other is there. That moment of blinding recognition in which desire appears in the image of its loss is a first and stunning apprehension of oneself as a separate being, but of oneself as threatened with annihilation, a first inscription of identity, perilously poised between being and non-being. The little pre-subject threatened in his being has here the first experience of his semblable "the one who is relating to his mother in a way that should be his, the one who is usurping his role" (ibid., p. 219). And it is this revelatory image of desire that constitutes the first apprehension of the object – as lost. On the side of the onlooking child then, a deathly pallor signalling "a sort of passionate self-destruction" (ibid.). On the other side an image of paradisal completeness, culturally symbolized in innumerable paintings of Madonna and Child but here an image which only became discernible in this blinding flash of loss. A foundational moment, a drama of the Imaginary, from which will be bodied forth the lineaments of the fundamental fantasy. Over the next few years this traumatic moment will come to epitomize what Lacan will call "imaginary castration", something far more devastating than Freud's matter of fact descriptions of the castration complex, and perhaps also more foundational, since in the tenth seminar *Anxiety*, he will assert: "everything starts with imaginary castration" (Lacan, 2014, p. 42). By then he will include other moments, other events, as capable of constituting this trauma. In itself this annihilating confrontation would seem to be without exit, other than murder or suicide. And indeed in life and in literature this is exactly what sometimes happens. Folk tales, balladry, small news items abound in "*passage à l'acte*" scenarios (like that of Little Musgrave) where the onlooking betrayed lover plunges his dagger into the rival and/or the faithless one. Over the next few years Lacan will go on asking the question of how continuity can be established following this level of devastation. Different answers will be proposed. Here the rescue is achieved by means of substitution, a substitution that will supply the necessary lineaments of the fundamental fantasy. The image of the other child is substituted for this "fundamentally pallid, and anguished" being which is the relationship of the subject in desire (ibid., p. 221). Here Lacan names this image of the other ego *i(a)* (ibid.). Three years later in the seminar on identification he specifies: "It is false to say that the being of which I am jealous is my semblable; he is my image in the sense that the image involved is the founding image of my desire" (Lacan, 1961–1962, lesson thirteen, 14 March 1962, p. 9). And an actual elective object is substituted for this impossible paradisal completeness (ibid.). We will have to wait until the seminar on identification for a much fuller exposition of how this comes about. For now, if the fundamental fantasy is a substitute formation with something like the Saint Augustine story as its underlay, we can certainly see why the subject is an evanescent subject when confronted too directly with the object of desire. Readers should note that at this point this is what the o-object is (later, particularly from the seminar on anxiety onward it will be object cause of desire). So it would seem that by bringing into play the operation of substitution, the fundamental fantasy in a sense, rescues the subject from the impossible devastation of this moment without for all that losing its electric intensity. As such it forms the algorithm specifying the desiring subject. Lacan will return many times to this topic over the next few years, complexifying what he has to say each time.

For now, he concludes this section of the seminar with a few summarizing remarks about the Ella Sharpe dream. What Lacan has, I think, successfully established in this section is the manner in which for this analysand, the fundamental fantasy is operative at a number of levels. In the first section of the seminar on the dream of the dead father, we saw the dream as a protective structure, interposed at a point of threatened collapse of this fantasy. Here the fantasy is that which subtends the analysand's symptom and appears in several different guises. It can be read in his conscious phantasy, it can be read in the dream, and here in his concluding remarks Lacan suggests that it can be read in his identification. In my view the evidence for this is not overwhelming, but interesting nonetheless. Much taken by this man's childhood compulsion to cut up the straps of his sister's sandals, and by the fact that he had very little memory before age 11, his sister's age at the time of the father's death, Lacan suggests that these straps are the o-object (like his car arousing a simple surge of unmotivated desire in him) (Lacan, 2019, p. 221). And his sister is the i(a) since there has occurred an imaginary alienation of himself in this sisterly personage (ibid., p. 223). This certainly strengthens Lacan's earlier privileging of the hood in the dream as vagina, sheath, representing the non-separation of masculinity and femininity in this analysand (ibid., p. 188). To a degree, Lacan seems to yield to a scatter-shot of brilliant surmises at the end of this section but he brings his listeners back to his primary insight, the very specific manner in which the aphanisis introduced in the first section, plays itself out here, in order to protect the subject from the unsustainable recognition that the woman is indeed "without having it". The aphanisis that is in question here is the concealment of "the object in question, namely the phallus" (ibid., p. 229). His wife is kept safely out of the game. And this man is trapped as a result since the most neurotogenic stance of all is not wanting the other to be castrated.

As we come to the end of this section let us call to mind again that this seminar on desire is a gateway seminar. This new focus on being will upend much of the masculinist bias of the Oedipus complex and impel Lacan in directions which eventually find expression in his twentieth seminar of 1971–1972 – *Encore*. The discovery of the efficacy of the double negative is a further impetus towards the daunting intellectual trajectory through topology, perspectivist painting, and mathematics in search of "something that thinking refuses" with respect to representation (Lacan, 1961–1962, lesson fourteen, 21 March 1962, p. 6). And the question of "the between", appears and reappears in sometimes readable, sometimes dauntingly obscure terms. It can look like what happens in the intense space between mother and baby. "Just as the ego is constituted in a certain relation to the imaginary other, desire is instituted and fixated in a certain relationship to fantasy" (Lacan, 2019, p. 173). This is a between place where the subject "through a lifetime of effort, tends to develop fully in something in which his being declares itself – desire, inasmuch as it is a reflection or effect of this effort, situates itself halfway to it" (ibid.). But it can also migrate into the positioning of the object itself. The desire of the subject, he tells us:

> Lies midway between a pure and simple signification – that would be owned by him, that would be clear and transparent to him – $s(A)$, on the one hand, and something closed and enigmatic that is not at all a fantasy, or a need, pressure, or "feeling," but that is always something akin to a signifier as such, $S(\bar{A})$, on the other hand. Between these two poles, there is the object. The object appears here in the form of an extremely clear and precise visual representation […]
>
> (Lacan, 2019, p. 181)

Baffling as this description is, it at least establishes that the o-object for now is tangible, has not yet begun to fly the nets of representation.

References

Cox Cameron, O. (2019). "The Phallus of the Fifties: Those Years of 'Tranquil Possession'", in, Owens, C. and Almqvist, N. (Eds.). *Studying Lacan's Seminars IV and V: From Lack to Desire*. London. Routledge.

Freud, S. (1900a). *The Interpretation of Dreams. S.E., IV, and V.*

Joyce, J. (1975). *Finnegans Wake*. London: Faber and Faber.

Klein. M. (1988a). *Love Guilt and Reparation*. London: Virago.

Sharpe, E. (1937). *Dream Analysis*. London: Routledge.

Soler, C. (2014). *Lacan – The Unconscious Reinvented*. London: Routledge.

Lacan, J.:

Lacan, J. (1977). *Écrits. A Selection*. (Trans.). Sheridan, A. London: Routledge.

The seminars:

——. (1961–1962). *The Seminar of Jacques Lacan, Book IX, Identification*. (Trans). Gallagher, C. Unpublished. www.lacaninireland.com

——. (1988a). *Freud's Papers on Technique, 1953–1954, The Seminar of Jacques Lacan, Book I*. (Ed.) Miller, J.-A. (Trans.) Forrester, J. Cambridge: Cambridge University Press.

——. (1988b). *The Ego in Freud's Theory and in The Technique of Psychoanalysis, The Seminar of Jacques Lacan, Book II, 1954–1955*. (Ed.) Miller, J.-A. (Trans.) Tomaselli, S. Cambridge: Cambridge University Press.

——. (1992). *The Ethics of Psychoanalysis. The Seminar of Jacques Lacan, Book VII. 1959–1960*. (Ed.) Miller, J.-A. (Trans.) Porter, D. London: Routledge.

——. (2014). *Anxiety, The Seminar of Jacques Lacan, Book X*. (Ed.) Miller, J.-A. (Trans.) Price, A. Cambridge: Polity Press.

——. (2017). *Formations of the Unconscious, The Seminar of Jacques Lacan, Book V*. (Ed.) Miller, J.-A. (Trans.) Grigg. R. Cambridge: Polity Press.

——. (2019). *Desire and its Interpretation, The Seminar of Jacques Lacan, Book VI*. (Ed.) Miller, J.-A. (Trans.) Fink B. Cambridge: Polity Press. Also (Trans.) Gallagher, C. Unpublished. www.lacaninireland.com

Chapter 4

Nine lessons on *Hamlet*

In the previous two sections I have adhered strictly to the delineations in Jacques-Alain Miller's published version of the seminar and also in Bruce Fink's translation. Here I have found it necessary for my commentary to overspill this delineation in order to balance out some of the important points made by Lacan in this section. A number of forays have occurred beyond lesson nineteen (Miller's boundary), extending as far as lesson twenty-two for reasons which I hope will be clear to the reader.

Section 3, lessons thirteen to nineteen, represent one of Lacan's most celebrated incursions into literature, his reading of *Hamlet*. Given the sometimes unseemly clamour of psychoanalysis to be recognized as a science, it is interesting to note that for both Freud and Lacan, what we might call "the first responders" were literary. As Ernest Jones reminds his readers; "the first, and almost the only person to appreciate the significance of Freud's earliest contribution to psychopathology, the *Studies on Hysteria*, was a writer, Alfred von Bergler. Bergler was Professor of History of Literature at the University of Vienna" (Jones, 1957, p. 450). In Lacan's case the Surrealists celebrated and acclaimed a doctoral thesis which had been coolly received by the world of psychiatry, and pretty much ignored by psychoanalysis. The Surrealists, however, were not the only "first responders". In the Anglophone world, in the late 1960s and particularly the 1970s when translation began to bring Lacan to the attention of the academic world, literature departments were the first to take up his teaching on the primacy of the signifier.

Lacan's relation to literature is, however, not straightforward, and perhaps to some extent mirrors Freud's own ambivalence. "Before the problem of the creative artist analysis alas must lay down its arms", said Freud in 1928, using a curiously agonistic metaphor to describe the relation between these two disciplines, and, appearing to situate psychoanalysis in a position of regretful defeat (Freud, 1928b, p. 177). Lacan – notably in this seminar on desire – is bolder than Freud. Freud made it clear that he was incapable of engaging with the crucial questions: what is literature? How does writing become art? Indeed he explicitly steered clear of them:

we have to admit that the nature of artistic achievement is inaccessible to us psychoanalytically [...] psychoanalysis can do nothing towards elucidating the nature of the artistic gift, nor can it explain the means by which the artist works – artistic technique.

(Jones, 1957, p. 444)

Lacan, on the contrary, occasionally pushes into this domain with interesting if enigmatic results. In this seminar, as we will see, he suggests that the relation between the literary artefact and the unconscious is a transversal one. Elsewhere, he expands on this, suggesting, though still in rather gnomic terms: "inasmuch as it is written, it (the literary work) does not imitate the effects of the Unconscious. The work poses the equivalent of the Unconscious, an equivalent no less real than it, as it forges the Unconscious in its curvature" (Georgin, 1977, p. 15).

That said, it must also be recognized that on many occasions, Lacan is guilty of what Derrida in "*Freud and the Scene of Writing*" has called the failure of psychoanalysis to address the literary signifier; a failure that takes the form "of a retreat from an analysis of the literary signifier into that of the literary signified" (Derrida, 1978, p. 230). A critique that sounds crushing, but as Andrei Warminski points out, pretty much everyone is guilty of this, and it is fair to say that this repressive gesture extends well beyond psychoanalysis and to a very great extent applies to most writing about literature. Writing in *Yale French Studies* nearly 20 years ago, Warminski accuses literary criticism of this same tendency to retreat from the literary signifier in favour of the signified:

> as though now that we know what language, text, rhetoric etc. are we can go back to the serious business (as usual) of teaching texts as sources and repositories of knowledge and value – useful historical knowledge, and instructive ethical religious and aesthetic value [...] what happens in literature is a text, and only a text happens.
>
> (Warminski, 1988, p. 264)

As we will see, this is a point Lacan makes in his lectures on *Hamlet*, but as we will also see when Derrida accuses him of illustrative or paradigmatic readings of literary texts, repudiation is rendered implausible by statements such as "I believe that taking up the topic of Hamlet can serve to bolster our work here on the castration complex" (Lacan, 2019, p. 235).

There are three places in Lacan's long career where the literary text is in the foreground of his thinking and his teaching. These are: the 1930s, the decade between 1955 and 1965, and 1975. The middle period to which his commentary on *Hamlet* belongs is, I think, the most thought-provoking in its attempt to explore via the literary text, the relations between the subject and what is beginning to delineate itself as the o-object. It also represents his most sustained and accessible reflections on the relations between psychoanalysis and art. But the 1930s deserve a brief background mention in that these are the years when Lacan seems closest to the world of literature. Indeed, 1933 marks his only known incursion into literary creation as such. A romantic and rather incantatory poem of his, entitled "Hiatus Irrationalis" appeared in *Le Phare de Neuilly* alongside contributions from such well-known Surrealists as Queneau and Asturias (Lacan, 1933b). Also in these years, in Paris at least, it is litera-ture that looks to psychoanalysis rather than, as is more usual, the other way around. Surrealism enthusiastically embraced Freud. (Freud did not respond in kind). Breton and his entourage were in search of a special language tuned to the unconscious. As Sarane Alexandrian puts it, they wanted to speak desire as fluently as one might speak Chinese, to swim upstream to the very sources of being and there to come upon the pre-history of metaphor (Alexandrian, 1974, pp. 191–192). They also insisted on madness as meaningful, with levels of fer-ocity that managed to penetrate establishment thinking. As a student of medi-cine Lacan formed part of a whole generation of young psychiatrists forced to re-think the problem of madness along these revolutionary lines. In 1932, the publication of his doctoral thesis in which he cites large swathes of his patient's two novels seemed to confirm the classically Surrealist thesis that the patho-logical is not meaningless but a mode of expression that has its own validity and indeed that "an equivalence between psychic states and discursive modes can be constructed" (Macey, 1988, p. 65). Exciting stuff indeed since what it implies is that the unconscious and its formations can be linguistically simulated and studied (ibid.). The young Lacan seemed to be bang on the button with respect to this loudly proclaimed Surrealist view and indeed a surprisingly interesting paper of his pre-dates the doctoral thesis. *Écrits Inspirés: Schizographie* examines the writings of a psychotic patient, Marcelle, in the hope that they may reveal specific thought disturbances and even more crucially may indicate the intimate mechanisms and the developmental stage of her illness (Lacan, 1931a). Lacan highlights the privileged position which these writings occupy for the patient, then turns his attention to their style and content. Marcelle's style will be scanned for disturbances which are verbal, nominal, grammatical, and semantic. Such an examination will demand a very close reading, and in fact this article contains the most minute and most sustained stylistic analysis of a written text ever undertaken by Lacan. In it, reference is made to three Surrealist writings but although Lacan acknowledges the similarity between Marcelle's writing process and that practised by the Surrealists, the article had been written in a medical context and the medical mould remains essentially unbroken.

But the year 1933 represents a kind of efflorescence where what Freud had seen as the rather agonistic relation between literature and psychoanalysis appears to have smoothed into conjoined amity, largely thanks to Lacan. His doctoral thesis *De la psychose paranoïaque dans ses rapports avec la personnalité*, had been published in late 1932 by a publishing house specializing in medical texts – *Le François*, and as such destined to fall immediately into the dusty oblivion usual in such circumstances (Lacan, 1975). It seems that Lacan himself had a hand in rescuing it from this fate. According to Jean Allouch he gave copies of his patient's poetic writings to Crevel, Fargue, and Eluard, prior to its publication. It was most likely as a result of this that in March 1933 extracts from these writings formed the front page of the first issue of a new Surrealist journal, *14 rue du Dragon* alongside a rave review by its editor, Joe Bousquet, praising in more or less equal measure, the poetic gift of the writer, her certified madness, and the fact that she has twice attempted murder. Two months later in an article in *Surréalisme au service de la revolution* Rene Crevel signals that he has read Lacan's thesis, and approves of both the poetic quality of Aimée's writing, and Lacan's innovative approach to his patient (Crevel, 1933). Indeed this rather incoherent article concludes by calling for someone – Lacan? – to replace Freud, portrayed as old and doddering among his collection of antiques: "What young psychoanalyst will take over?" (cited in Allouch, 1994, p. 627). A month later, Salvador Dali refers to "the admirable thesis of Jacques Lacan" in the Surrealist publication *Minotaure* (ibid., p. 629). And even more impressively Lacan himself is now being published by these virulent enemies of psychiatry. Dali's article is preceded by Lacan's "The Problems of Style and Psychiatric Concepts of Paranoiac Forms of Experience" an article whose title appeared to target the pith of the Surrealists' interest in the relations between language and madness (Lacan, 1932). However, as the reader will find in the course of this rather insubstantial paper, the actual linkage between psychic processes and literary tropes is not so easy to demonstrate, and in fact Lacan contents himself ultimately with pointing his readers in the direction of an examination of syntax rather than literary tropes as the key to the understanding of psychotic style.

Lastly, December 1933 saw the publication – again in *Minotaure* – of Lacan's article on the much commented double murder by the Papin sisters: a superb piece of writing, and arguably the finest example in all of his published work of his gift as a prose stylist (Lacan, 1933a). It is clear, terse, tense, combining the sustained narrative drama of the crime and its aftermath with a theoretical interpretation which is itself taut with tragic implications. Here too for the first time traces of the tragic vision which will so searingly penetrate the great middle seminars can be discerned.

Not until Seminar VI will he yield again to his fascination with those moments when the subject goes beyond some invisible limit, when something happens which cannot be inserted into ordinary teleological narrative. Here in 1933, the sombrely dramatic sentences with which he concludes his account of the Papin sisters makes it clear that this psychotic crime, like psychosis itself, opens onto the most profound questions posed by the human condition. It is their own anguish which the sisters abhor and annihilate in the couple that mirrors them, their own transgressive desire which drives them to literally penetrate the entrails of their victims in search of life's mystery.

In the 1930s Lacan's privileged position in the world of literature was largely predicated on his interest in the relation between madness and poetic creation and was not undeserved. In 1975 when he courageously, if less effectively, embarks on an exploration of Joyce's writing this topic is once again the central one. So his engagement with literature in the 1950s, adumbrated by that brilliant article in *Minotaure*, and to which the lectures on *Hamlet* belong, are in a category of their own.

The central theme in these middle years is tragedy. For three consecutive years in his seminar, Lacan turns his attention first to *Hamlet*, next to *Antigone*, and then to Claudel's trilogy, but these years also include his much celebrated seminar on "The Purloined Letter" and his lengthy commentary on two books on Gide. The latter, *La Jeunesse de Gide* was published at exactly the same time – April 1959 – that he was delivering his commentary on *Hamlet* in the seminar on desire. There is, however, surprisingly little overlap in their content, despite the fact that both form part of the stated project of this year's teaching which is a "re-writing of the object". His reference to "The Purloined Letter" in the introduction to the *Écrits* published almost ten years later allows the reader to see the distance traversed theoretically in the course of this decade. One would not expect the following remarks to appear in his 1955 thinking:

> For I decipher here in Poe's fiction, which is so powerful in the mathematical sense of the term, the division in which the subject is verified in the fact that an object traverses him without them interpenetrating in any respect, this division being at the crux of what emerges at the end of this collection that goes by the name of object *a* (to be read: little *a*).
>
> (Lacan, 2006)

But let us embark now on *Hamlet*. Given that the first part of this seminar, focussing on the dream of the dead father returns over and over to "the pain of existence when desire is no longer there", and to the devastation underpinning the birth of the subject, one might have anticipated the appearance of an actual tragedy in this year's teaching. Given too that in Sections 1 and 2, Lacan organizes what he has to say – and is explicit about doing so – by presenting a father, a son, death, and the relation to desire, *Hamlet* would seem to have been a part of the plan from the very start. Jean Michel Rabaté, however, suggests that its position in the seminar was more a matter of happenstance than of rigorous structure (Rabaté, 2001, p. 54). Lacan was brought to *Hamlet* less by the numerous Freudian allusions to this play than by the fact that in the middle of his 1959 seminar he was reading a series of texts by Ella Sharpe, above all her *Dream Analysis* (1937) and her unfinished notes for an essay on *Hamlet* (ibid.). Be that as it may, his very brilliant commentary fits seamlessly into this year's teaching. In the seminar he does not reference Ella Sharpe as inspiring his choice of *Hamlet* but insists rather that he was brought to these considerations by his own lengthy modulation of the opposition between being and having, which, he suggests, "echoes Hamlet's "To be or not to be"" (Lacan, 2019, p. 234). While this is debatable, it certainly underscores the new focus on being in Lacan's teaching which has its inception in this seminar, and the growing realization, fully expressed in *Encore*, his twentieth seminar of 1972–1973 some 12 years later, that "[T]o dwell on the verb 'to be' – [...] to produce it as such is a highly risky enterprise" (Lacan, 1999, p. 31). By then his stated project will have become: to redeem the verb "to be" from its tamed auxiliary role as copula, and to oppose to traditional concepts of being, in other words, those supported by the philosophical tradition "the notion that we are duped by jouissance" (Lacan, 1999, p. 70). So this new focus on being will have very far-reaching consequences for his later thinking. And while *Hamlet* may not have been part of the overall plan for the seminar Lacan begins by very smoothly linking it to the first lessons on the dream of the dead father. This is an absolutely essential alignment as we shall see.

Lacan's reading of *Hamlet* will be entirely his own, but as is customary in these years, he begins under Freud's umbrella, and as mentioned in the introduction to this book, a number of innovative moves can and do happen here. He starts with Freud's question: what in the unconscious corresponds to Hamlet's conscious procrastination? A question Freud answers himself in a classic outline of the Oedipus complex. Lacan sees this as "a first bridge thrown over the abyss that is Hamlet" and while he tells his audience that "it paves, as it were, the straight and narrow way we must simply go down in order to follow his lead", he is clearly eager to get past that bridge and to bring into play his own current preoccupations (Lacan, 2019, p. 237). So quite quickly and in keeping with the theme of the seminar, *Hamlet* is introduced as "a tragedy of desire", as well as "the drama of subjectivity". In contrast to Freud, Lacan's own question will be: what has to happen in Hamlet to make the final act possible? What can bring about "a sort of rectification of desire?" (ibid., p. 248). The commentary that follows will be organized around five moments in the play:

- The revelation of the ghost
- The collapse of the fundamental fantasy into its component parts
- Ophelia as o-object
- The desire of the Mother
- The graveyard scene.

In introducing the play to his audience, Lacan initially lists and briefly comments on these five moments, then returns in greater detail to each one, cutting in and out of them in accordance with the point he is making, but for the sake of clarity I will line up what he has to say on each one.

It is also important to note that in this section of the seminar, the o-object appears under a number of different guises. Lacan is in the process of thinking this new concept for the first time, and there is a sense of fermentation, at times resulting in bubbles of bafflement. Again prosaically I will make a list, so the reader can see lines of continuity running from the beginning of the seminar, alongside completely new and unelaborated concepts, some to be developed later, others never to be mentioned again.

The o-object is:

1. The imaginary support the subject manages to give herself at the point of fading or collapse, *"inasmuch as he falters in his certainty as subject"* (ibid., p. 366). (This is the most prevalent and central definition, in continuity with the rest of the seminar, and to be found everywhere in this section.)
2. The mathematical square root of −1. (This version is thrown into the mix here unelaborated. It will be developed at length in his 12th seminar *Crucial Problems in Psychoanalysis* (1964–1965).)
3. For the first time, no longer the object *of* desire but the object *in* desire. (This is the case in several places, but Lacan also continues to speak of the object of desire.)

These newly introduced ideas will be supplemented in the final section by the concept of "the cut" (ibid., p. 381), heralding years of topological demonstration, starting with the seminar on identification. This will be discussed at greater length in the last section of this commentary, as will another rather wonderful definition of this o-object as the analogue in the unconscious of the pronoun "I" (ibid., p. 368). This is a fascinating statement, barely elaborated and developed more fully in the seminar on anxiety.

Just as he was to do with Joyce some 15 years later, Lacan establishes his credentials as a commentator by gesturing to the wide swathe of secondary literature he has consulted in preparation for this task. He also impresses upon his listeners that an examination of *Hamlet* is by no means a side alley, a departure from clinical considerations. And, importantly, in lesson fifteen he justifies the appearance of this great tragedy in a psychoanalytic teaching, specifically a teaching on desire.

Over and over, like a leitmotif, Lacan makes the point that *Hamlet* is "a tragedy of desire", and in lesson fifteen, he expands this statement by embarking on a courageous and penetrating attempt to mine the questions that had defeated Freud about what happens in a work of art, and the relevance of this to psychoanalysis. This is one of the most sustained and important reflections on the work of art to be found anywhere in Lacan's writings. Taking some of his inspiration from Ernest Jones, he sets out his stall at a very clear distance from the naivete of other psychoanalytic writers, beginning, interestingly enough, with the exact same observation Warminski insisted on: "what happens in literature is a text, and only a text happens" (Warminski, 1988, p. 264). Yes, *Hamlet* is a tragedy of desire but Lacan insists on the signifierness of this. Hamlet is of course not a real person. He exists only through his discourse; in fact, strictly speaking "he is a mode of discourse" (Lacan, 2019, p. 273). What confronts the spectator is what Lacan calls, the organization of an illusion, and as he goes on to point out, an illusion is by no means a nothing. It produces something in the same way, Lacan suggests, as his own experiments with the concave mirror that can body forth a real image.

It is quite astounding that Lacan should have come so close to this recognition of the work of art as something in a particular relation to the inexistence that subtends human ex-sistence and even at this point of proximity should have found in the square root of −1 a more satisfying analogy for the o-object. These middle years of his teaching when he engages with literature are tantalizing in that he seems on the cusp of recognizing in the fictional gesture, the narrative act, the same properties that will fascinate him in the coming decades with respect to the zero, the vanishing point, and imaginary numbers. What he says of numbers in his twenty-second seminar *RSI* could just as pertinently and perhaps more colourfully refer to the work of art (Lacan, 1974–1975). Throughout that seminar, number is described as a semblance, created from nothing, which is also a highly effective mathematical entity. "It can happen" he says "that there is no root, that no root exists, and when it does not exist that does not upset us, we make it exist, namely, we invent the category of the imaginary root and what is more, that gives results" (Lacan, 1974–1975, 11 February 1975, lesson five, p. 27).

Here in Seminar VI, what is produced by the work of art, this organization of an illusion, touches us at the level of the unconscious, not because there is something in front of us that could really have an unconscious but because of the work of art itself, its composition and organization. This has nothing to do with any traces of the writer's unconscious which may be present but are of no real interest.

> What interests us and can allow us to structure certain problems is obviously based on the play's deepest plot, the whole of the tragedy, and its articulation as such. This is obviously something other than a fleeting revelation by the author about himself.
>
> (Lacan, 2019, p. 273)

Interestingly Lacan goes on to define what he means by the "organization" involved in the work of art as the superimposition of different planes "within which the true dimension of human subjectivity can find its place" (ibid.). A year later in Seminar VII – *The Ethics of Psychoanalysis* (Lacan, 1992) – speaking of Antigone he will invoke anamorphosis in this same context of superimposed planes (Lacan, 1999, p. 135). One will not find an image as such on the surface of the cylindrical *objets d'art* which were fabricated on the principles of anamorphosis. What occurs rather is that the superimposition of fragmentary images creates a series of layered screens out of which, viewed from a given angle, a certain form that was not visible at first sight transforms itself into a readable image. In a similar manner, as Lacan suggests in Seminar VII, tragedy is a form which can render perceptible a point in subjective existence which is on the very edges of representability. In this same seminar he uses the term "subsidence" to describe this process, a term that in English has much milder connotations than the catastrophe in question: "What occurs concerns subsidence, the piling up of different layers of presence of the hero in time" (Lacan, ibid., p. 265) and the "collapse of the drama back onto its premises" (ibid., p. 266). In Seminar VI: "[I]t is within the depth that is thus created that the problem of the articulation of desire can be posed in the fullest way possible" (Lacan, 2019, pp. 273–274). And it is here that we discover the presence of the unconscious – again not that of the author, but rather that of the spectator:

> If we are moved by a play [...] it is because of the space it offers us, owing to the multiple dimensions of its development, in which to lodge what is hidden in *us* – namely our relationship to our own desire.
>
> (ibid., pp. 274–275)

Lacan is insistent and goes on to amplify this statement:

> It is because this play furnishes the layering of myriad dimensions and organized levels – and in some ways, the maximum possible number of dimensions and levels – necessary to provide the space for what lies within us to resonate there.
>
> (ibid., p. 275)

Lacan builds a powerful case here, distancing himself from both applied psychoanalysis and psychobiography. In his paper on Gide, written at the same time, he had distinguished between applied psychoanalysis, possible only in the psychoanalytic setting and engaged in the psychoanalytic project, and the psychoanalytic *method* which involves the deciphering of signifiers without prior assumptions regarding the signified (Lacan, 2006, p. 747). What he is working on here, he tells us is psychoanalytic theory – a world apart from psychobiography: "Compared to the theoretical question whether psychoanalysis can adequately discuss works of art, any sort of clinical question is one that falls under the heading of applied psychoanalysis" (Lacan, 2019, p. 276). The question remains: how exactly will psychoanalysis discuss art, and these clear caveats must be set alongside Lacan's stated theoretical and non-art focussed intention with respect to *Hamlet*.

> I, for one, would like to broach the play on the basis of notions that I have managed to spell out here since the beginning of the year. For I believe they allow us to bring together in a more synthetic and striking way the various mainsprings of what occurs in *Hamlet*.
>
> (ibid., p. 239)

Nonetheless the central point being made in lesson fifteen is that insofar as the unconscious is in question, it will be the unconscious of the spectator. Hamlet is a character made up of the empty space in which our own ignorance can be situated, and it is this "situated ignorance" that renders the unconscious present. This, Lacan says, is what gives *Hamlet* its power and its import (ibid., p. 275). Very interestingly, Lacan extends the power of the play to engage the unconscious of the spectators to the actors who play this part. As he says, there are as many Hamlets as there are actors who play Hamlet. Those who succeed best do so because of something compatible in their own unconscious. Just as all of us "furnish the material that constitutes our relationship to our unconscious, namely, the signifier – [...] with our imaginary, that is with our relationship to our own body, for that is the Imaginary", so in an analogous fashion, "an actor lends his members and presence, not simply like a puppet, but with an unconscious that is truly real – namely, the relationship of his members to his own history" (ibid., p. 276). This of course, is a huge statement on several fronts, not least in its matter of fact definition of the Imaginary as the relationship with our own body, an interesting concept to keep in mind when reading the later Lacan as well as contemporary Lacanian theory on the Real of the body.

But – and this is the essential point Lacan wants to make in this sustained discussion of the relation between the work of art and psychoanalysis – none of this constitutes the crux of the matter. The crux is the performance of the drama as it was written: "the effect of *Hamlet* is essentially the way in which desire can and must find its place in the play as it was written" (ibid., p. 277). All through this section of the seminar Lacan keeps his audience tightly corralled to this central statement: *Hamlet* is the tragedy of desire. In lesson fifteen he wants us to know that it is so because of its composition and its structure.

So now let us look at this structure – at the five moments in the play around which Lacan situates his commentary. I am not entirely happy about taking these moments one by one as it cuts into Lacan's own particular weaving approach, no doubt with certain consequences, but it does at least stay close to the chronology of the play.

The revelation of the ghost

What Lacan wants to demonstrate here is that something essential to the normal functioning of subjectivity is smashed at this point. This is $\$\lozenge a$, the structure of fantasy. In the first two sections of the seminar he has been at pains to show the limit point to which this structure responds. In lessons one and two using Freud's term *Hilflosigheit* he describes the little pre-subject as without recourse faced with a specific encounter with the Other which is the *che vuoi?* This question "what do you want?" is one that puts the little pre-subject itself in question. As Lacan will say in the seminar on transference, "faced with this question [...] he loses the someone to whom desire is addressed – in other words himself" (Lacan, 2015, p. 217). At this point of panic something from the imaginary register comes to the rescue and this is the fantasy, closely allied at this stage in Lacan's thinking, to the ego. In the second section, his account of how the structure of fantasy comes into being is encapsulated in the Saint Augustine anecdote, where similarly it is at the point of threatened annihilation that the subject manages to bring in something to sustain her. Here in *Hamlet* Lacan's focus is on the collapse of this structure of fantasy, resulting from the ghost's revelation of limitless betrayal. Over and over in the first section on the dream of the dead father, Lacan had emphasized the vital importance of the "he did not know", stating unambiguously that "it is here – in this human fantasy, which is the subject's fantasy [...] that the subject maintains his existence, maintains the veil that is such that he can continue to be a subject who speaks" (Lacan, 2019, p. 94). Unlike this dreamer, and unlike Oedipus, Hamlet *knows*, and it is this *knowing* that sets the entire drama in motion.

What we saw in the dream of the dead father was a subject poised on the edge of an impossible knowing. In *Hamlet* this edge has given way. Not only does the father know, but from the ghost scene on Hamlet must founder under this impossible knowledge. As Lacan says of the ghost's revelation something is lifted, a veil that "weighs on the articulation of the unconscious line" (ibid., p. 296). What is laid bare is "the irremediable, absolute, unfathomable betrayal of love", a beyond of pact and of possibility identical to that evoked in Seminar VII for Oedipus and in Seminar VIII for Sygne de Coûfontaine (ibid., p. 297). Speaking of *Hamlet*, Lacan's language is stark and uncompromising. The betrayal is absolute. Everything that falls under the heading of good faith, loyalty and vows is thus presented to Hamlet as not merely being revocable, but as having actually been revoked (ibid., p. 402). The truth of *Hamlet* "is a faceless closed truth, a truth that can be bent in any direction one likes. As we know only too well, it is truth without truth" (Lacan, 2019, p. 299). When he broaches this event for the first time in the seminar in lesson sixteen, Lacan seems to equate this irredeemable betrayal with the notation which had made its first appearance in lesson seventeen of his fifth seminar *Formations of the Unconscious*, S($\mathbb{A}$): "the value of the play is that it allows us to accede to S($\mathbb{A}$)" (ibid., p. 297). It is important to note, however, the manner in which this statement will be modified and nuanced. In lesson sixteen, the betrayal evoked is the starkest possible, even side-stepping the ghost's own description of himself as "doomed for a certain term [...]" presumably therefore to the fires of purgatory. At every mention of the ghost in this seminar, Lacan plunges him repeatedly into unending hell. Futurity is foreclosed in this play, not just for the living but for the dead, one of the hallmarks of tragedy as Lacan will say in his discussion of Antigone a year later. Of *Hamlet* he says: "There is no trace in the whole play of an ascension toward something that might lie beyond this, some sort of redemption" (ibid., p. 298). What we have here is an absolute and unmodifiable version of the *me phunai*, which will be the defining feature of the tragic stance in Seminar VII.

Can this level of absolute bankruptcy be what is meant by S(A)? Yes and no it would seem. What is at stake Lacan says, is something so devastating that even pessimism constitutes a kind of veil, shielding us from its full impact (ibid., p. 298). At the same time it does not suggest that everything pertaining to the Other is valueless, and therefore, Lacan insists, it should not be read in the context of Absurdism. What S(A) actually says is that there is no Other of the Other – and for Lacan this is the big secret of psychoanalysis (ibid., p. 298). Because of this fact; "I have absolutely no guarantee that this Other, owing to what he has in his system, can give me back [...] what I gave him, – namely, his being and his essence as truth" (ibid., p. 299). At this point Lacan suggests that this failure is because the Other lacks a signifier (the usual, and depressingly monotonous one) but when he returns to this topic some weeks later, he grounds this assertion in an intersubjective drama between the small pre-subject and the Other, rooted in a tragedy that is common to both.

In lesson nineteen, he expands on this first discussion of the ghost's revelation, again identifying S(A) to a truth bereft of redemptive futurity but interestingly pointing up the flimsiness of the Oedipal promise upon which futurity depends. In the classic Oedipus "the truth about truth is expected from the father" who of course, cannot guarantee it any more than anyone else, but handing oneself over to the fragility of this myth is very different to the certain knowledge that the father is entirely without power, that he presents himself as the ghost does, in the most signifying form of A. Once again Lacan changes purgatory into hell to hammer home this point; the father "has been wiped away not only from the surface of the living, but from the recompense that should have been his [...] sent [...] into the bowels of hell" (ibid., p. 343). Over the next couple of lessons he will go on to make a distinction between the absence of guarantee, and this utter destitution, a distinction that will have important reverberations for future theory and will reappear in more definite form in his ninth seminar *Identification*. Here in lesson twenty he speaks of the impotence of the Other to respond to the demand of the little pre-subject in terms of "a common tragedy", one familiar to every parent. The Other cannot make it better, cannot fully protect the child, does not have at its disposal the wherewithal to comfort all distress. And yet the response of this Other is absolutely crucial. In "the tragedy that is going to be played out" (ibid., p. 371), the question remains "in what respect can we count on the Other?" (ibid., p. 372) Since no signifier exists that can guarantee any concrete manifestation of signifiers under the pressure of the subject's demand for a guarantor, what happens at the level of the Other is primordially something at the level of a lack (A) in relation to which the subject must situate himself (ibid., p. 372). As Lacan says in the following lesson, there is nothing philosophical about all of this. We are at the coalface of psychic life and the possibility or not of a trusting relationship when faced with the question: "To what degree and up to what point, can I count on the Other?" (ibid., p. 376). This is a notably different situation to that described by Lacan when he returns to the topic of the Ghost for the final time in lesson twenty-two. What is in question here is not the absence of guarantee, but rather that a guarantee has in fact been given, and this is the guarantee of "untruth" (ibid., p. 402). The absolute betrayal, the revelation to Hamlet that everything that falls under the heading of good faith, loyalty, and vows has been revoked is quite different from the fact that there is no signifier that could constitute a guarantee, for something is clearly guaranteed here, which is an untruth (ibid.). This is a crucial distinction, which will be more or less occluded by the primacy of the *me phunai* in Seminar VII but will be developed at length in Seminar IX. So the notation S(Ⱥ) is to be read at two very clearly distinguishable levels in this seminar, linked however by the term "tragedy" since at the more usual level, the impotence of the Other to respond adequately, its impotence as guarantor is troped as "a common tragedy". Three years later in the ninth seminar *Identification* it will be troped as something absolutely essential to ongoing existence. This response of the Other in Seminar IX oscillates between the "nothing perhaps" and the "perhaps nothing" which together constitute a question and a message. The *nothing perhaps* as question opens out onto possibility, onto the unforeseeable, while the *perhaps nothing* as message functions as uneasy reassurance, but in Seminar IX, Lacan insists on their intrication. Essentially no guarantee exists; approximation and insufficiency are the only things on offer and – crucially – this is precisely what gives us our world. "This Other who guarantees precisely nothing qua other, qua locus of the word it is here that it takes on its instructive incidence. It becomes the veil, the blanket, the source of occultation of the very place of desire" (Lacan, 1961–1962, lesson fourteen, 21 March 1962, p. 9). In contrast to this, what Lacan wants to show his audience in his commentary on *Hamlet* is the consequence of the unspeakable guarantee, the guarantee of unplumbable betrayal which is the revelation of the ghost.

The collapse of the fundamental fantasy into its component parts

In this seminar Lacan, week by week, is thinking the fundamental fantasy and the role of the o-object for the first time. In the first three sections, he presents three guises under which the fundamental fantasy functions as a brink phenomenon interposed to protect the subject from an unsustainable knowing. In the dream of the dead father it is captured, balanced on this brink. In the Ella Sharpe dream, we see it maintaining itself stably enough by underpinning an obsessional neurosis and in the last section on *Hamlet* it collapses into its component parts only to be re-installed towards the end in a momentary flash. It would appear that at the panic point induced by the helplessness which is now common to both the subject and the Other, something can be interposed, brought in, from the imaginary register. In the seminar on desire, this something is closely linked to narcissistic passion, to the narcissistic image. From the mirror stage onwards, Lacan's theorization of this image is marked by Heidegger's *Zukunft*, a being thrown forward into the anticipated fullness of futurity. Before we look at how this collapses in *Hamlet*, it might be useful to look at a celebrated literary enactment of how it comes about, in the hope that seeing it in the making so to speak, will allow us a clearer insight into its unmaking, as it occurs in *Hamlet*.

To this aim I shall examine a small speech from Shakespeare's *Henry V*. The scene is the morning of the battle of Agincourt. The English army is decimated by disease, drenched by months of rain, starved, and demoralized. What is relevant here is that it is precisely these elements of doom and disaster that "Harry" (the King) invokes to create the fabric of an immortal story. It is the material of destitution itself that will be woven into the texture of heroism, a tale that will resound and fill up the future with a glory that will make these ragged few the envy of all. The night before, Harry had walked through the camp, and been shocked by the proximity of his men to their own death. He had listened to talk about the arms, legs, and guts which would lie strewn upon this field where they are so hopelessly outnumbered. And it is from this baseline that he now speaks. In the imagined future remembrance, it is their scars, their wounds that will position these men as heroes:

> *Enter* King Henry.
> Westmoreland. O that we now had here
> But one ten thousand of those men in England
> That do no work to-day!
> King Henry. What's he that wishes so?
> My cousin Westmoreland? No my fair cousin:
> If we are mark'd to die, we are enow
> To do our country loss; and if to live,
> The fewer men, the greater share of honour.
> God's will! I pray thee, wish not one man more.
> [...]
> This day is call'd the feast of Crispian:
> He that outlives this day, and comes safe home,
> Will stand a tip-toe when this day is nam'd,
> And rouse him at the name of Crispian.
> He that shall live this day, and see old age,
> Will yearly on the vigil feast his neighbours,
> And say, "To-morrow is Saint Crispian":
> Then will he strip his sleeve and show his scars,
> And say, "These wounds I had on on Crispin's day".
> Old men forget: yet all shall be forgot,
> But he'll remember, with advantages,
> What feats he did that day. Then shall our names,
> Familiar in his mouth as household words,
> Harry the King, Bedford and Exeter,

> Warwick and Talbot, Salisbury and Gloucester,
> Be in their flowing cups freshly remember'd.
> This story shall the good man teach his son;
> And Crispin Crispian shall ne'er go by,
> From this day to the ending of the world,
> But we in it shall be remembered;
> We few, we happy few [...]
> (Shakespeare, *Henry V*, Act IV, Scene III)

A switchpoint has been effected here from the dereliction of death into the glory of future fame. What has been occluded is the spread of guts and arms and legs on the field. Harry's speech in transmuting the probability of annihilation into the possibility of an acclaimed identity as hero, also effects a switch at the level of lived time, the temporal zone that the subject inhabits. Time is now future-driven, but it is a very particular future tense, that of the future anterior – in other words who these men will have been. This precipitation is the hallmark of the narcissistic image which is thrown forward from this point into its own becoming. The exact opposite is what takes place in Hamlet's subjectivity following the revelation of the ghost. Paradoxically what Lacan had said in lessons twenty and twenty-one about the impossibility of guarantee, experienced as "a common tragedy" between the subject and the other, is also that which sets desire in motion:

> It is at this point that the subject brings in from elsewhere – namely, from the imaginary register – a part of himself that is involved in the imaginary relationship to the other. This is little *a* [...] It comes into play in a complex that we will call fantasy. The subject manages to prop himself up with this object at the moment at which he vanishes when faced with the signifier's failure [or: inability, *carence*] to answer for his place as subject at the level of the Other.
>
> (Lacan, 2019, p. 377)

As Lacan goes on to say, nothing will ever be able to make up for this failure on the part of the Other, much as we try with one attempt after another, one appeal after another ("But do you really love me?"); all the successive attempts which unbeknownst to us, actually end up weaving the texture of the life we will live (ibid., p. 372). What has happened in *Hamlet* however is of a completely different order. Instead of a non-response, a response has been unambiguously delivered. Very interestingly for the point Lacan wants to make, the play opens in a not unusual version of S($\bar{A}$), that of mourning. In the study group we used Kenneth Branagh's wonderful film production to stay in touch with the play, and the colour contrast at the beginning – the scarlet and white of the court as background to the sober compacted black figure of Hamlet in the foreground was a striking image of despair and of the loss of any will to live characteristic of profound mourning. Hamlet is outraged, full of pain and fury, but ultimately composed, compacted, coherent. After the ghost's revelation however, a suffering that had existed at the level of metaphor is catapulted into actuality. Before the revelation Hamlet could long to just dissolve; "Oh that this too too solid flesh would melt [...]" After it he in actuality, falls apart. The world order as such has been radically destroyed. The stability, pomp, and beauty we have just witnessed in the royal court rests upon an enormous web of horror and deceit and in consequence the stability of world and self is catastrophically undermined.

Ordinarily the structure of fantasy $\$ \Diamond a$ which sustains the subject, remains unconscious, but at certain points, which are more or less pathological, it goes beyond this. Where nothing holds any longer the components of this fundamental fantasy, $\$ \Diamond a$, ordinarily indiscernible and indivisible, surge into visibility. As Lacan says, something vacillates, allowing its components to appear (ibid., p. 320). While there are multifarious ways for this disaggregation to occur what happens here in *Hamlet* is that the subject is dissolved while the object is debased and degraded. In the first instance, the imaginary body is disrupted in its functioning. Hamlet cannot even dress, cannot recognize Ophelia, the one in whose presence, his face would normally have lit up. The ordinary vital functions of his body fail him – he is pale and trembling, disengaged, unable either to connect or disconnect. That which has been laid waste in Hamlet is his very life, the pith of his being which had been most vibrantly alive in his love for Ophelia. And it is in her presence that the degree to which he is unable to maintain himself as subject shows itself, initially in this bewildered loss of all bearings as Ophelia reports to her father:

Lord Hamlet, with his doublet all unbraced,
No hat upon his head, his stockings fouled,
Ungartered, and down-gyved to his ancle,
Pale as his shirt, his knees knocking each other,
And with a look so piteous in purport
As if he had been loosed out of hell
To speak of horrors – he comes before me.
[...]
He took me by the wrist and held me hard.
Then goes he to the length of all his arm,
And with his other hand thus o'er his brow
He falls to such perusal of my face
As 'a would draw it. Long stayed he so.
At last, a little shaking of mine arm
And thrice his head thus waving up and down,
He raised a sigh so piteous and profound
As it did seem to shatter all his bulk
And end his being. That done, he lets me go,

And with his head over his shoulder turned
He seemed to find his way without his eyes,
For out o' doors he went without their helps
And to the last bended their light on me.

([Act II, Scene I, pp. 77–100]
Lacan, 2019, p. 319)

Citing this description in full in lesson seventeen, Lacan suggests "that it would not be much of a stretch to designate this moment [...] as pathological" (ibid., p. 320). It is certainly akin to "those periods in which some sort of subjective disorganization irrupts" (ibid.). The impact of this world-changing shock has caused the imaginary distances between subject and object to be disrupted. In general we take these distances completely for granted but this disruption can be experienced in shock – when for example one is, out of the blue, diagnosed with terminal illness. Melanie Klein recounts a moving episode in her own life in the days following the sudden death of her son when she felt walls collapsing on her, streets looming over her. These of course are limit situations, but the whole tenor of this seminar is to insist on the fragile equipoise which allows the subject of desire to function:

In psychoanalytic experience, desire presents itself first of all as a problem [*trouble*] It disturbs [*trouble*] our perception of the object. We see this in poets' and moralists' curses: desire denigrates, disorganizes, debases, and in any case undermines the object, going so far at times as to even dissolve he who perceives it – namely the subject.

(ibid., p. 359)

Shakespeare's great tragedy offers Lacan impressive scope to develop this thesis, since what happens here is that the subject – Hamlet – is dissolved into madness and disarray, while the object, in this instance, Ophelia, is debased and degraded.

Ophelia as o-object

Lacan's commentary on *Hamlet* engages with and expands on the structure of fantasy more fully than heretofore and very unambiguously he situates Ophelia "at the level of the letter *a*" (ibid., p. 310), and as someone who functions as a sort of barometer of Hamlet's position with regard to desire (ibid., p. 244). The close relation between narcissistic eros and the object which supports the subject in his being, a relation prevalent throughout this seminar, is very visible here. As mentioned above it is in Ophelia's presence that Hamlet's loss of bearings is conveyed in the complete disarray of his self-presentation. And the great speech in which he declares his inability to go on living – what Lacan calls the pain of existence when desire is no longer there – is followed by a sustained attack on Ophelia which is a violent attack on livingness itself. Everything that Ophelia is; trusting, girlish, flowering in the beauty and promise of early youth, is pounded with fury. As Lacan puts it she is the bud and blossom of life as well as being the carrier of future life in her young body, and it is this that Hamlet pulverizes in his savage diatribe. "I loved you not [...] get thee to a nunnery: Why wouldst thou be a breeder of sinners? [...] God hath given you one face, and you make yourselves another" (Act III. Scene I).

Kenneth Branagh's production very brilliantly uses mirrors to enact Hamlet's distortion of everything he had loved in Ophelia, squashing her beautiful face into horrifying unrecognizability against the mirror of his pained rage. In turning his attention to Ophelia in lesson seventeen Lacan announces as his focus "the imaginary setting [or: regulating, *réglage*] that is brought about by what constitutes desire's prop" which he will go on to specify as the o-object (ibid., p. 309). From the very beginning of this seminar he had emphasized the indivisibility of the formula for fantasy. Here, having just allowed us to see the disaggregation of the $ in Hamlet he refers to the more or less fetishistic character of the object, going so far as to suggest that what is known as a fetish is perhaps one of the dimensions of the human world, and one that pertains specifically to psychoanalytic thinking (ibid., p. 313). The essential message of this seminar – "$ in the presence of little *a* [...] is the fantasized prop of desire" is repeated in order to ask, and to some extent answer, a question that will gladden the somewhat bedazzled reader; what does *a*, this imaginary other mean? (ibid.). While it remains always something necessarily opaque, he tells us, it is also always, "image and pathos", always tightly linked to the pain of exist-ence even in the case of perverse fantasy (ibid., p. 314). This statement shouldn't surprise his listeners, already outlined as it was in the dream of the dead father. Here he expands on his earlier formulation.

> fantasy as such is situated at the extreme point of subjective questioning – at its tip, endpoint, or reflection – inasmuch as, beyond demand, the sub-ject attempts to get his bearings anew [*se resaisir*] in the dimension of the Other's discourse in which he must refind what was lost owing to the fact of his entrance into discourse [...] what is involved is [...] not the level of truth but the moment of truth.
>
> (ibid., p. 314)

The central drama of subjectivity around which psychoanalytic theory circulates, has shifted majorly here from Freud's castration complex at the centre of the Oedipal event to something very much wider, and not initially sexed as such. We will see in greater detail how this is done in the final section of the seminar. What we find very often in attempting a close reading of Lacan is what I would call a sleight of concept, a shift in the underlying theoretical narrative. So here the object is not just something the subject draws from the imaginary register as defence in face of the desire of the Other, but is something of which this subject has been deprived:

> a specific object becomes an object of desire insofar as the subject is deprived of something of himself that has taken on the value of the very signifier of his alienation – and this something is the phallus – deprived of something that is related to his very life.
>
> (ibid., p. 327)

It is now this devastating loss that shadows the object with the "pain of existence" ensuring in Lacan's repeated phrase, that it is "image and pathos" (ibid., p. 312). This underlying drama, Lacan specifies, allows us to conceptualize in what respect this imaginary object can become the magnetizing lure around which, "what one might call the virtues or the dimensions of being converge" (ibid., p. 312).

While tomes could be written about the many avatars of the phallus that surge up in Lacan's teaching, the one that makes its appearance here is deeply interesting, and questionable only insofar as it sets itself up as unique (but see Cox Cameron, 2019, and Part III in this volume, for my critique of the phallus in Seminars IV and V). Here it functions as *the* signifying symbol of life, rather than *a* signifying symbol of life (ibid., p. 321). As a result, Ophelia flowering with promise, and carrying fecundity in her young femaleness, cannot in herself be this symbol but can only be a stand-in for the poor overworked phallus. Lacan memorably describes Ophelia as a bud ready to blossom, an image of life that bears all life within itself "bursting with life", and can only interpret this as the psychoanalytic equation Girl=Phallus. At the point where Hamlet looses his hatred on her, Ophelia is "the phallus, the phallus qua signifying symbol of life" (ibid., p. 321). A week earlier he had described what the phallus signifies as; "[V]ital turgidity – this enigmatic, universal thing that is more male than female" (ibid., p. 300). But is it? Why on earth would there be only one "symbol of life that the subject makes signifying"? Ophelia so powerfully interposes herself as one such symbol that Lacan recognizes implicitly that this vocabulary applies equally to her. Hamlet's attack shows "that woman is conceptualized here only as carrying the vital turgescence that must be cursed and stopped up" (ibid., p. 321).

What happens at this point is not unrelated to what Freud speaks of in "*Mourning and Melancholia*"; "the shadow of the object falls on the ego" (Freud, 1917e, p. 249). What we see in *Hamlet* is an intersubjective version of this intra-subjective drama. The attack Freud describes is an attack on one's own livingness. So for example after a break-up I berate myself – I was a fool, too trusting, too this, too that; I hate everything about myself. The most noteworthy feature of this mechanism is its ferocity. Ordinarily one's narcissistic relations with oneself are reasonably calm, or at least only intensify at specific points. In melancholia, not only are they reversed but hugely magnified. And this, Lacan points out repeatedly is what occurs in the reversal of Hamlet's love for Ophelia. The o-object as he had already pointed out in lesson five relates to the most intimate part of oneself, that which must not be exposed, even to oneself, and as he now says, in speaking of the phallus, to that which must be lost. While not every Shakespearian will agree with Lacan's reading, it is in fact very convincing. As we will see further on in the graveyard scene, it is only when Ophelia is definitively lost – dead in fact – that she is restored to Hamlet as o–object.

The desire of the Mother

Given the centrality of the structure of fantasy, and the place of the o–object in this particular reading of *Hamlet*, one might not have expected the major scene with Gertrude to form "the crux of the play", but this is how Lacan describes it. He very clearly spells out his departure from Freud here. What is in question is not Freud's incestuous, Oedipal, and rivalrous desire for the mother but the mother's own desire. A desire that in the first instance is described in terms rather different to that of the arcane terminology of say the graph – Gertrude is "a gaping cunt". At several different points in his commentary, Lacan insists that the play is dominated by the desire of this mother, and that the scene in Gertrude's room is the key to the whole drama, an insistence based on a curious misreading, but one that could be troped as brilliantly perceptive (ibid., p. 308). For Lacan everything hinges on Hamlet's final adjuration to his mother in this scene, but he, Lacan neglects or ignores the first line of this instruction:

QUEEN: What shall I do?
HAMLET: Not this, by no means, that I bid you do [...]

(Act III. Scene IV)

As a result of not reading this negative adjuration he sees Hamlet foundering, and defeatedly sending his mother back to her lustful ways, to what Lacan calls the instinctual voracity of this genital character. What are we to make of this reading which really cannot be said to be backed up by Shakespeare's text? It's positioning as central gives us pause. Lacan is insistent:

> This dimension is essential [...] In the sort of collapsing or caving in that manifests itself at the end of Hamlet's plea, we find the very model that allows us to conceptualize in what respect there is a waning [*retombée*] of his own desire, of his impulse toward the action he is dying to take, the whole world becoming a living reproach to him that he is not equal to his own will. If this action founders [*retombe*] in the same way as his plea to his mother does, it is essentially because of the dependence of the subject's desire on the Other subject.
>
> (ibid., p. 308)

He reinforces this assertion by adding unambiguously that "[T]his is the major accent, the very accent of the drama of *Hamlet*, what one might call its constant dimension" (ibid., pp. 308–309).

It can fairly be said that if Lacan has not read the first line of Hamlet's instructions to his mother, he has very accurately picked up on the hate filled jouissance of the imagery Hamlet uses, a jouissance that betrays a very real enmeshment in the mother's desire:

> Let the bloat King tempt you again to bed;
> [...] And let him, for a pair of reechy kisses,
> Or paddling in your neck with his damn'd fingers [...]
> (Act III. Scene IV)

The violent ambivalence audible here renders plausible Lacan's reading. Whether we his audience are convinced or not, this reading offers Lacan an important platform for an essential tenet of his teaching, and an essential element in the graph of desire. This is the primordial relationship with the first Other – ordinarily the mother, spelled out in several contexts in this seminar as elsewhere during these years. It is to this primordial subject, presumed to be omnipotent, that the baby's first demand is addressed. So this demand has to pass through the defiles of the signifier, or as Lacan puts it elsewhere, it enters an already structured world. As noted earlier in the first section, the so-called *che vuoi?* is two-way. Consequently it is in this already structured world that the little pre-subject has to orient himself, to locate himself. The Other's demand will have necessarily fragmented and fractured him, Lacan says, so if he is to succeed in locating himself, he must go through a fundamental stage in which what becomes *his* discourse is taken beyond the Other (ibid., p. 283). So he has to go "beyond the necessities of demand inasmuch as he seeks to find anew [*retrouver*] his desire in its ingenuous nature" (ibid., p. 283). Is this a different way of describing the Oedipus complex? Hard to say, although what is clear in Lacan's exposition here, is that everything hinges on Hamlet's relation to his mother's desire and that his subservience here entails the failure of the classic Oedipus complex. Commenting on this scene in the Queen's closet in which Hamlet berates Gertrude, and then in Lacan's reading, "caves in", he states; "there is no moment at which the formulation 'man's desire is the Other's desire' is more tangible or manifest, no moment in which it is more completely realized, no way in which it could more thoroughly cancel out the subject" (ibid., p. 286). Hamlet's initial address to the mother is in the father's name, urging her in the name of the social order and ordinary *bienséance*. As Lacan puts it Hamlet attempts to join up "with the level of the code or law ($\lozenge D$)" only to back down to the level of her desire, summed up as "she is simply a gaping cunt" (ibid., pp. 286 and 287).

While this is a bravura piece of theorization it in some ways seems extraneous to the overall movement of this aligning of the fate of the fundamental fantasy with Shakespeare's tragedy. This alignment follows what he had earlier called the double rule of three, defined in lesson thirteen as the two stages of the relationship between the subject and the more or less fetishistic object (ibid., p. 233). He will go on to describe three stages, centred on the collapse of this fantasy and its eventual restoration. The collapse involves the ghost's revelation, its effect on Hamlet, the rejection of Ophelia as love object, and her ultimate reinstatement in the graveyard scene. In other words, what we have listed here as the four other elements of Lacan's commentary on *Hamlet*.

The graveyard scene

This is the scene that turns the play around. We are suddenly going to see what was impossible become possible. Something happens here to which in Lacan's view, not enough importance has been attributed, and which Lacan describes in terms of the fantasy:

> This scene grabs him and offers him a prop by which his own relationship as a subject, $, with Ophelia − little object *a*, − which had been rejected owing to the confusion or compounding of objects − is suddenly re-established [...] this is the moment at which something happens that allows Hamlet to take hold of his desire anew.
>
> (ibid. pp. 288–289)

Having described the scene between Hamlet and Gertrude in her closet as "the crux of the play" he nonetheless sees the graveyard scene as that which shows "on which point all the avenues of the play's articulation converge" (ibid., p. 289). Lacan sees what happens here as the exact correlate of Hamlet's violent rejection of Ophelia as love object, the moment when despite the sheer savagery of this laying waste, the fundamental fantasy manages to re-install itself albeit momentarily. This is the place where Hamlet takes the bit between his teeth, and extraordinarily, names and proclaims himself; "This is I, Hamlet the Dane" (ibid., p. 289). In this moment, the sight of Laertes leaping into the grave to take the dead Ophelia in his arms galvanizes Hamlet "and offers him a prop by which his own relationship as a subject, $, with Ophelia − little object *a*, which had been rejected [...] is suddenly re-established" (ibid., p. 288). And it is this suddenly re-established fantasy structure that is momentarily going to make a man of him. For Lacan this is the moment where Hamlet can lay hold again of his desire. But how is this done? Lacan's answer is simple; by way of mourning.

> It is to the extent to which Ophelia has become an impossible object that she once again becomes the object of his desire [...] The fact that the object of desire is impossible is just one of the especially manifest forms of an aspect of human desire.
>
> (ibid., p. 335)

This leads into an extended exploration of the relation between mourning and the object in/of desire. Referencing Freud's work on mourning, Lacan suggests that this new concept, the place of the object in desire, can greatly expand Freud's theorization. And this it turns out, is what his study of *Hamlet* is about. Lacan is explicit; "Our analysis of *Hamlet* is designed, in the end, to help us make headway in this realm" (ibid., p. 346).

Making mourning central to what he has to say about the o-object is an immense step on Lacan's part, jolting his audience out of abstraction into immediacy. At several different moments in his commentary on *Hamlet* he reminds his listeners that "it is by means of mourning that we see the object come into view" and that "with the question of mourning and the object, we have arrived at the heart of the problem" (ibid., p. 287). Indeed it is by exploring some of the consequences of mourning that he feels enabled to open up effective and fruitful insights not otherwise accessible. These are insights that bear on the question he has been raising in different guises with his audience for the past several months: What relationship is there between "what I have formulated in the form of ($\lozenge a$), concerning the constitution of the object of desire, and mourning?" (ibid., pp. 334–335). So how does he answer this crucial question? Not with entire clarity of course, but in one of the extraordinary throwaway remarks he sometimes makes he suggests a very good reason for this lack of clarity when he opines that:

> mourning coincides with an essential gap, the major symbolic gap, the symbolic lack – in short the point x, of which the dream's navel, which Freud mentions somewhere, is perhaps but a psychological correlate.
>
> (ibid., p. 340)

And here we must ask the question; is a gap a representation or an absence of representation? Mourning takes all of us into that gap, without of course any effort on our part to do more than live it, but Lacan in this section of the seminar is working very hard to conceptualize the status of the object at its heart; "an existence that is all the more absolute in that it no longer corresponds to anything that exists" (ibid., p. 336).

He assesses his attempts in this respect as "tilling this ground [here] by plowing a series of concentric rows" and, significantly, finds himself taking a first step away from the usual parameters of representation (ibid., p. 346). Having once again in lesson eighteen repeated that what is involved with respect to this object is profoundly enigmatic, since it is fundamentally a relationship to something that is hidden or occulted, he rather tentatively hazards a mathematical metaphor – an imaginary number – the square root of minus one (ibid., p. 327). This is an analogy that apparently surges up out of nowhere in this seminar, but one that will have very far-reaching consequences. Here what is notable is Lacan's hesitancy. This is a *mere* mathematical metaphor, put forward with reserve:

please allow me a formulation that came to me [...] but don't take it as a doctrinal formulation, take it at most as something designed to give you an image – it is insofar as human life can be defined as a form of arithmetic in which zero would be an irrational number.

(ibid., p. 327)

It is an altogether brilliant analogy and what he says of it here is pretty much identical to what he will say of it in *RSI* almost 20 years later. As an imaginary number, the square root of −1 cannot in itself correspond to anything real but its entire function must nevertheless be maintained. Here in the seminar on desire he specifies the relevance of this metaphor to the topic in hand, since this is equally true of "the relationship between the object and the hidden element – which is the subject's living prop – inasmuch as, taking on the function of the signifier, it cannot be subjectified as such" (ibid., p. 327).

The appearance of this mathematical formulation in the seminar, followed a few weeks later by the introduction of "the cut", is a harbinger of directions to come. But these rather abstract pointers make their appearance in a seminar that over and over, cuts to the quick of human pain, and will find in mourning the most important and relevant access to an appreciation of the constitution of the object of desire in fantasy. In some ways this is classic Lacan – the reason he exercises such magnetism on those who spend years of their life trying to read him. The collision of dense abstraction with the pith of pain speaks to the unrepresentable at the heart of human experience that Freud tried to encompass when he spoke of the navel of the dream. Here in Seminar VI Lacan has already presented three dramatic and searing instances of what he calls the vertigo of pain, intolerable loss; the dream of the dead father, the cataclysmic loss experienced in the Saint Augustine anecdote and Hamlet's subjective collapse (ibid., p. 336). Now in lesson eighteen he generalizes this focus, making it clear that the mourning in question is not that experienced in the several deaths that punctuate any lifetime, but in a very particular death; that of the person "essential to you". In his biography of Freud published two years before this seminar, Ernest Jones had quoted Freud who had made exactly this point following the death of his beloved little grandson in 1923:

He (Freud) told me afterwards that this loss had affected him in a different way from any of the others he had suffered. They had brought about sheer pain, but this one had killed something in him for good.

(Jones, 1957, pp. 96–97)

For Freud, this loss was much more unbearable than his own cancer and he confesses to experiencing the first depression of his life. This touching incident recounted by Jones allows us to contrast the utter devastation described by Freud at this loss in 1923 against the far more liveable, almost workaday processes outlined in *Mourning and Melancholia* four years previously. The mourning Lacan speaks of here is of this second order and *Hamlet* offers us some access to it:

> The subject succumbs to the vertigo of pain, and finds himself in a certain relationship to the missing object that is, in some sense, illustrated for us by what occurs in the cemetery scene.
>
> (ibid., p. 336)

It is the irrevocability of loss, piercing the everyday accumulations of living that ordinarily mask it, that allows this object to appear in its absoluteness. For Lacan this is what provokes Laertes' action. Laertes jumps into the grave, out of his mind, and embraces the object whose disappearance is causing him such grief. It is clear that the object here has an existence that is all the more absolute because, in Lacan's words "it no longer corresponds to anything that exists" (ibid., p. 336). As with the square root of minus one, but in a more urgently immediate context, what is in question is a specific type of inexistence. And Lacan's remarks about Laertes' action could be expanded a little to make a further point. It is the imago of loss presented by Laertes' leap into the grave that spurs Hamlet in turn into the intensity of his grief and into re-inhabiting his own being; This is I, Hamlet the Dane. Lacan focusses on the mirror stage element of this rivalry with Laertes which is indeed present in Shakespeare's text, but it is also frequently observable at funerals that the person suffering the loss is in something like a state of subjective cancellation, numb, mechanical, and barely present, while others who were themselves in that situation some time ago, now, seeing imaged the trappings of death, are loosed into paroxysms of grief. This also forms part of the power of art and is an everyday instantiation of the problematic relation between representation and the o-object which will push Lacan down topological and mathematical pathways over the coming years.

But what he says of the o-object here is; it is image and it is pathos. There is nothing remotely abstract about this. The devastation of mourning which involves "a veritable, intolerable loss to human beings, gives rise in them to a hole in reality [*réel*]" (ibid., p. 336). Lacan is specific:

> the truly intolerable dimension of human experience that comes with mourning is not the experience of your own death, which no-one has, but that of the death of another person, when that other person is essential to you.
>
> (ibid.)

And his description of what happens at this point is deeply interesting. We have seen from the beginning of this seminar that the *Hilflosigheit* invoked by Freud is for Lacan that of both the subject and the big Other, and he has repeatedly described how the subject must bring something in from his imaginary texture to sustain him at this point. But now it would seem that when this structure, that of the fundamental fantasy is smashed by the death of the essential one, the big Other takes it upon itself to actively intervene at the level of the Symbolic. The hole in reality renders mourning not unlike a psychosis where the hole occurs in the Symbolic. Similarly to psychosis, "what we have here is the signifier that is essential to the structure of the Other", in other words, presumably that which gives me my world, and without which my world implodes (ibid., p. 336). The insufficiency of the Other at this point of intolerable pain mobilizes the entire signifying system, calls into play ritual, ceremony, public acknowledgement, happenings that clearly cannot fill this hole, but signal its enormity by a concerted excess of representational ploys.

> Funeral rites have a macrocosmic nature, since there is nothing that can fill the hole in the real with signifiers unless it is the totality of the signifier itself [...] The work of mourning presents itself [...] as a palliative for the chaos that ensues owing to the inability of all the signifying elements to deal with the hole in existence that has been created by someone's death. The entire signifying system is brought to bear on even the slightest case of mourning.
>
> (ibid., p. 337)

For very good reason says Lacan; for in the absence of these representational devices supplied by ritual at the level of the symbolic order, all kinds of rogue representations at the level of the Imaginary may proliferate, notably ghosts. And here Lacan gestures to the insufficient and abbreviated funeral rites in *Hamlet*.

What is one to think of Lacan's "synthesizing" of the mechanism of mourning with the loss of the phallus in the castration complex? (ibid., p. 346). At one level this is a brilliant move since in both instances Freud describes a seemingly impossible loss being managed by way of identification on the part of the subject. So something very important is being said about an originary loss constitutive of subjectivity. The question is how exactly is one to define the phallus here? Lacan bases what he has to say on Freud's 1924 paper, *The Dissolution of the Oedipus Complex* in which Freud pits the narcissistic attachment to the penis over against the danger of incestuous triumph, with the victory going to the narcissistic preservation of the penis, which is preserved yes, but also paralyzed (Freud, 1924d). This is clearly stated and clearly paraphrased up to a point by Lacan: "Stated otherwise [by Freud], the subject lets go of what was most important to him – namely, the love relationship [...] because [...] of his narcissistic relationship with [...] the phallus" (ibid., p. 347). But rather astoundingly "the upshot is the loss of the phallus experienced as a radical loss that no satisfaction can plug up" (ibid., p. 347). It seems to me that the other avatars of loss invoked by Lacan in this seminar function more effectively than does this one. What is in question is a loss that is absolute. The subject is deprived of something that is related to his very life, something upon which all the dimensions of being itself converge and this is what here is called the phallus (ibid., pp. 312, 327). What his audience needs to grasp, and Lacan repeats this definition at least three times, is that the 0-object is in a substitutive relation to the phallus. Having asked the question how does the object become the object, he proffers this substitutive event, while admitting that what is going on here is profoundly enigmatic: "the object – which is the object of desire solely insofar as it is one of the terms in fantasy – takes the place […] of what the subject is deprived of symbolically […] namely, the phallus" (ibid., p. 312). It is owing to this that the object takes on the place that it has in fantasy, in other words presumably its very specific intensities. This formulation allows us to conceptualize

> in what respect this imaginary object finds itself in a position in which what one might call the virtues or the dimensions of being converge on it; it goes so far as to become the true decoy [or: lure, *leurre*] of being that the object of human desire is.
>
> (ibid., p. 312)

This powerful observation is immediately followed by invoking Simone Weil's miser and his relation to what is too intimate, too close, to be brought into focus. It seems to me that Lacan's own telling of the Saint Augustine anecdote in the previous section offers a much more searing instance of devastating loss and the finding of the substitutive prop that will maintain the subject in existence than does this one.

Eventually in the final lessons, Lacan will (somewhat) clarify what he is thinking here about the relations between the o-object and the phallus, suggesting that the phallus is the object of castration and the o-object its effect (ibid., p. 368). This statement will however be itself de-stabilized by further theorizations before the close of the year.

In focussing as he does on the fact that Hamlet can only fulfil his destiny, can only strike the mortal blow when he is himself mortally wounded, Lacan touches for the first time on a territory he will examine more fully the following year. This is the "between two deaths". Throughout his commentary he has reminded his audience of the procrastination that marks Hamlet's relation to time all through the play. But also, by repeatedly drawing the attention of his audience to this brief space between two deaths, in which Hamlet kills Claudius and everything comes crashing down, he invokes what Terry Eagleton calls the time specific to tragedy, which is *kairos*, a time zone that has exited *chronos*, defined as the gradual passage of historical time, and is instead outside of history (Eagleton, 2003). This is the between two deaths, the charged time, devoid of futurity, in which Hamlet can at last act (Eagleton, ibid., p. 181). What happens in the cemetery scene, to some extent also happens outside time, not as a deliberate act, but rather as a revelatory flash. In the instant that Laertes takes the dead Ophelia in his arms, Hamlet sees, and for the first and only time in the play, names himself: This is I, Hamlet the Dane. Momentarily because it is not possible otherwise, as the o-object appears in a lightning bolt of recognition, the "I" which Lacan will call its analogue can say itself.

If as Jean Michel Rabaté has suggested, Lacan's commentary on *Hamlet* in this seminar was more a matter of happenstance than a thought out plan, the reader can only applaud happenstance. One may not agree with everything he says, but this section of the seminar remains an extraordinary achievement. Lacan is detailed, attentive, impressively insightful. Extraordinarily, almost everything he says is both a totally valid reading of the play and a brilliant exposition of the teaching on desire with which he is engaged. As Patrick Guyomard argues in *La Jouissance du tragique* Lacan's domain *is* tragedy (1992). Certainly this is true for the great middle years of his teaching. And these years are where one will find his finest incursions into literature, something earlier readers might have foreseen when reading his brilliant article on the Papin sisters in Minotaure back in 1933.

References

Alexandrian, S. (1974). *Le Surréalisme et le rêve*. Paris: Gallimard.

Allouch, J. (1994). *Marguerite ou l'Aimée de Lacan*. Paris: E.P.E.L.

Crevel, R. (1933), "Notes en vue d'une psycho-dialectique", in, *S.A.S.D.L.R.* Paris: Éditions des cahiers libres, 5, 15 mai, pp. 45–52.

Derrida, J. (1978). *Writing and Difference*. (Trans.). Bass, A. Chicago: University of Chicago Press.

Eagleton, T. (2003). *Sweet Violence: The Idea of the Tragic*. London: Wiley & Sons.

Freud, S. (1917e). Mourning and Melancholia. *S.E.*, *XIV*. pp. 237–258.

Freud, S. (1928b). Dostoevsky and Patricide. *S.E.*, *XXI*. pp. 173–196.

Freud, S. (1924d). The Dissolution of the Oedipus Complex. *S.E.*, *IX*. pp. 173–182.

Georgin, R. (1977). *Lacan*, Lausanne: L'age de l'homme-Cistre.

Guyomard, P. (1992). *La Jouissance du tragique*. Paris: Aubier.

Jones, E. (1957). *Sigmund Freud, Life and Work*. London: Hogarth.

Macey, D. (1988). *Lacan in Contexts*. London: Verso.

Rabaté, J.-M. (2001). *Jacques Lacan*. New York: Palgrave.

Shakespeare, W. (1979). Henry V, in, *Complete Works*. London and Glasgow: Collins.

Sharpe, E. (1937). *Dream Analysis*. London: Routledge.

Warminski, A. (1988). "Reading over Endless Histories: Henry James' Altar of the Dead". *Yale French Studies*, 74.

Lacan, J.:

Lacan, J. (1931a). "Écrits 'inspirés'; Schizographie", in Lacan, J. *De la psychose paranoïaque dans ses rapports avec la personnalité, suivi de premiers écrits sur la paranoïa*. Paris: Seuil (1975).

Lacan, J. (1931b). "Structures des psychoses paranoïaques", *Semaine des hôpitaux de Paris*, juillet, pp. 437–445. Republished in *Ornicar?*, 44, printemps 1988, pp. 5–18.

Lacan, J. (1922). "Le problème du style et la conception psychiatrique des formes para paranoïaques de l'expérience", *Le Minotaure*, 1, p. 68. (Also in *De la psychose paranoïaque dans ses rapports avec la personnalité*. Paris: Seuil, 1975, pp. 383–388).

Lacan, J. (1933a). "Motifs du crime paranoïaque: le crime des sœurs Papin", *Le Minotaure*, 3/4, pp. 25–28. (Also in *De la psychose paranoïaque dans ses rapports avec la personnalité* Paris: Seuil, 1975, pp. 389–398).

Lacan, J. (1933b). "Hiatus Irrationalis". *Le Phare de Neuilly*, 3–4, 1933, reprinted in *Magazine litteraire* 11, 1977, p. 121.

Lacan, J. (1975). *De la psychose paranoïaque dans ses rapports avec la personnalité, suivi de Premiers écrits sur la paranoia*, Paris: Seuil.

Lacan, J. (2006). *Écrits. The First Complete Edition in English*. (Trans.) Fink, B. New York: W.W. Norton & Co.

The seminars:

——. (1961–1962). *The Seminar of Jacques Lacan, Book IX, Identification*. (Trans) Gallagher, C. Unpublished. www.lacaninireland.com

——. (1974–1975). *RSI The Seminar of Jacques Lacan. Book XXII. 1973–1974*. (Trans.). Gallagher, C. Unpublished. www.lacaninireland.com

——. (1992). *The Ethics of Psychoanalysis. The Seminar of Jacques Lacan. Book VII. 1959–1960*. (Ed.) Miller, J.-A. (Trans.) Porter, D. London: Routledge.

——. (1999). *On Feminine Sexuality, The Limits of Love and Knowledge, 1972–1973. Encore. The Seminar of Jacques Lacan, Book XX*. (Ed.) Miller, J.-A. (Trans.) Fink, B. New York & London: W.W. Norton & Co.

——. (2015). *Transference. The Seminar of Jacques Lacan, Book VIII*. (Ed.) Miller, J.-A. (Trans.) Fink, B. Cambridge: Polity Press.

——. (2019). *Desire and its Interpretation, The Seminar of Jacques Lacan, Book VI*. (Ed.) Miller, J.-A. (Trans.). Fink B. Cambridge: Polity Press. Also (Trans.). Gallagher, C. Unpublished. www.lacaninireland.com

Chapter 5

The dialectics of desire

The last section of the seminar, lessons twenty to twenty-seven, is both a recapitulation and an expansion of the central tenet of this year's teaching; the new notation of the subject of desire as $\$\lozenge a$, which is also the structure of fantasy, with all that this entails. Despite rather dismissively referring to the previous section as "a humungous digression" the shadow of *Hamlet* falls on this recapitulation and it repeatedly refers to the processes involved with respect to the subject and the Other as "a common tragedy" (Lacan, 2019, pp. 430, 376). The year is 1959 and psychoanalytic thinking is dominated by object relations theory and the British school. This dominance allows Lacan to draw a clear demarcation between the object as it functions in this school of thought and the entirely new object he has introduced, that which sustains the subject in the fantasy. With respect to this o-object Lacan is of course breaking new ground week by week, and as a result brilliance and incoherence are frequently intertwined in the definitions proffered. As in earlier lessons, the o-object continues to be theorized as the vital support of the subject at the point where he is without resource. But in anticipation of future seminars it is also identified to "the cut" as it occurs in topology, to the "not-One", and also to the subject as "counting", all of which analogies will be further developed in his ninth seminar *Identification*, while the "something symbolized by nothing" presages the lengthy explorations of the vanishing point and the origins of zero in his twelfth and thirteenth seminars *The Object in Psychoanalysis* (1964–1965) and *Crucial Problems* (1965–1966), respectively. What will perdure through all the seminars of course is his haunting definition of this o-object as the nothing beyond which "the subject will seek out the shadow of that life of his which he at first lost" (ibid., p. 373). A provocative direction not pursued in this seminar is its description as the analogue in the unconscious of the "I" in conscious living (ibid., p. 367). Four years later in Seminar X, this "analogue" is a now unambiguous assertion; "right where you say *I* – that is where, at the level of the unconscious, the *a* properly speaking is located" (Lacan, 2014, p. 103).

However, this section extends well beyond recapitulation and anticipation. It carefully, explicitly, and effectively ties all this newness in with solid Freudian positions. It also introduces these newly theorized concepts into the clinical field. In pursuit of this latter aim the structure of fantasy $\$ \Diamond a$ is demonstrated in the various guises in which it is lived by the hysteric, the obsessional, and the psychotic, and – at much greater length – by the pervert, or more accurately in perverse fantasy. The radically new elements of this seminar, in particular the introduction of "the cut" in this last section will dominate what he has to say about this latter, and considerable space is given to an examination of the cut as a structural feature of perverse fantasy, which surprisingly is ultimately linked to sublimation when, as is his wont, Lacan ends this seminar by referencing some of the major themes to be explored in the following year.

An unobtrusive but pervasive feature of this last section is Lacan's tentativeness. Often in reading Lacan, one has to grapple with mantric statements, apparently unamenable to questioning. Here on several occasions Lacan describes the terms he is using as not the best, lacking in rigour, and "allowing himself to be ridiculous" (ibid., pp. 417, 367, 421, respectively). On one occasion he tells his audience that the class has perhaps been the most difficult of all he had ever given, refers to what he is doing as mental gymnastics, and encourages his listeners to follow him along these austere pathways (ibid., p. 388). What we encounter here is his own struggle to think along these "austere pathways", and his concern that his listeners may not be able to follow. Very different to the high-handed obscurantism in which he sometimes seems to indulge. The great American scholar Shoshana Felman kindly shared a text with me in which she describes this tentativeness as a feature of Lacan's later teaching. Written for *Le Monde* in 2001 to commemorate the 20th anniversary of Lacan's death, but never published, this text describes Felman's weekly meetings with Lacan after each lesson of his twenty-first seminar *Les non-dupes errent* of 1973–1974. In these meetings Lacan would be discouraged, downhearted, admitting that although he had worked all night on the seminar, he had been unable to put anything coherent together. Felman in turn would admit that for the first hour she had understood nothing, but that always, before the end, she would glimpse something enormously innovative and stimulating, which she would then spell out to an amazed and delighted Lacan. This is an anecdote to keep in mind as one wades into the cascade of difficult ideas here. One approach, perhaps reductive, but I think useful is to note that there are two primary thrusts in this section – a forward thrust into radically new territory, and a backward one legitimating and incorporating this newness into existing psychoanalytic theory. And within these, a robustly repetitive consolidation of what the year has produced. A very inadequate attempt will be made to treat these elements separately, and to interrogate the Freudianism claimed for some of this newness.

Consolidation

So let us start with the manner in which these last lessons of the seminar drive home the points made earlier concerning the fundamental fantasy. However helpful (and on occasion, accurate) it may be to read this as a relationship between subject and object, Lacan warns his listeners against such a reading: "It does not designate a relationship between the subject and the object; it designates fantasy, insofar as fantasy sustains the subject as desiring – [...] at a point beyond his discourse" (ibid., p. 454). Could we say then that the formula $\$ \Diamond a$ is a way of writing the subject of the unconscious? If so this newness can be firmly located on the established terrain of psychoanalysis. And indeed this proves to be the case. "This notation signifies that the subject is present in fantasy as the subject of unconscious discourse" (ibid.). At a number of points in this last section Lacan subverts the more conventional way of reading this formula as indeed representing a relationship, while at other times, he appears to underwrite it. But neither of its terms is to be privileged over the other because the status of the object is now very different to earlier formulations:

> It is no longer simply a question of the function of the object as I tried to formulate it for you two years ago, nor is it the function of the subject [...] which is distinguished [...] by a vanishing of the subject insofar as he must name himself. What interests us is the correlation between the two.
>
> (ibid., pp. 412–413)

It is in the correlation that this crucial drama is embedded. "The correlation is such that the object has the precise function of signifying the point at which the subject cannot name himself" (ibid., p. 413). This insistence on indivisibility undermines the binarism central to Western thought and presages an important direction in the work of the later Lacan. Traditionally in Western thought, the two end terms in question, subject and object, are not just set up as separate entities, but especially since the seventeenth-century promulgation of scientific methodology, as actively opposed to each other. From the outset of this seminar Lacan has taken issue with this opposition, in order to introduce the very specific intrication of subject and object which finds expression in the formula for the fundamental fantasy. Fast forward to *Encore* some 14 years later when he will aver that: "the reciprocity between subject and object *a* is total" (Lacan, 1999, p. 127). Here in lesson twenty-one of Seminar VI, he is thinking this out, repeating that the subject of the unconscious is not to be found at either of the end terms, but is to be located in the interval, the between-space, in other words, "*inter-esse*". Lacan puns on the phrase "*il l'intéresse*" suggesting that this phrase catches the content of his teaching that day. This can take the reader into all kinds of surmise. Insofar as she is desiring, interested, which is one of the most accessible ways we can recognize the desiring subject – interested in this and that – the status of this subject, Lacan punningly but tellingly suggests is "*inter-esse*", to be between (ibid., p. 388). This is perhaps a more accessible way of thinking about the gap or the cut, concepts that Lacan then goes on to introduce.

We know that Freud too gestured towards this between-space. In an important footnote near the end of *The Interpretation of Dreams* he talks of how difficult it was to get analysts to shift their attention from the manifest to the latent content of the dream and bemoans the fact that now they have become fixated on this latent content, instead of realizing that the activity of the unconscious is to be located between the two (Freud, 1900a, p. 506). In his most recent book *C'est à quel sujet*, Guy le Gaufey comes back repeatedly to this status of the subject as relative. Quoting from the writings of the eighteenth-century philosopher, Maine de Biran, whom Lacan also invokes on occasion, Le Gaufey tries to envisage a relation between two elements which are distinguishable without being separate, or perhaps a connection between two necessary elements of the same fact (Le Gaufey, 2009, p.26). And as mentioned in Chapter 1, in the seminar on the psychoses three years earlier, Lacan referred to the existence in older grammatical forms of a voice which was neither active nor passive but positioned between the two, and known not surprisingly as the middle voice. With increasing complexity from Seminar VI onward, this middle space will be theorized as the cut, the gap, the interval, the slit. Much of this theorization will be bafflingly abstract and is best read with Seminar IX (*Identification*) to hand although we will attempt further on to trace the directions adumbrated here. But there are also easier ways of approaching "being" (*esse*) in this seminar.

As is the way with puns, the "*esse*" of *inter-esse* turns out to be multi-directional. Lacan in this section again explicitly announces his new focus on being, pointing out to his listeners at the beginning of lesson twenty-three that he has "foregrounded the term "being"" (ibid., p. 407). And *esse* (to be) can also be heard as the interrogative *Est-ce?* – a notation of the very first coming into being of the subject, what Lacan calls "the subject in abeyance" (ibid., p. 376). This S, Lacan says, "is the id [*Ça*], and in an interrogative form. If you add a question mark, S is in fact articulated as *Est-ce?* ['Is it?' or 'Is this?']" (ibid., p. 376). Throughout the seminar this primordial drama has been heavily weighted by Lacan. A weighting that as suggested earlier, constitutes a perceptible departure from strict Freudianism in that it appears to be at least as central and as crucial as the Oedipus complex deemed by Freud himself to be the defining phenomenon of childhood (Freud, 1905d, p. 226). How can this departure be made to look like a non-departure?

Can the o-object be Freudian after all?

Lacan's focus is the subject "*in statu nascendi*", the subject at the point of his coming into being. This drama which has already been sketched out more than once in earlier lessons is here summarized as "the subject's first position, grasped in the act of the first articulation of demand. Its necessary counter-weight is the position of the real Other, rA, insofar as it is all-powerful in responding to this demand" (ibid., p. 374). The significance and eventual fall-out of this drama cannot be overstated as Lacan goes on to say. It "is the basis on which the principles of the child's history are built [...] the mainspring of what is repeated at the deepest level of his destiny; this is what commands his behavior's unconscious modulation" (ibid., p. 376). Assertions that leave no doubt about its impact, and that seem to shunt Lacan out of the Freudian camp. As noted earlier, in the midst of abstract formulae indicating what is going on, Lacan repeatedly insists on the concreteness of all of this "there is nothing more concrete than this [...] it is something primitive that is established in a trusting relationship" (ibid., pp. 375–376). Lacan is often criticized as someone who high-handedly theorizes at lofty heights far removed from the suffering encountered in the clinic, and in fairness that is how it sometimes looks. One of the reasons this gateway seminar, *Desire*, is so deeply interesting is that we can see how, at the point where dauntingly abstract concepts begin to be formulated, they do in fact cut to the quick of the human condition. Lesson twenty-one is a case in point. The crucial question of the little pre-subject just evoked: to what extent can I trust this Other runs aground on the impotence of this big Other. This Other can only respond in the name of "a shared tragedy". The little pre-subject will not find the answer,

> for at this level he encounters in the Other the hollow or empty space that I formulated by telling you that "there is no Other of the Other"; that no possible signifier can guarantee the authenticity of the series of signifiers.
>
> (ibid., p. 377)

This predicament can clearly not be without consequence, and Lacan is unambiguous. "This is why the subject depends so essentially on the Other's goodwill" (ibid.). The point has been made elsewhere in the seminar. The reader will recall that in the commentary on *Hamlet*, two different levels of this drama were evoked. Here the more usual level, that undergone by every subject is evoked, in a manner that is stark and unadorned. It is precisely at this juncture between question and non-answer that the o-object comes into being: "it arises at the very place where the S wonders what he truly is and what he truly wants" (ibid.). So the *Est-ce?* is no abstract question. "The subject manages to prop himself up with this object at the moment at which he vanishes when faced with the signifier's failure [or: inability, *carence*] to answer for his place as a subject at the level of the Other" (ibid.). What is clearly in question here is the primordial drama with "the maternal Other" (ibid., p. 372), and it is her inability to respond that sets the foreverness of desire in motion. "Nothing real on the Other's side [...] can ever make up for this, except by a series of additions [...] that will never be exhausted" (ibid., p. 372). This unappeasable longing is what becomes encapsulated in the o-object, and this Lacan says is in fact its core function. The word Lacan uses is *l'os*, the bone, translated by Fink as *hitch* (ibid.), and by Gallagher as *core* (p. 261). Both translations work well. The term will reappear 27 years later in Seminar XXIII *The Sinthome* where the neologism "*l'osbjet*" is used to designate the o-object (Lacan, 2016, p. 132).

So is this drama more crucial than that produced by the Oedipus complex? The two narratives can certainly not be mapped onto each other in a point by

point way. Notwithstanding this difficulty Lacan will go on to create a degree
of overlap in this last section of the seminar. He will be able to do this because
over the course of the year the narrative around this primordial drama segues
convincingly into language resonant with the dereliction proper to castration.
It is in fact the threat of this dereliction that spurs the o-object into being.
A shield is needed against the pain of existence "when all desire disappears from
it" (ibid., p. 115). For the dreamer in the dream of the dead father, Oedipal
rivalry had functioned effectively against exposure to this pain, but now with
the father gone the son can only continue to protect himself in the dream fantasy by switching the necessary ignorance to the father himself. But there is no
sense here that this is a process necessary for the humanization of desire, such
as posited in Freud's Oedipus complex. Also alongside this poignant reading of
the dream of the dead father, another image permitting us to access something
of what is in question in the o-object is repeatedly evoked. This is the miser's
treasure, and Dalio's blush – the relationship to the most intimate element of
ourselves, something too close to know, too disabling to be able to bear. An
image that will reappear two years later as a way of introducing the o-object is
agalma (Lacan, 2015, p. 134). And in lesson twelve of Seminar VI yet another
narrative is introduced. The Saint Augustine story profiles a revelatory image of
desire that constitutes the "first apprehension of the object, insofar as he [the
subject] is deprived of it" (ibid., p. 219). On the side of the onlooking child his
deathly pallor signals a "sort of passionate self-destruction" (ibid). On the other
side an image of paradisal completeness, becoming discernible for the first time
in this blinding flash of loss. How to exit this annihilating impasse? According
to Lacan the rescue is achieved by means of substitution, a substitution that will
supply the necessary lineaments of the fundamental fantasy. The image of the
other child is substituted for this barred subject who is "fundamentally pallid
and anguished", and is named once again by Lacan as ego: "He does so by sub-
stituting the other's image, i(a) – namely, the successive identifications that will
come to constitute the ego – for himself" (ibid., p. 221). And an actual elective
object is substituted for this impossible paradisal completeness (ibid.). Here the
fundamental fantasy is a substitute formation, as it also is in the dream of the
dead father, but these are not Oedipal scenarios.

As the seminar progresses the emphasis on the helplessness of the little
pre-subject which spurs the o-object into being remains, but the dereliction
involved is not only its spur but a crucial element of the cost of this transac-
tion. The little pre-subject must lose what is most essential to his life. "He must
make up for this inability [defaut] through personal sacrifice" (ibid., p. 367). An
alternative suggested by Lacan's phrase in French – payer de sa personne – would
be: must pay with his person (ibid). This paying of something that is taken at
his own expense is named "the pound of flesh", and, although Lacan announces
himself as tentative here, is very specifically identified with castration. "The
subject who pays the price necessary to be able to locate himself as faltering
is thus brought into the dimension that is always present whenever desire is

involved: having to pay for castration" (ibid.). The question then is: how is the non-response of the Other to be aligned with the threat of castration? This is done at several different points, and with perhaps several different levels of success.

It turns out that this non-answer, the inability of the Other to respond, troped repeatedly as "a common tragedy" is not a generalized powerlessness (see pp. 371, 375, 376). It is because this other does not have the phallus at its disposal – the phallus as vital turgidity. (Since the phallus pops up under such a plethora of different guises it is always worth noting which one is currently in play). In lesson twenty when the topic of paying the price that is castration is evoked, Lacan, to the joy of the reader asks: what is the phallus? (ibid., p. 368). At last we will know! What follows could not have been anticipated. Referring to a case history by Felix Boehm, one of the early analysts, the phallus Lacan evokes here is not a phallus at all, but very specifically "an evagination [...] the turning inside out of the vagina" (ibid., p. 369). There is no ambiguity here: "the phallic appendix seems to be made from the externalization of the insides" (ibid.). What Lacan is referring to is the fantasy of Boehm's homosexual patient, but given his earlier descriptions of the o-object as somehow capturing the most intimate part of oneself, that which cannot be shown even to oneself, this bizarre image does indeed have a certain relevance.

> What can we say about this fantasy if not that the phallus presents itself here in a radical form, inasmuch as its function, in the end, is to show on the outside what is on the subject's imaginary inside?
>
> (ibid.)

Nonetheless, while complying with these criteria and obviously effective for Boehm's patient, this does seem a rather far-fetched version of the omni-presence of the phallus in psychoanalytic theory. The reader may feel similar reservations a few pages further on when the role of the phallus is aligned with "whatever sticks out" (ibid., p. 386). As he says here the phallus is not the only appendage to stick out, but – and the androcentric bias is what *sticks out* most in this reasoning – "the relationship of the subject to himself that makes him most apprehensive – namely, that of tumescence – naturally designates the phallus as the object that is most often offered up to the cutting function [...]" (ibid.). This statement is situated between, on the one hand, a very forced link between castration and the o-object, and on the other, a very interesting link between the phallus and narcissism.

The forced link assigns functions to the o-object which it has not had up to now and will not have again. The title of this lesson, lesson twenty-one, is "In the Form of a Cut", so it is to be expected that the language of mutilation should be brought into play around the castration complex. "When we turn to the castration complex, we find another form of little *a*, which is mutilation" (ibid., p. 384). In terms of separating the subject from some part of himself, the concept of mutilation is congruent with what we have heard so far. However, identifying the role of o with "the power to be different and better" seems forced (ibid., p. 385). Initiation rites, designed "to transform the subject", to give to desire "a function with which the subject's being can identify and by which it can be designated as such [...] a fully fledged man" seem very distant from the other ways in which the o-object has come into being (ibid., pp. 385–386). It looks as if different theoretical processes are being compressed into the same mould here. Since the o-object is being broached for the first time in this seminar, the fact that this should be done via a series of concentric and unaligned narratives is in itself not problematic, but we are of course at liberty to assess the respective valences of these narratives. We must also recognize that the non-aligned narrative is the hallmark of the unconscious. Shards of story, Freud tells us, are jammed up together like pack ice (Freud, 1900a, p. 341). And it is the inception of unconscious knowledge that Lacan is trying to circumscribe in the theorization of this new concept. At this edge, he tells us, the unconscious begins: "Another dimension begins here where it is no longer possible for the subject to know either who he is or where he is. Any and all possibility of naming himself ends here" (ibid., p. 378). That description stands starkly at variance with the placid stolidity of initiation rites that designate the subject as "a fully fledged man" and "in their fundamental function [...] play the role of little *a*" (ibid., p. 385).

Rather hilariously given the pervasiveness of its popping up in the seminar, Lacan reacts with surprise to the accusation of phallocentrism (ibid., p. 477). In this section, however, where he is trying to find a place for the o-object in the castration complex, the connection he makes between the phallus and narcissism, even if androcentric, is interesting and convincing. (This connection will be made again later in the seminar). From the very first lesson onward Lacan had suggested that narcissism or narcissistic eros is what comes to the subject's rescue in the crisis of *Hilflosigkeit* engendered by the drama in question. And from the beginning he signals a complexification here. While the subject defends himself with his ego ... he also "constructs something with the other that, unlike specular experience, is flexible" (ibid., p. 19). This point is repeated throughout the seminar: it is narcissism that offers the subject a prop, a solution or solution pathway to the problem of desire. And in lesson twenty-one he draws a parallel between the fragility of the phallus, its unsureness as to whether or not it can perform, and the mirror stage, which brings into play the fragility of the "I". The same (the apprehension about tumescence) "is true of the function of narcissism as the imaginary relationship of the subject to himself" with specific reference to the mirror stage (ibid., p. 386).

Lacan was clearly aware of his departure from strict Freudianism in this seminar. In his subsequent major theorization of the o-object in his tenth seminar *Anxiety* he goes some way towards reconciling the originary drama so heavily weighted here, and Freud's castration complex by referring to this originary drama installing the fundamental fantasy as a kind of imaginary castration.

"Everything starts with imaginary castration" he says, and widens out the various forms this may take, with the result that the Saint Augustine anecdote cited in Section 2 is just one of several scenarios embodying "the fracture that occurs when the libidinized image of the *semblable* is approached, at the phase of a certain imaginary drama" (Lacan, 2014, p. 46). The particularity of the scenario is in every case, decisive. "Hence the importance of the mishaps of the *scene* which for this reason is called *traumatic*. The imaginary fracture presents all sorts of variations and possible anomalies [...]" (ibid). He will also suggest in *Anxiety* that there are two kinds of imaginary identification (ibid., p. 37); "*i(a)*" and the more "mysterious identification [...] *a*" (ibid.,) referring his listeners back to the graveyard scene in *Hamlet* where this o-object is designated without any ambiguity whatsoever (ibid.). Here in this section of Seminar VI, the reader will note the very first indication of this bifurcation in the Imaginary: "At the outset, it is the other's image that serves to prop up the subject, at least at the point at which he qualifies as desire. Later comes the more complex structure known as fantasy" (Lacan, 2019, p. 422). In both *Identification* and *Anxiety* these two forms overlap to a degree since the o-object "is usually masked beneath the *i(a)* of narcissism and misrecognized in its essence" (Lacan, 2014, p. 335).

As mentioned in Chapter 2, in the years that follow, the close alliance of the o-object with narcissistic eros so strongly established in Seminar VI will dissolve in a search for a non-narcissistic, non-specular entity which can fulfil this function, but the often poignant insights explored in *Desire* are not invalidated by this move. For now Lacan appears to privilege "the extreme, imaginary point where the subject's being resides, as it were, in its greatest density", and the merging of the drama that installs the fundamental fantasy with Freud's castration complex is cleverly if not altogether convincingly achieved (ibid., p. 424).

In this final section of the seminar a number of new, highly abstract, and difficult concepts are broached for the first time. On the one hand Lacan introduces all of this newness in order to push the minds of his listeners onto radically new territory. But on the other he insists that he is simply elucidating classic Freudian positions. Considerable time is spent on this linkage to Freud. So in the midst of grappling with "the cut", the "not-One" and the subject as "counting" the listener is comforted with the familiarity of the *fort/da* anecdote, a reading of *Wo es War soll ich warden* that is truer to Freud than the usual one, and a realization that Freud was already on the track of the o-object with his insistence on the navel of the dream as the authentic location of the unconscious. To some extent this is a lure, a tamping down of the big differences that are beginning to open up between Freudianism and Lacanianism. But it also establishes very valid connections. So for example when speaking of aphanisis, the aphanisis of the subject at the height of desire, he repeatedly makes it clear that we are on the terrain of the unconscious, Freud's terrain. And at several points, at the moment that he pushes his listeners to think this topologically, he vaults them back into Freudian familiarity.

Even the newly introduced cut is not un-Freudian:

> The subject's being must be articulated and named in the unconscious, but in the end, it cannot be. It is solely indicated at the level of fantasy by what turns out to be a slit, a structure based on a cut.
>
> (ibid., p. 424)

And Freud too knew this:

> Let me remind you that we find a trace of the notion of the disappearance of the subject in Freud's work when he talks about the dream's navel as the point at which all the dreamer's associations converge only to disappear. At that point, they can only be related to what he calls the *Unerkannt*. This is what is at issue here.
>
> (ibid., p. 424)

The *fort/da* anecdote too turns out to be a model for the relations between S and o, *fort/da* being a game where the subject grasps himself in the moment of his disappearance: "I am now going to indicate what I would like to convey to you regarding the relations between $ and *a*, by first providing a model of them, which is no more than a model: *fort/da*" (ibid., p. 415).

And earlier, when making the same point, speaking of the moment where S tries to designate himself as the subject of unconscious discourse, Lacan proffers this "I" as the true reading of Freud's *Wo es War soll ich werden* (ibid., p. 378). Freud's *ich*, Lacan tells us, refers not to the ego as is often supposed, but to the personal pronoun "I": "What designates to us the place [...] of the I that must come to light? The index of desire, precisely speaking [...] desire sustained by the co-existence and opposition of two terms, $ and little *a*" (ibid., p. 378). A week earlier using a term which rarely occurs in his vocabulary Lacan had said of the pronoun "I" that it is the *analogue* of the o-object (ibid., p. 367), suggesting that just as the I is occupied only momentarily by each speaker in the instant of speech, and often conceals itself under the safer "we", the anonymous French "*on*", or other locutions, this same place is occupied in the unconscious by the o-object. The I is invoked more than once in this context. In lesson twenty-four he states, "Where *it speaks* in the unconscious chain, the subject cannot situate himself in his place, or articulate himself as *I*. He can only indicate himself qua disappearing [...] as a subject" (ibid., p. 424).

Another instance of embedding the new directions of this seminar in existing theory occurs in lesson twenty-one when Lacan rather dauntingly announces that he will now consider "the formal properties of object *a* in the structure of fantasy" (ibid., p. 382). He then goes on reassuringly to tie these to analytic experience and will list "a certain number of shared properties of the different forms of this object that are already known to you" (ibid.). It is worth noting here that although this direction will prove extremely fruitful in future work, Lacan is hesitant, questioning the legitimacy and the rigour of this approach, but justifying it by the need "to start from already familiar terrain" (ibid.). An interesting venture too in light of his earlier assertion that what he is calling the place of the object in desire "is completely new territory" (ibid., p. 346).

There are, he tells us three types of o-object that have heretofore been identified and located in analytic experience: "a, φ, and d" (ibid., p. 382). Interestingly even at this early stage, Lacan signals that this list is not a closed entity. The first of those listed, the pre-genital object translates as two objects, breast and shit. These will turn out to be exemplary in terms of what Lacan wants to show. The second, the phallus will be problematic. The third, the delusion, while inciting him to repeat what was said in earlier seminars will be convincingly justified as an instance of how the subject, at breaking point, draws something from his own substance in order to be able to bear the hole or absence of the signifier "at the level of the unconscious chain" (ibid., p. 383). Lacan does not lean here on the fact that the psychotic's response – to draw something from the Imaginary to supplement the hole in the Symbolic – is pretty much identical to the manner in which the origins of the fundamental fantasy are theorized in this seminar.

Earlier in the seminar when introducing Ophelia as o-object Lacan had recognized as "right-minded" the current psychoanalytic focus on object relations, while suggesting a degree of confusion with respect to "the theorization of the object as a so-called pre-genital object" (ibid., p. 310). Now returning to this topic, he finds in the breast and the shit, very effective exemplars illustrating how the cut might function. "What nourishes the subject is cut off from him at a certain moment […] and there is […] at the other end of the tube, the object he ejects and that is cut from him" (ibid., p. 383). It is because they are susceptible to the cut that these objects become eroticized. "Owing to this, they serve as props at the level of the signifier where the subject turns out to be situated as structured by a cut" (ibid.). One can see that even if this statement is not altogether clear, there is something convincing being said, and the breast and the shit, along with "the voice", "the nothing", and "the look" will form part of a list of o-objects in future seminars, a list that Lacan will always connote as not exhaustive.

At this point in *Desire*, the phallus is on the list, leading him onto strange terrain. As mentioned above, identifying the role of o with "the power to be different and better" seems altogether at odds with what we have heard thus far (ibid., p. 385). Lacan himself seems aware that these few pages on mutilation and initiatory rites, constitute a bizarre outcrop, and rather lamely justifies it with: "You must have noticed the ambiguities that revolve around the function of the phallus since I first began trying to broach it with you" (ibid.). Yes, as it happens we *have* noticed. The forced and unconvincing nature of this link has been discussed above (see also my essay "The Phallus of the Fifties: Those Years of 'Tranquil Possession'", Cox Cameron, 2019; Part III in this volume.).

The phallus will not remain on future listings of o-objects. Indeed it is surprising to see it here since Lacan, a week before, had drawn a clear distinction between phallus and o-object, pointing out that the phallus is the object of castration and the o-object is its effect (ibid., p. 368). But overall this tying in of the o-object to existing Freudian "objects" will prove extremely fruitful in opening up future theoretical and clinical directions.

An important factor in integrating the new elements of this seminar into existing structures relates to the clinic. In this last section, Lacan demonstrates the clinical relevance of its new focus, showing how the fundamental fantasy underpins phobia, hysteria, obsessional neurosis, and perverse fantasy, if not perversion itself. Much of what he has said up to now about the structure of fantasy $\$ \lozenge a$, has focussed on its two end terms. Here in this evocation of the clinic, the importance of the middle term, the need for something interposed, takes centre stage. As he puts it in lesson twenty-five, the notion of distance is so essential that it is perhaps after all, truly ineliminable from desire itself (ibid., p. 439). Speaking of phobia and of little Hans he re-introduces the scenario he had evoked in the very first lesson this year – that of the helplessness of the little pre-subject, faced with the desire of the Other. Having "no recourse" here in this "the simplest form of neurosis" (ibid., p. 425) is what causes the phobic object to be interposed: "[T]he phobic object is situated between the subject's desire and the Other's desire, and it fulfils a function of protection or defense there" (ibid.). Readers will recall that in lesson one it is the ego that performs this function. It is interesting to see the symptom now occupying this position, and also to see that the initial tragic resonances of this situation are somewhat alleviated. There is an answer to hand to the question: "can the subject (the subject who in the structure of fantasy is juxtaposed as $\$$ to a) find something that lightens his load [...] find something that sustains his presence, find something to latch onto?" (ibid., p. 426). The answer is yes. "At the onset of the whirlwind of fantasy, on the verge of the point of loss or disappearance indicated in the structure of fantasy, there is something that holds or stands firm" (ibid.). This turns out to be the symptom. Not a simple or self-evident answer, underpinned as it is by the repressed drive but nonetheless a slight modification of the tragic vision which has permeated this seminar. We are still very far from the *savoir faire* and the *bricolage* with which the subject patches up the deficits occasioned by this confrontation with the desire of the Other in Seminar XXIII *The Sinthome*, but the phobic, hysterical, and obsessional responses sketched here are not only possible but widespread, standard, and un-tragic. The focus is on the middle term, on what functions as maintaining distance between the $\$$ and the o-object. Up to now a lot of time has been spent in elucidating what is meant by each of the two end terms and as noted earlier Lacan had suggested that the gap between the two is where the subject is to be found. Here it is not the *inter-esse* that is emphasized but an actual saving distance. "Given that the object in fantasy is connected to the Other's desire, the goal is not to approach it" (ibid., p. 427). The subject now is not just without recourse, but exposed to a dangerous jouissance which could open "the true abyss of desire" to him (ibid.). It appears that the classic manoeuvres of both the hysteric and the obsessional are in fact responses to this danger. "The subject can sustain his desire when faced with the Other's desire in two manners: as an unsatisfied desire – that is in the case of hysteria – or as an impossible desire, which is the case in obsession" (ibid., p. 427). Once again, and rather to the reader's surprise, the highly innovative concept which is the structure of fantasy has been smoothly inserted into existing psychoanalytic orthodoxy. In fairness not uninterestingly, and although Lacan doesn't spend more than ten minutes making this point, he does complexify it somewhat, indicating how the hysteric tends to occupy the place of the o-object playing her part in the game "in the form of she who is at stake [...] [T]he obsessive, on the other hand, has a rather different position. He stays outside the game" (ibid., p. 428).

Cutting into the Freudian fabric

With respect to hysteria, obsessional neurosis and psychosis (via what he says of delusion) as o-object there is a sense that even though it is convincingly achieved, Lacan is simply traversing old ground and bedding down new ideas in what has been said already. Something else is happening with perverse fantasy. A noticeable amount of time is devoted to it in this final section, and readers will recall that in lesson seventeen, Lacan had also privileged it as bodying forth something essential of what he is in the process of exploring.

> As strange or bizarre as fantasy in perverse desire may appear to be, desire is always in some way involved [...] in a relationship that is always linked to pathos, to the pain of existing as such, of existing purely and simply, or existing as a sexual term.
>
> (ibid., p. 314)

In contrast with his bedding down of the structure of fantasy for neurosis in familiar theory, perverse fantasy is aligned with the most difficult theorizations of the year, and is introduced in lesson twenty-three via a consideration of "being" and its relation to "the least signifying of signifiers – namely, the cut" (ibid., p. 408). The cut of course had already been invoked in the context of neurosis but as discussed above, linked to known Freudian "objects". Here the lead in to a theorization of perverse fantasy is via a concentrate of the most opaque ideas of this year's teaching. The cut now is not just the cut but as mentioned above is identified with "being" itself: "Being is the same thing as cutting" (ibid.). This new focus on being is one of the perceptible innovations of this seminar and is presumably not entirely independent of the philosophical zeitgeist, which saw the publication of *Being and Time* (Heidegger, 1927), *Being and Nothingness* (Sartre, 1943), and *Being and Having* (Marcel, 1949). In the notes to this seminar Jacques-Alain Miller references Lacan's interest in being and the One to his (Lacan's) interest in the work of Etienne Gilson, the well-known Thomist scholar. In the first instance in this seminar "being" as we have seen is *Esse – Est-ce?* the primordial interrogative position with respect to the first Other which inaugurates subjectivity. But it is also the cut, and identifying being to the cut appears to embark Lacan on a direction very different to any of the above works with the possible exception of Sartre, since nothingness is also certainly in question for Lacan.

Although Lacan is specific in distinguishing perverse fantasy from perversion itself this section ranges comprehensively over exhibitionism, voyeurism, masochism, and … homosexuality. This latter "perversion" elicits his most phallocentric commentary, although to see the phallus as "the essential signifying element here" hardly marks it out from every other possible scenario at this stage of Lacan's thinking (ibid., p. 466). Also invoking the manner in which the pervert copes with the dilemma of being and/or having, brings Lacan up against the essential problematic shadowing this whole theory. Just as in the course of the previous year's seminar, the successful traversal of this dilemma via the Oedipus complex resulted in "real women" always being "a little lost", a bit astray in the head (Lacan, 2017, p. 179), now it turns out there is "an odd similarity" between the woman's unconscious formulation, and that of the pervert (Lacan, 2019, p. 449). A theory that convincingly sketches out the humanization of desire and its glitches for men but shunts women towards psychosis and perversion must surely be in need of an overhaul. Were there murmurs among his audience in 1959? We know from Gallagher's translation that this lesson, lesson twenty-five, was greeted with prolonged applause. In the very last lesson, however, he notes that some people may have got the impression that his conception of desire was "phallocentric" (ibid., p. 477)! It would be difficult for anyone who entirely agrees with everything Lacan says in this seminar, or for anyone who does not, to altogether rubbish this impression, and in fairness Lacan recognizes this, and goes on to justify this phallocentrism by referring to Kleinian theory. As often happens there is a sleight of concept at work here. Klein's focus is the penis, not the phallus. However, the phallus is not the most interesting element in what Lacan has to say in this section about perverse fantasy.

The week before in lesson twenty-two, Lacan had made a few relatively accessible observations about the cut, such as that reality is not a continuum but is made up of cuts, and had also seemed to suggest that it is a way of speaking about the unconscious: "the sort of cut constituted by the fact that the subject *is* not in a certain unconscious discourse, and that he does not know what he is in it" (ibid., p. 397). These mild remarks then ushered in a number of brief mantric statements of such opacity that a week later in his introduction to perverse fantasy he follows his initial comments on being with an admission that these earlier statements may have been "circumlocutory, not to say confused" (ibid., p. 408). In classic Lacanian style, he then goes on to massively complexify his "clarification" by invoking the "not-One" and "the subject as counting", themes barely adumbrated in this seminar, to which he will return three years later.

Let us for the moment stay with his take on perverse fantasy, since it receives extensive treatment in these last lessons of the year. For the reader, a more accessible point of entry into what will follow is his observation earlier in lesson seventeen that in contrast to neurosis where the accent falls on the first term, $, in perverse fantasy, "the entire emphasis is placed on the strictly imaginary correlative [...] little *a*" (ibid., p. 314). Lacan then goes on to discuss exhibitionism and voyeurism, before turning his attention more briefly to masochism, and as mentioned above, homosexuality. The most thought-provoking observation he makes concerns the aphanisis of the desiring subject at the climax of perverse fantasy, and its disappearance into the activity itself. Generalizations are dangerous of course, but this is demonstrable in Freud's own example, in "A Child is Being Beaten", where personhood has been struck out at both end terms, and only the act of beating subsists with its accompanying jouissance. Lacan wants to show this structure at work in exhibitionism, since in his view it best exemplifies the subject as being nothing more than the cut. He begins with a few accurate remarks about the preference of the exhibitionist for a public space, a dangerous setting, and the essential fantasized complicity with the one looking, or in the case of the voyeur with the one looked at. What the exhibitionist shows, however, is not *something*, but a kind of *nothing* – a glimpse, a flash, seen/not seen. "[w]hat is glimpsed in a certain relationship to what is not glimpsed is what I quite crudely call a pair of pants that opens and shuts" (ibid., p. 418). Lacan's recognition of the glimpse and its power is hugely significant and will be developed at length in his eleventh seminar *The Four Fundamental Concepts of Psychoanalysis* (Lacan, 1977). Here, since his focus is the cut, he is more interested in the opening of the pants, what he calls the slit in desire. "The subject designates himself in the slit" (Lacan, 2019, p. 418). As is his wont, Lacan repeats this statement a number of times, seeing it as true for both the exhibitionist and the voyeur. Can that be true in every single case? "Isn't it obvious to you that, in both cases, the subject is reduced to the artifice of the slit? This artifice occupies the place of the subject [...] [I]insofar as he is in his fantasy, the subject is the slit" (ibid., p. 419). And the obvious question presents itself. Does this relate to the woman's sexual organ, described by Lacan as what is, "according to our field, symbolically the most unbearable" (ibid.). A question best left aside for now Lacan says.

Thinking of a couple of scenes of perverse fantasy as they occur in literature I find helpful Lacan's expansion the following week of what he means by "the subject is the slit". Now in lesson twenty-four, the slit or gap is something that is both a hole and a flash in the Real (ibid., p. 423). Not unlike the masochistic fantasy explored by Freud, "the subject is indicated here in his activity", and nowhere else (ibid.). In this context we might re-read the famous Nausicaa episode in Joyce's *Ulysses* or the aeroplane scene in Dermot Bolger's *Emily's Shoes*. At the height of both these fantasies the subject has disappeared. In Lacanian language "an aphanisis of the subject occurs at the height of desire" (ibid., p. 424). Joyce's Nausicaa is a wonderful staging of the complicitous fantasy that pushes both participants to orgasm. The exhibitionist (and narrator) is Gertie McDowell who creates out of the masturbating Bloom, the smouldering hero of penny romance. "Whitehot passion was in that face, passion silent as the grave, and it had made her his" (Joyce, 1975, p. 476). Gertie's fantasy, centred as it is on the desiring onlooker is also a wonderful instance of what Lacan calls the structure of desire in perversion. "For what he aims at is the Other's desire, reproducing the structure of his own" (ibid., p. 420). And at the moment of orgasm there is no subject, only the flash – in this instance the flash of fireworks exploding over Sandymount Strand:

> And she saw a long Roman candle going up over the trees [...] and she let him and he saw and she saw that he saw [...] because he couldn't resist the sight of the wondrous revealment half offered [...] And then a rocket sprang and bang, shot blind and O! then the Roman candle burst and it was like a sigh of O!
>
> (Joyce, 1975, p. 477)

It is always interesting to test Lacan's mantric statements against clinical or literary examples. Not to prove that they are universally true, but to look at instances where their accuracy can be measured. This small episode in *Ulysses* would seem to show something of the aphanisis of the subject in favour of the object at the height of desire which, Lacan suggests, is particularly visible in perverse fantasy. This is the central point Lacan is making in stating that the subject here *is* the slit, the hole, the flash. The flash seems a brilliant way of catching the experience of vanishing, of evanescence. As Lacan says of the exhibitionist, "he is nothing but the flash of the object people speak of [...]" (ibid., p. 423). And the anamorphic cylinder invoked a year later in Seminar VII offers a very convincing instance of this something situated in a region that is between presence and absence, something only glimpsed in the flash, the twirl of the cylinder, revealing an image not to be found among the blurs of its inert surface (Lacan, 1992, p. 135).

Interestingly, in putting forward these observations, he tells his audience that he is deliberately putting to one side the role played in this economy by "the good old phallus of yesteryear" (ibid., p. 421). Something Joyce certainly does not do in the Nausicaa episode where a version of the phallus can clearly be seen profiled against the evening sky. Here writing the subject as cut on the blackboard, Lacan now says the same of the barred subject as he had previously said of the o-object – it too is the square root of minus one (ibid.).

At this point in the seminar Lacan diverts into the demonstration of how the o-object functions in phobia, hysteria, and obsessional neurosis discussed above, and then in lesson twenty-four returns to the phallus in one of several extended riffs on this topic. Generally speaking the reader of Lacan will have noticed that his signature serpentine approach can make it difficult to keep the different strands of his argument separate. This section is a good example of an interweave of a number of approaches which are not necessarily congruent in relation to each other. He begins with the assertion that in both neurosis and perversion the phallus plays a key role adding that what we are dealing with here is the phallus as signifier, "not purely and simply an organ" (ibid., p. 429). The Levi-Straussian cultural argument about the law of exchanges is then invoked but with a twist that would have surprised Levi-Strauss, since it is here that the highly charged subjective drama of "to be or not to be" will be played out. "In the law of exchanges – defined by the fundamental relations that regulate desire's interreactions in culture [...] – the subject presents himself qua phallus" (ibid., p. 430). Not the phallus just described – signifier of the law of fertility – but marker of a crisis, where "the subject can no longer get his bearings [...] in desire, starting at a certain moment: he is no longer, he fails to be" (ibid.). And it is here that he meets – not the phallus, but "the phallic function". This term will progressively replace "the phallus" in future seminars but the terminology here is far from clear. Here the subject undergoes a specific sequence summed up in terms of "being the phallus", "loss of bearings", and "encountering the phallic function". Lacan then recalls Ella Sharpe's patient whose dilemma is described as having to choose between being completely taken up by the devouring desire of a woman or being no-one. This is an interesting take on a certain subjective plight – to be it or be no-one, and then if you are it, not to have it. A plight that produces the first appearance in Lacan's teaching of the *vel*, which will feature largely in Seminar XI.

> If you will allow me to use a so-called logical sign, the V which is used to designate the "either/or" of disjunction [...] there is a choice to be made. Either "not to be it", not to be the phallus, and disappear, fail to be. Or, if he is it [...] if he is the phallus for the Other in the intersubjective dialectic, "not to have it".
>
> (ibid., p. 431)

It would seem that Freud's being or having, and Shakespeare's to be or not to be, have meshed in a very thought-provoking and clinically interesting manner here. A few sentences sketch how the subject might exit this dilemma. On the one hand there is a cryptic and un-illuminating evocation of the "not-One", by which "the barred subject in desire's fundamental structure designates himself" (ibid.). On the other this exit can be achieved by the most reasonable and most obvious truth to be gleaned from the castration complex, spelt out by Freud – the fact that all human beings are beset with a radical inadequacy: "the subject remains in an inadequate position, that of peril as regards the phallus in men, and that of absence of the phallus in women" (ibid.). In terms of interweave, what we have seen so far in this small section of lesson twenty-four is the phallus as signifier of the law of fertility, as focus of an existential crisis – to be

or not to be – as marker of inadequacy, and now lastly identified with the narcissistic image. "I am talking about the narcissistic drama, the subject's relation
to his own image" (ibid., p. 431). This, Lacan says is what is involved for Freud
in the fear of losing the phallus or of not having or missing a phallus. Lacan
spells it out in perhaps inadvertently masculinist terms, "In other words the ego
is involved […] the subject is afraid of losing what constitutes his privilege in
relation to the other" (ibid., p. 432). Indeed! As mentioned above, however, the
connection between the phallus and narcissism, even if androcentric, is a lot
more plausible than some of the other claims made for it. Of the very many
avatars of the phallus that surge up throughout this seminar the Kleinian bad
object, raising its head in lesson twenty-five, is one of the most unexpected. It
should be recognized, however, that Lacan's reading of Klein is in fact close,
careful, and complexified here. He not inaccurately relates Klein's depressive
phase to his own mirror stage in terms of creating an inside and an outside
(ibid., pp. 443–444). And as Lacan does here, Klein does indeed speak of the
bad internalized object as anxiety provoking (Klein, 1988, p. 3). In Klein however, this object is not subjected to the Freudian dialectic of being or having
delineated here by Lacan: "if the subject is the bad object, he does not have
it; insofar as he *is* [*est*] identified with it, he is forbidden to *have* [*ait*] it" (ibid.,
p. 445). Also throughout Klein's work, the bad object is always open to a plurality of identities. It is breast, faeces, father's penis.

But the purpose of this brief digression on the phallus (in line with Lacan's
own digression) is simply to offer the reader an example of the several different
registers which frequently are simultaneously in play in Lacan's expositions – a
certain sleight of concept thanks to which ideas become legitimated and render
it difficult to see how exactly this happened.

The place of perverse fantasy in this seminar is interesting. Jacques-Alain
Miller in his blurb on the back of the French edition notes that Lacan praises
it, even perhaps eulogizes it. Already in lesson seventeen he had elevated it,
giving it serious status as linked to the pain of existence. In the last lessons of
the year it serves as a privileged instance of the fundamental fantasy in terms
of the cut, and at the very end of this year's teaching, as Lacan leans forward
into the themes of next year it is further praised since it is seen as withstanding
the moralizing normativity he will go on to excoriate in Seminar VII: "perversion represents […] a protest that, with regard to conforming, arises in
the dimension of desire, insofar as desire is the subject's relation to his being"
(ibid., p. 484).

In terms of future directions in Lacan's mode of approach to the unconscious, will the reader find much help in this last section of *Desire* with respect
to the cut, the not-One, the subject as counting itself counting? Of these three,
only the cut receives sustained attention. What Lacan says of it, in part, links it
to known concepts, in part is concentrated in a couple of opaque and mantric
paragraphs, and in part (where it links to the not-One) opens onto difficult but
exhilarating considerations.

As mentioned earlier, it is linked to known concepts by remarks that reality is not a compact continuum but is made up of cuts, that Plato compared the philosopher to a good cook able to carve a joint of meat correctly, that cuts create something new, all rooted in the everyday (ibid., p. 397). A moment later the cut is other, a psychoanalytic entity since it is that which inaugurates the unconscious itself when Lacan speaks of "the relationship between the subject and the sort of cut constituted by the fact that he *is* not in a certain unconscious discourse, and that he does not know what he is in it" (ibid.). It is also that which creates the forms of the o-object known to psychoanalytic theory – oral, anal, genital, etc. All of this is graspable and convincing. But that Lacan is pushing out towards something significantly more complex is evident in the mantric paragraphs with which he introduces perverse fantasy and what he has to say about being and the cut (ibid., pp. 398, 408). Readers of the later seminars will know how Lacan's prose can spiral away into impossible punning. There are really only two places where this occurs in *Desire* and they occur in the context of "being" and "the cut" and "the subject as counting", both in the process of being thought for the first time and both awaiting lengthy and complex elaboration in the coming years. Without the relevant later seminars in hand the puns on the subject as "counting" (ibid., pp. 409–410) resist unpacking. However, I think he succeeds in taking the reader some distance into new territory when he says that what is at stake in "[T]he subject as real insofar as he enters into the cut, the advent of the subject at the level of the cut, his relationship to something that we must call the real, but which is symbolized by nothing" (ibid., p. 398) pushes psychoanalysis onto very new territory, that of the nothing, this "prop of non-being" (ibid., p. 457).

For Freud, the navel of the dream, unknown and unknowable, is nonetheless *something* not nothing, an inextricable tangle but not outside the parameters of representation. As are Lacan's quotients and remainders. But the thrust of the seminar as of those to come will be the search for what one might call a negative entity. Or perhaps a nega*tived* entity? In lesson nineteen Lacan had spoken of lack as putting something in reserve "in the form of nihilation" (*une forme néantisée*) (ibid., p. 347). In his search for a specific type of nothing, Lacan has not yet found what he is looking for. In this context it is hard not to think of Beckett's similar quest in *Watt*, published a little earlier in 1953, where the protagonist has to accept "that a thing that was nothing had happened, with the utmost formal distinctness" (Beckett, 1953, p. 73). And Lacan too will pursue formal versions of this negative entity. The seminar *Identification* will see him examine Kant's four nothings, and seemingly settle on the *nihil negativum* as the one most suited to his purpose, the one least susceptible to the complicities of the Imaginary in attempting to circumscribe what is now meant by the o-object. This will be further elaborated in his fourteenth seminar *The Logic of Fantasy*:

> The signifier does not designate what is not there; it engenders it. What is not there at the origin is the subject itself. Primal repression [...] does not

bite on anything, it constitutes absolutely nothing, it accommodates to an absolute absence of Dasein.

(Lacan, 1966–1967, lesson of 16 November 1966, p. 8)

A nothing that *is*, in other words, to quote the great Wallace Stevens (Stevens, 2006, p. 9). Here the cut and its relation to being seems to be a first approach to this vast topic, and Lacan invokes the work of art as bodying forth the essential cut constituted by his existence – namely the fact that he is here and that he must be situated in the cut (ibid., p. 401). This statement can doubtless be read in a number of ways. For me it recalls George Steiner's description of the work of art as situated at "the exact synapse where being at its most vivid – joins with extinction" (Steiner, 2001, p. 30), a conjunction of being and nothingness. In every case Steiner says, the work of art could *not* have been and therefore "carries within it the scandal of its hazard, the perception of its ontological caprice" (ibid., p. 29).

Is this what Lacan meant? Some of what he says of the cut seems to identify it to the concept of aphanisis already much elaborated.

> The subject's being must be articulated and named in the unconscious, but in the end, it cannot be. It is solely indicated at the level of fantasy by what turns out to be a slit, a structure based on a cut.
>
> (ibid., p. 424)

This point is also on occasion described as a prop, and indeed as both: "in fantasy, the object is the imaginary prop of a relationship involving cutting with which the subject must prop himself up at this level. This leads us to a phenomenology of cutting" (ibid., p. 396). It sometimes looks as if it is also a way of theorizing the inception of the unconscious signifying chain, described in the earlier part of the seminar as fragmented:

> the true function of symbolization must be located in the foundation of the cut. A cut is that by which the current of an early tension, whatever it may be, is taken up into a series of alternatives that inaugurate what one might call the most basic machine.
>
> (ibid., p. 457)

Similarly while being is identified to the cut, it is also defined in a manner that aligns it with a description of the unconscious:

> something in the subject is articulated that is beyond any possible knowledge he may have [...] articulated like a discourse [...] Now, a discourse cannot be sustained without some sort of prop, and it would not be going too far to qualify this prop with the term "being".
>
> (ibid., p. 381)

Lacan then goes on here to describe a discourse where the subject fundamentally misrecognizes himself:

> The harder he tries to broach this chain and to name or locate himself there, the less he can do so. He is only ever there in gaps or cuts. Every time he tries to get his bearings there, he is only ever in a gap. This is why the imaginary object of fantasy with which he then tries to prop himself up is structured as it is.
>
> (ibid., p. 381)

I bring these different statements together here to show that Lacan's thought, at the end of this seminar, is in a ferment of newness shooting out in directions later pursued.

The not-One and the subject as counting receive less attention in these final lessons but will prove foundational in later theorizations of the o-object, in particular those involving the dual semiotic character of the vanishing point and of Frege's conceptualization of zero, both of which play a double role, since they are simultaneously the essential support of what they create – picture or system of numbers – and a constituent element of this same entity. The first outlines of this future theorization are visible in the statement: "It is impossible to structure human experience […] without beginning from the fact that human beings count and count themselves" (ibid., p. 409), and perhaps also in his digression on Klein's "bad internalized object", as "both part of the subject and not part of the subject" (ibid., p. 444).

It is, however, clear even at this early stage that what is touched on here is at the heart of his thinking when in the last moments of the seminar he compares psychoanalysis to "a narrative that would itself be the locus of the encounter at stake in the narrative" (ibid., p. 485).

I am acutely aware of not doing justice to this brimming last section of Seminar VI. Although it is much more readable than some of the later seminars, a colleague, who like me has taught it a number of times, recently compared attempts at elucidation to digging a hole in the sand. Ideas pour in over other ideas, insights corroborate or negate other insights, changes of register make it difficult to keep one's footing. The overall effect is I would say, one of exhilaration, but adequate commentary is not made easy. Carving in to Lacan's weaving approach in order to indicate certain directions may prove enraging to lovers of this seminar. While it has had obvious advantages for the commentator it has also made complete inclusivity impossible. As we near a conclusion I would like to draw the reader's attention to two deeply interesting comments made by Lacan which have not been integrated into the above discussion. (There are inevitably others.) The first is the clear distinction he makes between drive and desire in the final lesson, where in contradistinction to later seminars he appears to minimize the importance of the drive:

This drive, call, or pressure is only of interest, exists, is defined, and is theorised by Freud inasmuch as it is caught up in the unusual temporal sequence that we call the signifying chain [...] Desire is not this sequence. It is a mapping of the subject with respect to this sequence.

(ibid., p. 476)

A statement worth noting in light of future directions.

The other set of remarks to which he returns more than once in this section, could be read as an expansion of points made in Section 2 with respect to the Saint Augustine anecdote and to his regular invocation of Klein's paper "Symbol Formation and the Development of the Ego". Here in lesson twenty-five, Lacan suggests that the neurotic finds a way to live and bear the annihilatory threat of the fundamental fantasy ($ in conjunction with the o-object), by finding a substitute to occupy the place of desirer. "In his desiring function, the subject elects a substitute. This is the crux of neurosis" (ibid., p. 451). The obsessional manages not to be the one who enjoys; the hysteric manages not to be the one who is enjoyed. Lacan is specific: "The imaginary substitution that is at work here is a substitution of the ego for the subject" (ibid.). For this reason, the neurotic seems to be pitched into the realm of misrecognition, living the fundamental fantasy in terms of demand rather than desire, and either always demanding *for* someone else or demanding *something* else. But the ego also takes the place of the person from whom one demands something: "Nowhere more easily than in the neurotic does this separate ego come to take the place of the separate object that I designate as the earliest form of the object of desire" (ibid.). Is this how we fall in love? According to Lacan it is an effective way of creating a permanent obstacle to one's desire, since it is easier to put someone else in the position of desirer and devote oneself to fulfilling their demands. Lacan describes this manoeuvre as the barred phallus in the presence of an object "that I will write in the most general form of an object of desire – namely, in the form of the imaginary other in which the subject situates himself and finds himself anew $\Phi \lozenge i(a)$" (ibid., p. 452). Here the barred phallus has taken the place of the barred subject in the formula for fantasy, and this brilliant theoretical/ clinical *tour de force* was – not unreasonably – greeted with prolonged applause by Lacan's audience.

References

Beckett, S. (1953). *Watt*. London: Calder and Boyars.
Freud, S. (1900a). *The Interpretation of Dreams. S.E., IV, and V.*
Freud, S. (1905d). *Three Essays on the Theory of Sexuality. S.E., VII.* pp. 123–146.
Joyce, J. (1975). *Ulysses*. London: Penguin.
Heidegger, M. (1927/2000). *Being and Time*. Oxford: Wiley & Sons.
Klein, M. (1988). *Envy and Gratitude*. London: Virago.
Le Gaufey, G. (2009). *C'est a quel sujet*. Paris: Epel.

Marcel, G. H. (1949). *Being and Having.* London: Dacre Press.

Sartre, J.-P. (1943). *L'Être et le Néant.* Paris: Éditions Gallimard.

Steiner, G. (2001). *Grammars of Creation.* New Haven and London: Yale University Press.

Stevens, W. (2006). *Collected Poems.* London: Faber and Faber.

Lacan, J.:

The seminars:

——. (1964–1965). *The Object in Psychoanalysis. The Seminar of Jacques Lacan, Book XII.* (Trans.). Gallagher, C. Unpublished. www.lacaninireland.com

——. (1965–1966). *Crucial Problems in Psychoanalysis. The Seminar of Jacques Lacan, Book XIII.* (Trans.). Gallagher, C. Unpublished. www.lacaninireland.com

——. (1966–1967). *The Logic of Phantasy, The Seminar of Jacques Lacan, Book XIV.* (Trans.) Gallagher, C. Unpublished. www.lacaninireland.com

——. (1977). *The Four Fundamental Concepts of Psychoanalysis.* (Ed.) Miller, J.-A. (Trans.) Sheridan, A. Hogarth Press: London.

——. (1992). *The Ethics of Psychoanalysis. The Seminar of Jacques Lacan. Book VII. 1959–1960.* (Ed.) Miller, J.-A. (Trans.) Porter, D. London: Routledge.

——. (1999). *On Feminine Sexuality, The Limits of Love and Knowledge, 1972–1973. Encore. The Seminar of Jacques Lacan, Book XX.* (Ed.) Miller, J.-A. (Trans.) Fink, B. New York & London: W.W. Norton & Co.

——. (2014). *Anxiety, The Seminar of Jacques Lacan, Book X.* (Ed.) Miller, J.-A. (Trans.) Price, A. Cambridge: Polity Press.

——. (2015). *Transference, The Seminar of Jacques Lacan, Book VIII.* (Ed.). Miller, J.-A. (Trans.) Fink, B. Cambridge: Polity Press.

——. (2016). *The Sinthome, The Seminar of Jacques Lacan, Book XXIII.* (Ed.) Miller, J.-A. (Trans.) Price, A. Cambridge: Polity Press.

——. (2017). *Formations of the Unconscious, The Seminar of Jacques Lacan, Book V.* (Ed.) Miller, J.-A. (Trans.) Grigg. R. Cambridge: Polity Press.

——. (2019). *Desire and its Interpretation, The Seminar of Jacques Lacan, Book VI.* (Ed.) Miller, J.-A. (Trans.) Fink B. Cambridge: Polity Press. Also (Trans.) Gallagher, C. Unpublished. www.lacaninireland.com

Chapter 6

Conclusion

Lacan's question in the final lesson; is desire subjectivity? vaults us back onto impeccably Freudian terrain, echoing as it does, Freud's earliest papers in which he describes the unconscious as a rejected nucleus (Freud, 1895d, p. 289):

> Desire is both subjectivity – it is what is at the very heart of our subject-ivity, what is most essentially subjective – and at the same time its opposite, for it opposes subjectivity like a resistance, a paradox, or a rejected, refutable nucleus.
>
> (Lacan, 2019, p. 474)

The alert reader will know that as well as vaulting us back, it also vaults us forward into daunting topological demonstrations.

For the moment Lacan takes leave of his audience by outlining the themes of next year's seminar – *The Ethics of Psychoanalysis* – in which the themes of the good, of moralizing normativity with its attendant dangers and banalities, of the limits and the seductions of conformism, and importantly of the rehabilitation of sublimation as the full expression of a drive and not just its pallid substitute – all outlined here – will be explored. But Lacan's question here – is desire sub-jectivity – will reverberate powerfully throughout the teaching of the coming year. And in its concluding lessons, the place of desire with respect to traditional morality will be memorably marked out:

> Traditional morality concerned itself with what one was supposed to do insofar "as it is possible", as we say, and as we are forced to say. What needs to be unmasked here is the point on which that morality turns. And that is nothing less than the impossibility in which we recognise the topology of our desire.
>
> (Lacan, 1992, p. 315)

In fact all of this great seminar *The Ethics of Psychoanalysis* with its exploration of courtly love and its stellar reading of Antigone – all of it culminates in the cru-cial and terrifying statement that "the only thing one can be guilty of is giving ground relative to one's desire" (ibid., p. 321). Terrifying because irremediable. "Something is played out in betrayal if one tolerates it […] You can be sure that what you find there is the structure of giving ground relative to one's desire" (ibid.). Lacan is trenchant: "There is no way back. It might be possible to do some repair work, but not to undo it" (ibid.).

This ethical call – truly a clarion call – stands altogether at variance with the slippage in psychoanalytic practice which Lacan criticizes in the final lesson on *Desire*. This is a slippage in the direction of that moralizing normativity he will go on to excoriate in next year's teaching. As he astutely points out here, it is not so much that analysts' interpretations go in this direction as that this perspective is what gives them their bearings, ultimately seducing the analyst into seeing his/her version of normality not just as the norm but as the ideal – "an ideal of normality […] that turns the analyst's ideals into the final standard that the patient, in concluding […] is encouraged to rally around" (ibid., p. 473). These biting remarks made in 1959 still command attention. More recently they have been echoed with respect to analytic institutions, who fall prey in their assessment of suitable candidates to what one critic has called the diagnostic fallacy of endorsing conformism and the values of a moralizing indoctrination: "I refer here to a buried assumption in some of these processes that if you do not think like me you must be mad or in need of more analysis (of the type valued by my group or sub-group)" (Steiner, cited in Frosch, 1997, p. 7).

Lacan began this seminar by asking the question, what is desire, and insisted on its unamenability to orderly description. Here at the end of the seminar he again insists that "no desire ever fails to present itself as problematic, dispersed, polymorphous, contradictory, and, in short, far from any oriented coaptation" (Lacan, 2019, p. 474). And he is equally insistent on the failure of considerable swathes of psychoanalytic practice to engage with this fact. On the contrary he says: "everything in the way in which psychoanalytic experience is currently formulated is designed to veil the meaning of desire and to make us turn away from it" (ibid). Presumably, even 50 years later, we are not meant to read these words with complacency.

Reading forward a little, one gets the impression that Lacan himself fully appreciated the importance of this seminar on desire, and that even after the seminar on ethics it continued to function as a point of reference in his thinking. In the seminar on transference, we see him consulting his notes of two years earlier, and unusually quoting himself word for word with reference to his reading of the Ella Sharpe dream: "'This phallus' – I said, speaking of a subject caught up in the most exemplary neurotic situation, insofar as it was that of *aphanisis* brought on by the castration complex – 'he is it and he is not it'" (Lacan, 2014, p. 232). While one encounters many oft-repeated mantric phrases throughout Lacan's teaching, it is very rare indeed to have an entire paragraph from a previous seminar repeated verbatim in this manner. What he is at pains to remind his listeners of is the slippage of the verb "to be", first mooted in *Desire*: "Language allows us to perceive the interval between to be it and not to be it in a formulation into which the verb to be slips; he is not without having it" (ibid.). And again the exact same phrase is used, one that appears nowhere else in the seminars: "It is around the subjective assumption between being and having that the reality of castration is played out" (ibid.). He then goes on to quote the paragraph in question in full, telling us not only of the significance he ascribes to it, but of the meticulous preparation and careful notes that underpinned Lacan's impressive life work.

The radical departures in his thinking announced at the beginning of this seminar have been amply introduced. This is not to say that Lacan's signature serpentine approach has been abandoned, and that certain concepts such as the phallus will not live on while mutating significantly over the coming years. It is, however, certainly true to say that "being" has been foregrounded where previously the opposition being/having held sway, the big Other is now barred, the o-object has begun to be profiled, tragedy is now at the forefront of psychoanalytic experience, and loss is radical since this o-object is already defined as the nothing beyond which "the subject will seek out the shadow of that life of his which he at first lost" (ibid., p. 373). Lacan will theorize this o-object in many different ways in the coming years, but his insistence on its electric intensity here should give us pause. It is, I think, not wise to read the seminars as a linear progression from insight to increased insight, and to discard earlier formulations as outpaced waystations in a journey to some kind of truth. This seminar stands apart from all the others and its often poignant insights are not invalidated by later departures onto more abstract terrain. Lacan's teaching is often characterized as intellectualist, but Seminar VI, *Desire and its Interpretation*, focussing as it does on the far reaches of human suffering, constitutes one of the most passionate pieces of writing in all of psychoanalysis.

References

Freud, S. (1895d). *Studies on Hysteria. S.E., II.*
Frosch, S. (1997). *For and Against Psychoanalysis.* London: Routledge.

Lacan, J.:

The seminars:

——. (1992). *The Ethics of Psychoanalysis. The Seminar of Jacques Lacan. Book VII. 1959–1960.* (Ed.) Miller, J.-A. (Trans.). Porter, D. London: Routledge.
——. (2014). *Transference, The Seminar of Jacques Lacan, Book VIII.* (Ed.) Miller, J.-A. (Trans.) Fink B. Cambridge: Polity Press.
——. (2019). *Desire and its Interpretation, The Seminar of Jacques Lacan, Book VI.* (Ed.) Miller, J.-A. (Trans.) Fink B. Cambridge: Polity Press. Also (Trans.) Gallagher, C. Unpublished. www.lacaninireland.com

Part II

The lectures

Chapter 7

Lecture I
17 December 2016

I don't know if some of you saw an amazing documentary they made a few years ago about one of my absolute heroines Dervla Murphy the intrepid cyclist. The documentary makers said that it was like filming wildlife, she's about 80 and they couldn't keep up with her. But they said the one thing about her was that she had no interest in the documentary – she didn't give a fuck – it could go out to the people of Ireland but she would never look at it.

[laughter]

So I'm going to try to do that. Fire away with this so long as I don't know.

CO: Good strategy!

I have to start by saying that I do consider this reading group to be heroic. I think it is a heroic but a really necessary undertaking to read these seminars right through from beginning to end. You're greatly to be commended. You probably know already since you're on Seminar VI that reading Lacan is a little bit like finding yourself as an insect on a *Moëbius* strip – that you move from seminar to seminar using the same concepts, the same vocabulary, but imperceptibly moving into entirely new meanings; it can be quite hard to realize – this is the place where he moved … As we will see today this seminar is where he begins with the o-object; here we have the first intimation of what will become the o-object. So there's going to be a break between what you did last year, in Seminar V, and Seminar VI this year. These seminars are so incredibly wordy, reading them can be a bit like standing under an avalanche; not only can you not think clearly but it's quite possible that you can't think at all. So it can be hard to see, even though these changes are written on the page, it can be hard for us as readers to actually see these changes as they happen. For this reason I think it's useful to start with an overview as we're doing this morning.

There are certain important innovations in Seminar VI; the first being, of course, the appearance of the o-object, this is where the o-object begins its life and will develop really over the next 20 years.

The second one is the status of the big Other. The big Other was much more the guarantor and something solid that you took your bearings from in the first five seminars now it begins to be the failing big Other, the Other who doesn't have the answer. The symbol for this failing big Other appears somewhere in Seminar V, but the concept begins to be really developed here in Seminar VI. So that's the second big innovation. And the third one is the being/having opposition which was very big in Seminar V – the man *has* it and the woman *is* it. That opposition begins to be drained somewhat of its power with the emphasis moving from having to being in this and subsequent seminars. So those three I would say are the big changes that happen in this seminar. The bizarre thing about this semi-avalanche – Seminars IV, V, VI, and VIII are particularly wordy; they are immense – is that it turns out that these seminars are very tightly structured. You mightn't see that the first time around. So you have today's topic which is lessons one to seven, the drama of the dead father, then lessons eight to twelve, the Ella Sharpe client whose main thing is again the presence of the dead father in his life, then lessons thirteen to twenty-one, Hamlet and the dead father – a father, a son, death, and the relationship to desire – and lessons twenty-one to twenty-seven is Lacan trying to kind of justify all this and give you the clinical implications. So it's … even though it's an immense fall of words on your poor mind, it's actually very tightly structured.

In lesson one he even sets out the programme for the year very clearly. On page 1 he says: we will ask ourselves what desire is. So that's what he sets out to do. And then he says further on – on page 7 – I've been following the pagination in Cormac's translation, and the reason I've got the table here is not to place a barrier between me and you but because my copy is in such a state that if I open it on anything other than a flat surface it will all fall apart – this is not because I am such an amazing scholar but because it's so badly bound!

[laughter]

Anyway on page 7 he says our aim this year is to define what fantasy is so that's very clear in lesson one. And he's going to more or less stick to that in spite of several other byways and pathways. There is a shift as I was saying from the metonymical object of Seminar V to what we have now – the object that is the vital support of the subject. But metonymy stays in there too and this is why these changes are hard to see in Lacan. He doesn't actually drop one and pick up the other, he slithers along with one and it kind of takes a new direction – this is what the o-object will be in Seminar VI: the vital support of the subject. But note that in Seminar VI – and this will change – it's an object which is very tightly tied to the narcissistic image and therefore it's not yet the object which is outside of representation. Which it will become. So here it is very much tied to the narcissistic image. From next year on in Seminar VII with *das Ding* he will start looking for something that is outside the ambit of representation but nevertheless in some way fuels or founds representation. That search will start in Seminar VII and will continue via the topological seminars, especially Seminar IX where he's looking for – again to escape representation – he is looking for something that functions but doesn't have a specular image. This is a little misleading. In Seminar IX if you line up the Klein bottle or the *Moëbius* strip or any of the topological models he uses ... if you put them in front of the mirror you will see something – you won't see the inversion, the normal specular image, but you will certainly see an image. So while Lacan will say he's looking at stuff that has no specular image, that's a little inaccurate, this is stuff that has a specular image that's eccentric, or doesn't fit within the normal rules of representation.

LM: **He makes a big thing of the specular image coming from the mirror image ... why is it so important that there's no specular image? Is it to talk about the uniqueness of human subjectivity?**

I think, what he's doing, and it won't be in Seminar VI, but he's moving toward something that is pre-subjective ... you know that Freud in his paper on negation – where Lacan takes a lot of stuff – talks about pre-subjective, early phases, and Lacan is looking at these stages ... eventually the o-object will be somewhere for example between the breast and the mouth, so it's neither the one nor the other but in a between-space. That is one of the things he's moving to ... and for some bizarre reason he progressively kind of takes against the Imaginary, which is strange because so much of clinical work – so much of the way we all live is in fact dominated by the Imaginary dimension – you know if you take the Imaginary out of it how do you manage to live your life? And you can see for example in Beckett's work what happens if you try to take the Imaginary out. You end up with, instead of a person, a voice. But there is progressively in Lacan's seminars that kind of suspicion of the lures of the Imaginary. These lures are certainly there. But Lacan's distancing is a bit excessive in so far as we can't live outside of the Imaginary. So after this seminar, *Desire*, there is a moving away from the Imaginary and ... also if I can go down a byroad ... [laughs] that I love dearly [laughs] ... we should ask: what Imaginary? In an article I read and have never been able to find since, the author suggests that ever since Coleridge's writings on this topic, there has been a tendency to define the Imaginary as something that is unitary and summative. And Lacan, who bases the Imaginary on the discoveries of the mirror stage, is totally in this camp. But if, for example, you read a page of *Finnegans Wake* the Imaginary functions quite powerfully, although in a fragmented and non-summative way. And if you read say Colette Soler's book exploring and defining the Real unconscious that's what she's talking about. So it is very likely a mistake and an inadequate definition of the Imaginary to think that it is One and that by its nature it tends towards and adds up to coherence and sense. The Imaginary can function and does function outside of those parameters. In dreams, for example, you know ... there is a fragment that is not going to add up to a whole, and that's one of the things that Freud massively struggled with in *The Interpretation of Dreams*. As a nineteenth-century man he liked the fragments to add up to a whole. His well-documented passion for archeology offered him wonderful instances of this. If you found a shard of pottery you could have the key to a whole civilization. On the contrary, the twentieth-century notion of the fragment is something that doesn't add up to anything; it can just exist in its own right. So I think again Liz in answer to your question that the notion of the Imaginary is inadequate and I might suggest in this context that people take a look at the Anna Livia pages in *Finnegans Wake* where you can see a splintered Imaginary in action. The dinkel dale of Luggelaw, the river, Anna Livia's hair "deepdown and ample like this red bog at sundown", fragmented images that pulse in and out but do not actually add up to anything.

KM: Can I ask Olga ... Does that mean that we have to distinguish all the time between the Imaginary and the fantasy?

No ... I think it means that we need to take in as part of the Imaginary the fragmented pulsing imagery in its fragmentariness and to do the same thing with respect to meaning. You know that for some reason the notion of non-sense is predicated on sense being summative and coherent whereas sense actually isn't either of those things in the joke or in the dream. So you never have complete non-sense. Like if I hear a joke in Chinese that to me is complete non-sense and I'm not going to be able to laugh because there's no hook for my amusement to latch on to. But what I normally hear in terms of non-sense-jokes is little tiny bits of sense jumbled in together to make that little explosion called laughter, to make fun the way a child will do. Little shards colliding, jostling, not summative. But the joke wouldn't impact on me at all if something wasn't provoked in me. And nothing will be provoked in me by the Chinese language. So something in hearing the word, or the half word is provoked. Not provoked enough to add up to anything ... just a pulse. And that is, what the later Lacan begins to focus on but I think the vocabulary ... again, the dissing of the Imaginary, the dissing of meaning is a bit silly. Because I think it's a different configuration of the Imaginary, a different configuration of meanings – meanings that don't add up but just caress you or pulse something in you, just make a little impact.

SM: It's like a subjective response to something?

Yeah. But like I say, if it was in Swahili unless one of the sounds of Swahili touched your fancy ... But there is something that is touched in one that doesn't have to exit in a concept. So it's all of that that the later Lacan kind of realizes that he's left out, and goes back on in the coming years.

Okay. So again then, Seminar VI is a kind of transitioning seminar. Lacan's thinking will be moving in the directions outlined but this is step one. Now in the opening lesson if you recall he does a sweep through poetry and philosophy and he already in that sweep — although it is dense enough — puts in place what he wants to say about this new type of object. Which is the point he makes on page 7 or 8 in your text — the non-opposition of subject and object. And that's the big change. Grammatically we can't speak at all without clear distinctions between subject and object. And normally what we encounter is the opposition between subject and object. This is what Lacan is trying to undercut now. He will go on to progress this under-cutting over the next few years so incisively that by the seminar on anxiety in 1963 he will declare that the term object itself is inadequate, insufficient, and inaccurate. In the seminar on anxiety he says,

> to designate this little object with the term object is merely a metaphorical use of this word, since it's borrowed from the subject-object relation, from which the term object is constituted … but this object of which we speak under the term o-object is precisely outside any possible definition of objectivity.
>
> (Lacan, 2014, p. 86)

So he's trying to say: we're calling it an object but guess what guys, it's not. This is what is in question during these years. So you have the first outline of this in lesson one alongside two bursts of complexity which are the graph of desire and the enunciating/enunciation divide. Central to these lessons, however, is the initial sketching out of the structure of fantasy. I think sometimes when I'm reading these seminars — and I could be wrong — I think that when Lacan is on the verge of discovery and is excited about new insights that some kind of inhibition comes over him and he goes into a snow storm of other concepts before he comes to the point. I get that impression and I could be completely wrong. He could be telling us something we really need to know. But you do sometimes see him approach something new and interesting and then siphon off into a whole load of extremely difficult dense stuff as if he can't quite cough it up. But that's just my response. And in the main what he siphons off into repays attention.

So briefly let's look at those two bursts of complexity. We'll take the easier one first which is the distinction between the enunciating subject and the enunciation. Now I think it's useful to remember that during these years Lacan was working every Sunday morning with Benveniste who was also working and writing on this topic. For both men this can be summed up as an examination of the way the subject, the speaking subject, is captured in language. So in the first instance you have Saussure as a major influence on Lacan's thinking on this topic and then also Damourette and Pichon and I brought this along for anyone who reads French — it's Damourette and Pichon's article on negation … it's so often quoted that it might be useful to have the original. It is very useful generally to familiarize oneself with Lacan's sources. Otherwise you've no idea if what he is saying is actually in the original or if he is putting a completely different spin on it. Benveniste, Damourette, and Pichon, they were very much his influences regarding the place of the subject in language. More I think – a little bit more than Saussure. Benveniste, published his major work *Problems in General Linguistics* in 1966, a tremendously interesting study. Even the chapter titles are illuminating. If I were to recommend just one for your attention it would be "Subjectivity and Language". Really excellent. But he also has a chapter on something Lacan alludes to in the seminar on the psychoses: the history and the roles of the active and passive voices in the verb, as well as a chapter on the functions of the verb *to be* and the verb *to have*. You can see how close all of this is to what preoccupied Lacan in his seminar. Furthermore, Benveniste has something on the nature of pronouns, the relative clause, the relation of the person in the verb, the role of the I. As we will see further on in this seminar, Lacan, using a term that is fairly unusual for him will say of the o-object that it is the analogue in the unconscious of what the I is in conscious speech. Isn't that an interesting notion? So the kind of linguistic background to Lacan's teaching is not at all dry linguistics. Who knew that grammar could be riveting?! Central to our work is the question: how does the subject speak? As it happened when I was reading Benveniste for the first time, I was also reading Bleuler – his book on schizophrenia – which is really, really interesting since it describes in detail the daily manifestations of the psychoses among patients before there was treatment; how they could manage their bodies but also how they could manage their words, and the absence of the I in psychotic speech, was very remarkable indeed. He had one patient who only spoke – if you can imagine doing it – in past participles! Now if you decided "I'm only going to speak today in past participles" I think you'd probably have a silent day trying to think of them. And as we will see further on in this seminar Lacan is going to talk about somebody who only speaks in the infinitive. Do you remember the poem "*Être une belle fille*"? – to be a beautiful blonde in lesson five? Something is being said that is not amenable to first-person speech. So Benveniste is not a dead end shall we say.

LM: ... **the way the form, or demonstration of hysteria has changed I wonder if the language of the psychotic has changed I wonder if you still see the absence of the I or is there something else?**

Absolutely. I think there are a lot of psychoses where there isn't an absence of the I. It's there in speech, but it's not there in agency. You know like, the I is not absent say in Schreber's speech but everything is done to him, he is always at the receiving end of what happens. So it's absent in terms of agency. So yeah a lot of jumping on the bandwagons in the 1950s – we have discovered the answer to psychosis: no metaphors – all that is too rigid. It's not even true.

AB: **They talk of a different kind of intentionality in psychotic subjects.**
LM: **I'm saying that I think this is influenced by epoch and if you think of Trump's "I will make America greater ..."**

And yet at the same time even though it's influenced if you take the example of Trump, the pronoun I – and Benveniste talks about this he says – it is the way we take hold of the code. The code is out there, language is there, the way each subject takes hold of it is via the I. But that in itself is not a simple thing. We don't like, for example, somebody who goes I, I, I, so there is already a resistance, and we also find, and this is really interesting clinically, the points in a narrative where there is a switch to the second person – "I went into the pub and you know the way they'd be looking at you..." You know? So something is too hot for me to actually say as I. It is likely that the I remains always somewhat hot. What Benveniste says about it is that unlike the word chair, for example, there is no lexical entity that corresponds to it. I, Benveniste says, is the instance of discourse, it exists and designates something in the moment that I say I. That's the I who is speaking. So Benveniste puts the I and the you in a place apart in terms of the code which is language. These are the hooks by which the person takes on the code, takes possession of it so to speak. He also says there are a whole lot of other spaces in the code that only refer to the speaking subject and I'll just briefly go through three of them.

There are the indicators of deixis, which is here, now, today, yesterday. Those only have meaning in terms of the speaking subject.

Then certain verbs: I feel, I believe. "I feel it's going to rain today", so I take a declarative sentence, an enunciation, and I make it into an enunciating by the "I feel". I appropriate, I capture it.

Third, the performatives: I swear, I promise. As Benveniste says these have no extra-linguistic existence. Their entire substance is in the saying.

In his article on the verbs to be and to have, Benveniste writes interestingly about the predominance of the verb *to be* over the verb *to have* when it comes to expressing possession. In most languages including Irish, it is far more common to say "it is to me" rather than to say "I have". *Tá sé agam*: I have it. *Tá gúna nua agam*: I have a new dress. And similarly in many other languages. Even in the Latin forms, *habeo* and *mihi est*, the *mihi est*, is far more prominent he says. It would seem that it is during this time when he was working closely with Benveniste that Lacan's emphasis shifts towards being and focusses less on the being/having opposition. (Not of course that this latter disappears in these years).

Anyway, what Lacan is trying to establish here is the distinction between the enunciation and the enunciating. These are the grammatical ways in which this distinction can be established. But if you think about it yourselves, tonality, which Lacan doesn't but will later talk about – the jouissance of language and the jouissance of the voice functions equally here. You know yourselves in enunciation, if I want to apologize to somebody and I say Sor-EEEE – you know, there's an enunciating in that enunciation. It's perfectly obvious that I am not fucking sorry! At all! So, as I have put it, grammar is not the only place where an enunciating subject can appear. It can appear in the tonality and it can also appear in phraseology. For example, if you have Eileen Dunne saying on the Nine O'clock News: "Welcome to the Nine O'clock News", that's enunciation. And then if she goes on: "Can you fucking believe the water charges are back?" You know, there is a presence of the enunciating subject there. So there are many many places where this happens, and that's what you're listening for in the session, among other things, of course. We have to sensitize ourselves to the distinction between the two levels. There is a brilliant example of this in one of Ian McEwan's novels which is *Enduring Love*. What you get at the beginning is the psychiatric report, so a complete and thorough enunciation, and then you get the enunciating, the novelistic account where the subject is captured in all this stuff. So the distinction is not as hard to figure as it might appear in Lacan's explanation. And it is worth listening for in the clinic. Certainly that switch from I to you is always interesting. And in those other places where the enunciating subject is in the speech or alternatively, and you can get this with an obsessional, where the enunciating subject is rigorously kept out of the speech and you're going to be given a so-called objective account of what happened. It'll be interesting in the film festival which we're doing on documentary to see where documentary pretends to be an enunciation, "this is what happens ... etc". That'll be an exercise for us – discerning the distinctions, especially under certain types of officialese.

How are you doing on the graph of desire? Mercifully for some of us, Lacan narrativises this graph in lesson one and I think the problem – and Freud had the very same problem in *Early Papers* and I think in *Studies in Hysteria* – is the sheer complexity of what he is trying to get across. Freud had been hoping to show that memories, leading back to original trauma, might function like – I think he called it pearls on a necklace – that an analysis might proceed back from one to the other. But essentially what both Freud and Lacan are trying to describe in early experience is an impossible mesh. In trying to encompass something of this process the graph of desire is obliged to create succession where there is actually simultaneity. Lacan is against the developmental thing, the accents on the different activities may change: the new baby is oral, but not just oral, the baby is anal, the baby is shitting as well as feeding. So they are all happening; also, this baby is being touched and embraced by the mother. So everything happens more or less at the same time for the little pre-subject, and it's very difficult to give a successive account. Importantly, however, Lacan mentions the question of anteriority. We cannot begin to get a grasp on how anteriority is at work in the subject. If you think about it: you have been listening in the womb ... You have been listening to these voices for a very long time before you start to know their voices, before you know that they're your people and registering – registering what? For example, a particular voice calms everything down here, a particular voice panics everything around here. So all of that is layered, layered, layered, in the pre-knowledge that eventually becomes – who knows what – some kind of underlay to subjectivity. When Lacan says this is retroactive, he hardly begins to cover the ground. It is so retroactive that we have no access to how early our experiences began to impinge on who we become. In later life we can sometimes see how this retroactive knowledge functions along with the surprised recognition it can bring about. You can often say: well, I'm no longer in love with that person, Jesus, when did that happen? And you mightn't have even noticed. So many of our states of mind and heart are burgeoning unseen alongside what we think we think. The graph of desire is an attempt at registering some of these early processes, and precisely because so much is happening Lacan hangs more and more on this graph so that it becomes alarmingly overloaded.

CO: I just had a moment of that simultaneity right now when you said Freud said something about pearls of … I wrote down graph of wisdom because the expectation, you know … because you could have said pearls of wisdom! So that is I suppose something when we've looked at and tried to understand the different moments of the graph and sketching them in each seminar and also trying at the very same time to not allow ourselves to get too, too bogged down with you know following not so much the text that accompanies the graph but the graph itself. What does this line mean? What does that line mean? But actually just that, trying to come to an understanding that there is something that he's desperately trying to say here but that it is actually happening all at once.

Absolutely, happening all at once and the other thing is what he leaves out, which again if you look at a new-born you see – the fleetingness of these experiences – you know, a baby will focus for four or five seconds and then it's gone. So the discontinuity of experience … I remember watching my daughter seeing the purple of a cotton wool roll and reaching her hand out and then forgetting what her hand was there for and dropping it. And extraordinarily I saw the same thing when my mother was dying. She would lift her hand to do something and then not quite remember what her hand was doing there and drop it.

So the fleetingness and discontinuity which we encounter in dreams, and which is why dreams are so important – and also I should say, having a raised temperature is very important. You know the mad world you inhabit when you have a high temperature? That's really important because again you're accessing those early phases of the fleetingness, the jumbledness of primal experience… so Lacan is trying to take all of that and make something more schematic of it. But you have to include all this chaos to be realistic. Of course, we don't know how much the baby knows about the code. It's likely the baby has already got some words and knows a whole lot of things about voice from early on. What Lacan wants to is point out is the extra weighting that is put on needs by demand in each mother/baby relationship. This is a hugely important observation. It's not the whole truth, but it's a big truth. The baby quite early will realise – without realizing it of course – that crying is a complete pain in the ass to the mother, the mother does not want a crying baby, or that crying is great for the mother because she recognizes – I am the one who can soothe this baby so please cry please let me do this for myself. Or I remember supervising somebody who is a child analyst and where the mother was saying she loved the baby to cry so she could just not feed it. So the baby's cry and the response it elicits bear a particular imprint … And I remember in Womens Aid, a baby who smiled, smiled, smiled, because that's what the mother wanted … this baby was never changed … her nappy was never changed … we discovered … I can't even tell you what we discovered but – a smiling sweet baby. So the imprint… is going to happen. Not just the cry but how it is heard. However, Lacan leaves something out here, something immensely important. Rather amazingly, the baby is not always altogether at the mercy of this drama … babies can resist or respond in unexpected ways to demand.

The baby with that mother who just wants to soothe it, won't be soothed. Cries and roars all through the night and won't let the mother feel she has the answers. So you have the baby's resistance to the demand of the mother, and the baby's resistance even to the code. You know these extraordinary stories of twins who develop a private language and they just fecking won't enter the code, or you have other babies who enter the code but who remain at the baby stage and refuse to move on. So its a two-way thing; the enormity of the imprint of demands on needs as Lacan is saying is for sure true but that there can be varying levels of resistance from the baby. What Lacan is saying is that the baby has to enter the defiles of the signifier – that's what happens to the cry. And again if you're around a new-born its really interesting to notice the difference between the wild helpless panicked, almost unbearable, crying of the absolute new-born, and then the cry "I want you", the cry that is specific, that's already targeting, already focussing. Lacan talks about the appeal for a presence; so the cry that is initially completely unfocussed, has some kind of imprint put upon it but then also becomes "I want you", "I want you here". So again a very interesting observation, because it has to be lined up against real life and real babies. Much of what he is saying is true, but it's by no means the whole story. And Lacan says that it's at this point that the baby hears the *che vuoi* "what do you want?" from the mother and again this is entirely two-way; Lacan only sees it in one direction, which is the baby hearing what do you want? And there's the poor fecking parent screaming: what do you want?

CO: Yeah, yeah absolutely.

It's a completely two-way thing; this poor parent is in despair, or anybody minding the baby. What is it that the baby bloody wants?

CO: But there's huge anxiety around that … and ambivalence.

Absolutely.

CO: Because this tiny thing is larger, larger than life.

Absolutely.

CO: And it becomes the praying mantis in Seminar X.

That's right. I'm reading a lovely little novel at the moment – can't remember the title of it, the mother she's so exhausted and she's saying, she's lying there, and she's saying just let the spoon go across the room into the baby's mouth so that I don't have to move, you know … so all of that drama. Obviously Lacan didn't like babies very much or maybe didn't spend much time looking after them!

[laughter]

However there's a huge criss-crossing at this point in the graph; it's much more a mesh than a graph, but this is the place bizarrely enough where the o-object first comes in around what Lacan says is the baby's kind of staggering or faltering under this question from the mother: what do you want? Come up with something. What do you want? So he talks about the original helplessness of the baby – in lesson one, 12 November 1958. *Hilflosigheit*. In face of the original *Hilflosigheit* which occurs because the little subject is without recourse, has no answer to give to this question. At this point Lacan says – something intervenes and he says on the next page, this something is specifically linked to the specular image. It is insofar as something intervenes at this stage, which is the specular experience, and unusually he announces that he's going to say something completely new about the specular image. A couple of lines down he says: we are going to rediscover a completely new way of using it in a context that will give it a completely different resonance. Unusual for Lacan to signal that he's moving into a new reading, though not unheard of … so it is the specular image that is going to come in here to save the subject at the point where the subject is without recourse. And we will have this scenario repeated over and over in the seminar. It is then an imaginary element which will guard against helplessness by constructing something and that something is the fantasy. He spells that out here. And he's going to take us over this terrain a number of times. Several times we're going to see that the o-object is what sustains the subject at a crisis point, and several times it's going to be linked to the Imaginary and to narcissistic passion. So what he says in this seminar is not going to be invalidated by later seminars in the move away from the Imaginary because in lived experience the o-object is very often incarnated in the other and you often only know that this other has been the o-object for you at the moment of radical loss. So the question of the Imaginary is really close to how we live, actually live.

CO: So Olga can I ask something … so at this stage in the game so to speak … these particular bits that you're pulling out for us and you're saying that the o-object, we need to think of it as, and he says it, that it comes in at these kind of crisis points …

He called it a panic point …

CO: And then immediately after that, and we did highlight that when we were reading this particular section that this is where he for the first time introduces the function of the fantasy which we go on later on to call the fundamental fantasy. But I'm just wondering, it's a curious way to think about the fundamental fantasy as sustaining the subject but also sort of recuperating the subject at a point of crisis.

Well, like I say he goes through this on a number of occasions, particularly in the dream of the dead father he's going to expand on it. By and large, as he says, we are protected from what he calls the pain of existence which invades us at those moments when everything that sustained us is stripped away. This is a place that we don't and can't inhabit in ongoing time. In fact, Lacan suggests in his commentary on the dream of the dead father that it is actually the ordinary irritations of life that protect us from this. One can think of the father as annoying: he was the rival and he was all sorts of things. But when he dies, or when the person dies, and that could be a partner, a child, all that they are, or have been, in terms of sustaining your existence stands forth. I think with the formula for the fundamental fantasy, the three elements are in some kind of balance and they are held in balance by the diamond. You know, you're both involved in your desire and you push away from it. The o-object is not supposed to stand on its own but it does in mourning … I think I might have got away from your question Carol.

CO: No, it's ok, just wondering about this weird idea that the fantasy – taking it to its most literal endpoint – that the fantasy is the thing that sustains us at times of crisis… but what we often find clinically is that at times of crisis, the fantasy is gone out the window.

That's right, but no, the fantasy sustains, we bring it in originally, it sustains us, but when the o-object gets out of kilter, it's gone.

CO: Okay.

So it's there, it's something that we have originally, that we'll never get to know, the original drama where we have put something in to keep us from psychical collapse and that something is the o-object, which we can incarnate variously with all kinds of things in our work, in our lives, in a 100,000 … but when it goes, everything goes. You're absolutely right there. Everything goes.

LM: So the o-object is fantasy …

The o-object is *in* the fantasy; it's there in a sustaining way, but also there is a protective distance, the diamond protects you.

SM: The fantasy frames the o-object ...

Yeah, and keeps you going. Exactly, and with successive avoidances. So I live my life thinking I will be happy when such and such happens... I remember when Cormac [Gallagher] was doing this seminar with us, we were at the end of the two year course and the new intake was applying and he was saying, so many people were ringing me up and saying "my desire will be fulfilled, I will be happy if I can get on this course" and somebody in the class said, "and I'll be fecking happy when I'm off it".

[laughter]

Cormac wasn't a bit pleased [laughs]. So, but yes, successive avoidances and obstacles ... we put in.. you know... when this is done, I'll be a happy person. Then it's done and you're not a happy person. But at times of gross, enormous loss, none of that works. The fantasy structure collapses. None of that works. Ok. So we'll look at it then in the dream of the dead father.

Lacan really starts his commentary on the dream of the dead father in lesson five and I think its page 55 in your books, the place where he talks about the panic point. An important point he wants to make concerns our existence as speaking beings. Not only is man alive but he has to think about his existence, so you have this double layer. In Seminar IX he talks about the subject as caught between vital immanence you know which is just the body living, and epos or saga, so not only are we living but we tell ourselves about our living. So I'm alive and I'm thinking: I'm really happy to be alive, or I'm not, or I wish ... We are caught between those positions and this is what he's saying here. Not only are we alive and we have to think about our existence because this is who we are, but the relationship between the subject and the object is such that the object cannot be the correlate of one of the subject's needs but is something that props the subject at the precise moment at which the subject has to face his existence. This is not a philosophical moment but one of existential crisis, happening at a moment of crisis, what Lacan calls a panic point (page 84), where the subject must grab hold of something, and he grabs hold of the object as object of desire. So at this point you need to attach yourself to something ... and it is precisely as he says to the object as object of desire that one attaches oneself. This is a very new and striking innovation with respect to what the object might be. At this panic point something is brought in and I think it's the same page or the next page, – I love this bit here where he talks about this something that is too close to yourself to see; way too intimate for you to see and also too close to you to be able to bear reference to it. Remember he talks about the miser and his box and he says, you know, we have to laugh at that because that hits home a little too hard for all of us, so we have to make a joke of it ... Geraldine?

GC: Would you say that's the person and the conditions of their own possibility?

Their own possibilities, but their own very intimate possibilities. What is it that so touches me that I really wouldn't be able … it would be too hot for me to talk about … so what Lacan says here is that ridicule or making a joke is one way of distancing oneself from it. Another way which I think he talks about, I think its Dalio in some play … is the sudden blush. Remember the moment in *Ulysses* where Stephen is in the newspaper office. He is very easily seduced by language and when somebody quotes from Seymour Bush − never even heard of him − seemed to be a lawyer in Dublin at the time − but somebody quotes from him a very flowery passage and Stephen blushes because he is seduced by the beauty of these phrases … something in him is targeted to the point that he can't actually keep his composure. This is another instance − the place where you lose your composure, you forget what you were going to say, you're a bit staggered in the conversation, something has been said that makes you lose your place. So that's what he's kind of targeting in these very early outlines of the o-object and then he uses this poem … yes Sarah?

SM: Is this to do with what he's going on about with affect?

Affect, yeah. Absolutely. And the thing about affect, and again, this in one of my cranky things. I think that Freud slightly queered the pitch making such a divide between idea and affect. I think that affect exists definitely all by itself but the only ideas that stick long enough to affect my unconscious will have some punch of feeling. Like, my unconscious probably won't be affected by trying to read Theodore Adorno you know … which I find very hard … but my unconscious will be hit by an idea in a novel so if you think even of the example that Freud gives of the girl who is molested in the sweet shop in the "Project", my unconscious is only going to be constructed if something in me is targeted and that something is not going to be my intellect alone. So yeah I think that is why he goes on about affect.

And so here we have it again, the most intimate part of oneself, is what Lacan calls it, on that page, so not just specular, even though he is still saying specular but you can see the enriching of this concept here.

CO: So the blushing, the effacing, the disappearing, the embarrassment …

The embarrassment, or the inability to say it in the first-person, the fact that I cannot actually use the I …

MK: Something closest to the greatest secret …

To the greatest secret, yes something like that. The secret of my being that I don't really consciously let myself know.

CO: Perhaps what later on Miller will call extimacy I suppose.

Yeah, yeah, except, I think Lacan captures much more, the feelingness of it here, these lessons are quite poetic compared to some of the others. I think in these seminars he gets to the intensity of the experience much more than he does earlier or later. I find the seminars between VI and XII, even VI and XIV which are very much close to actual devastation, actual pain, actual loss of presence, in other words, experiential stuff, maybe dramas of the Imaginary, but that we remember and we know about. And we'll see further on, castration will not be so much simply the Symbolic necessity of earlier seminars so much as the absolute devastation of one's being, so maybe that's why I like these seminars.

CO: And isn't there a great connection here between this seminar and Seminar X?

Oh completely! They're sisters ...

CO: They're sisters, ok!

Oh yes, desire and anxiety are sisters definitely!

CO: Well, he does make a huge thing of desire and anxiety in seminar X and then the embarrassment here ...

That's right...

CO: Yeah.

And the embarrassment here is actually better than in anxiety because this is how we really are embarrassed. That we lose our place in the conversation, that we are devastated with ourselves and continuity is broken, I can't remember what I was saying and still less can I save myself and go on saying it.

PO'C: There was a great instance of that in the Nobel prize ceremony for Bob Dylan ... Patti Smith sang a "A Hard Rain's Gonna Fall" in his honour and a little way into the song forgot the words, just froze, and even though she was clearly very embarrassed she found the reaction to her made it okay for her to continue.

That's really interesting. I must look at that. Is it on Youtube?

[Yes and it is on Facebook.]
IM: But there was something banal, maybe something trivial but about exposing her own lack and people loved her.

But this is it Ivana, exposure, so the o-object becomes exposed. And you can't, you lose your place, like I say, like Stephen in the newspaper office. Once that happens, and it's completely unpredictable, you can't know what will do that to you until it happens.

IM: But there's also what Sarah was saying between idea and affect, how close would that be to the bird girl in "Portrait of the Artist" ... and it's also interesting if you look at Gertie McDowell and Leopold Bloom ... you know ... I mean they are always these elusive figures producing very strong physical ... if you want.

Absolutely yes.

IM: Affect at the same time, without, as you were saying ... so the object is between the breast and the mouth and the representation of that lost object ...

Absolutely well I mean there are so many ... I think what I find about the successive theorizations in Lacan ... the ones that speak to you which don't of course invalidate the others, and I think here this particular incarnation of the o-object I find speaks to me which doesn't mean that I won't read the later stuff and see those "between" places. Here it's not so much "between" as incarnated in the other and we'll see ... I don't know if any of you saw this paper I gave in Toronto where I talked about this – Mallarmé has a poem about the loss of his son – and it's in the dream of the dead father – what one mustn't know – and this is again the structure of the fantasy. What I cannot know I give to the other to know. In Mallarmé, the poem is really beautiful. The child was 8 years old when he died, every single night the father dreams that the child has come back and that the child doesn't know that he's dead and he, Mallarmé, must not tell him because if the child was told, then he would know and be dead, but in that dream space he can be there and alive so again its ... what I like about the seminar is that it ties in very strongly to very intense experiences. These are Lacan's tragic years, for some reason or another. Why they are his tragic years? Mainly he was fighting with the IPA ... but they are his tragic years, if you look at VI with Hamlet, VII with Antigone, VIII with Claudel, and IX and X he's moving out of it but during those three years, his best meeting, his best encounter with literature is definitely through tragedy. He's always saying – including in Seminar V – that he's going to talk about comedy but he actually never does. No more than in Seminar X when he says this year I'm going to take you through *Inhibitions, Symptoms, and Anxiety* and there's never a sentence about it after that! But that's fine; he's lecturing.

AB: What about the business of the non-signifiable or non-representation at this time ...

He hasn't moved into the non-representable at this point. He does at one point speak of it as we'll see but not specifically in connection with the o-object. He talks about a turning point in *Hamlet* which is outside representation. This is the moment in the duel when Laertes' poisoned weapon is suddenly in Hamlet's hands. So he's getting there, and he will be there big time in Seminar VII but he hasn't got there yet.

What he's looking at here then is what can be learned from intolerable pain, the pain of existence when there nothing to mask it. And he says on page 63 about the *me phunai* which I always pronounce differently to Dany [Nobus] the "better not to have been born" which again he has been talking about since Seminar II using the correct reference, using *Oedipus at Colonus* correctly. In Seminar II he recognizes that it is the chorus who make this statement. A year later he will use this quotation again but now these words are uttered by Oedipus according to Lacan – a powerful misquote which will occupy centre stage in future years.

So now onto the dream of the dead father.

Lacan tries to stay within the Freudian interpretation; one of the things he's trying desperately to do this year is to stay within the armature of Freudian theory while actually moving quite a bit away from it. In his later years he'll be quite happy to say he is Lacanian and not Freudian, but in these years he wants very much to be Freudian. However, he actually suggests something very different to Freud in this commentary on the dream of the dead father. Lacan's reading is far more about the "he did not know" than the "as he wished". So the accent is on the "he did not know". Now, as I was saying, this is not at all an uncommon dream. Freud doesn't seem to have known that this is actually a common dream that occurs not in the case of all mourning, but is often reported when the person who has been lost is the person who has taken the place of the o-object. Here Lacan will use Trotsky's dream. Mallarmé uses this beautiful poem about his 8-year-old son – I remember having these dreams myself – the person is back and you're absolutely, the dreamer is absolutely delighted but then I remember that he has died and I'm about to say it to him and then I realize: no if you say it he'll go. And the shock of that thought generally speaking would be so intense that I would wake up. So I was very taken when I found it in Mallarmé and when I find it in the clinic, and I do hear it from time to time. This then is not an uncommon dream. As Lacan will say about the Trotsky dream, when the dead person appears it is not just that they don't know they are dead but it is essential that they must not be told. Mallarmé spells this out: what you do not know/no I will not/Tell it/to you – for then you/would disappear. He says it absolutely. Paul Auster who translated this work says in his introduction to the English version that these fragments written by Mallarmé are not poems *per se*, that Mallarmé wasn't able to write, but that what he had written down were the shards of a poem he was too broken to put together. A French scholar found the fragments a couple of years after this seminar and then Paul Auster has translated them. They are so bang on what Lacan is trying to say here that I thought I would include this excerpt. On page 80 Lacan uses the

Trotsky dream – the dreamer mustn't tell the dead person – and it's back to what Carol was saying earlier that we need a fantasmatic structure – whatever our fantasmatic structure is – to shield us from the unbearable pain of existing when it's stripped down to its bare elements. So normally the formula of fantasy keeps this screen in place; the everyday ups and downs, the everyday securities, keep me from fully knowing just what this person is to me, but in death that's completely stripped away and you can't go on in any shape or form … and bizarrely the dream – Lacan is saying – those dreams are a kind of protection because here it's the other who doesn't know the unbearable thing. That's the point he's making. Rightly or wrongly, but that is the point he's making. So it's too unbearable to know; the one who has died or vanished mustn't be told. According to Lacan this is always found in dreams of this kind. Lacan seems to know that this is a common dream although Freud doesn't seem to know this. It is because the dreamer has hit this low point and Lacan says this; the subject knew this pain – the one to whom the "he did not know" refers is the dreamer – but this ignorance is actually needed, because if the child knew, as Mallarmé says, then he would indeed be altogether lost to his grieving father. Lacan then links this drama to castration. On pages 64 and 65, he links the dream to castration and he says that the fantasy which is here the dream – the dream is a version of the fantasy – allows the subject to live somehow and on page 65 he says it is the only thing that the dreamer can hold onto, the veil that ensures he can continue to be a subject who speaks. This is the last sentence in this lesson. And as I was saying – here is where castration begins to be equated in this seminar to utter devastation and not just to symbolic necessity, because if you remember Seminar V, it was much more a matter of symbolic necessity; the mother needed to be castrated in order for the child to live. It wasn't associated with absolutely not being able to go on another step. So this is a big change and this will be developed over these seminars to the point that in *Anxiety* (Seminar X) he will say that what everything starts with is imaginary castration. He is going to be looking at some primal trauma, a trauma that more or less almost does the subject in, which will enter the subject's world and form the substratum of what will be symbolic castration. In *Anxiety* he links this event very much to his famous Saint Augustine story where what you see/look at, abolishes you. You look at the image of this, your mother, with the new baby in her arms and you as subject are annihilated and abolished. That is what he is going to be linking castration to. This is very very different to Freud. And he says in *Anxiety* that this kind of founding event varies for each subject – there isn't just one – the Saint Augustine anecdote is a specimen story, but we each have our own; the moment of falling out of our existence, losing our place in existence is specific to each one of us, maybe not recuperable in memory, but that moment where I might not be is always a possibility: I am, but maybe I might not be able to go on being. You can see it very much in the performance arts, where you know Pauline, what you were saying about Patti Smith, will I be able to carry it off can I put a presence there that is sufficient to manage or can I not? That would be an analogue of what he is talking about.

CO: Olga can I ask something …

Please.

CO: It really just concerns that last paragraph that you just quoted from lesson five because we did see when we looked at this that this was a really like heavy-duty important piece.

Yeah.

CO: And, but in particular, and for people who haven't read these early seminars before because the notion that he crystallizes here about the object its very different to the one that has become almost banalized in lots of different versions of Lacan.

Oh, absolutely yeah.

CO: About the object cause of desire and so on and so forth because this object is absolutely predicated on the other, sorry … "that the object as such, namely that it is with the other that we try to identify" so in other words, this is the object, understood as the product of identification with the small other … so.

Well, it's a version of that …

CO: A version, so.

But it is not just that, it is opposed to identification, it is taking support from an image, so it's a little move away, he stays within the vocabulary, but it is a little move away from that.

CO: Because you know you were saying the Saint Augustine example, of course, the baby, the child doesn't vanish as subject without first realizing his place, the place that he held has been taken up or usurped by another. So it requires the identification, perhaps, with the other?

I'm not sure that it does. I think that there's a simultaneity. You see. And what you see lets you know that you have already lost it.

CO: So seeing is equivalent to the identification?

No, with the loss.

CO: With the loss?

At the moment that I recognize this image as my world, there's no way back it's lost, it's gone. So I think the accent is more on the loss. Some identification can come afterwards. Falling out of one's existence. It's a version of anteriority. By the time I see, there's no going back; this is it. It's done. And the o-object comes into being. There is only the lost object, no other, which Lacan has always said in fairness to him. Always the lost object. So while I may have greatly loved whomever I have lost who would also have gotten on my nerves and so on but then the time I fully realize what it is I've lost, it's lost. And that can be, I remember hearing somebody when her o-object was much closer to her self-image, somebody who in her own view was the lynchpin of the office, without her there'd be nobody, kept the whole show on the road and one day she over-heard, she overheard people talking about what a pain in the ass she was, how she was so out of touch, when was she going to retire, and her universe fell in, caved in. So what sustains you, I suppose that's the question. And not one that you can answer; you can never know what sustains you, alas, until it's gone. And then you know. An irremediable quality, not to be got back and you only know it's gone when it's gone.

CO: "Don't it always seem to go ... you don't know what you've got 'til it's gone ..."

I was just thinking that Carol! Absolutely, that's right. But Lacan leans on the tragic import, which of course is there and I think that's why I like this seminar.

PO'CONN: Olga I was just thinking about an example of what Carol was saying, a client who had been bereaved young, his wife had died, but he would frequently dream about her, but in a subsequent session he was talking about a work presentation – I mentioned this in my paper to the group – and he said: "I know my subject very well". I said, you know in psychoanalysis we talk about the subject as the person, and in that moment he burst into tears and he said: "my wife interpreted everything for me, since she died, I don't feel like I exist". So it really brought a lot of that together.

Hmm. Yes, that's why I like this seminar. Because it's right on the button. With the most harrowing of human experiences. Yeah. And much more than ... you know Lacan kind of lets his guard down a bit. You know, you hear that poetic side of him which you don't always hear. You'll be glad to hear I'm almost finished.

As I say, a version of castration occurs. And imaginary castration is very close to the *me phunai* profiled in the Saint Augustine story. In lesson six he is saying that the father protected him from this knowledge. The dream he says then is a kind of a veil. So the ordinary ups and downs of life protect you. He uses three terms there: protection, defence, and a necessary ignorance. And he talks about that dream as the slender footbridge that keeps the dreamer from knowing his devastation. Yes Sarah?

SM: I'm just wondering if it's in the ups and downs that's where our ambivalence comes in in mourning so that for somebody you love but also hated and now that's gone … where does that go …

Well in a way I always think of it in *Henry V* when Falstaff dies, and Henry says a wonderful thing which is "I could have better lost a better man". That says it all. You know we don't just love someone because somebody is good, but we love somebody because we love them. Or even what Montaigne said about his friend – *Parce-que c'etait moi, parce-que c'etait lui* – because it was me, because it was him. So the particularity and intensity of love which as Lacan will go on to say in *Encore* (Seminar XX) is inseparable from hate.

IM: When my aunt's husband died – she's 87 – he died when he was 84 and I called her – I was in Ireland she was in Serbia and you know to express my condolences I asked her how she felt and she said: "I miss our fights so much".

[laughter]

Absolutely, that's right, that's right.

IM: It's what sustained their … the pain of existence – which is in the end the only sign of existence when you're so old.

Absolutely. That's what we were talking about on the way over, Kevin (Murphy) and myself, about aphanisis … Jones considers it differently. Lacan invokes aphanisis even as he segues into the phallus here, but he's saying again that we live and we have to think about our existence so in terms of desire and our *élan vital*, our energy for life, we have that but also we think about it. And we worry about it and we are pleased or displeased about it so this is … yes Geraldine?

GC: As Saint Augustine says – we are questions to ourselves.

Yes, we are questions to ourselves, so it's not enough that I am you know a desiring person but I have to also ask myself am I desiring enough am I desiring too much how is my desire today … and he says that is why we set up these successive avoidances. We keep our desire going, because we keep unsatisfied. That's one of them, that's one of the ways that we do it. So it's necessary for us to keep it going and we would worry if it were gone. When Jones brings it in, it's a short book, and worth reading, Jones talks about it as the death of desire – the subject's desire. Lacan will move it along in this seminar, so it becomes the vanishing of the subject. There's going to be if you like, a morphing of that concept through the seminar. It begins as the death of desire but will be actually the elision of the subject that he will move it towards. We will finish up then for today with a brief foray into the phallus (laughs).

CO: The first of many.

[laughs]

The first of many, absolutely. Again as you all know I find this difficult but I also find exceptional the ability of this phallus to morph into all kinds of other different things. The idea or concept which has been shunted into definition under the heading "phallus" is usually good, so very often what he's saying is true, but we need to ask: "but why would that be the phallus?" He begins his discussion with three questions. First of all, the subject asks himself – he doesn't say if the female subject asks herself – does he have a big enough phallus, yes I do thank God, so that's one question. The next question is, this phallus which is essential to the subject which could be what will sustain me, it doesn't, presumably, it doesn't have to be a penis (so could it be called a vagina?), and then the third one does the subject have or have not the absolute weapon. These three questions. Are they specifically masculine questions and if they're not, to what might they refer? Are these questions different to asking do I have whatever it takes and which I might have to ask myself not in general but in specific pertinent terms like here this morning, do I have whatever it takes to do this work, and also he goes on, and says exactly the same thing about the pre-eminence of the phallus as he has said earlier about the double layer of "the subject's lived experience" on page 101:

> What psychoanalysis shows us is that the desire to live is as such subjectively put into play in the subject's lived experience. This does not merely mean that human experience is put into play by desire … but that the human subject takes desire into account and counts on it.

This is now linked to the phallus. In speaking of the *élan vital* and the fear that this might fail one, a reference to the phallus is valid enough, but it would make more sense to recognize that this is simply one instance of this dilemma: can I do it or will I be up to it? Here Lacan goes off down the road of the Oedipus complex and then he goes again into another segue about Freud's silliness about women. Then about page 76 he talks about – very interesting – the identification to the image of the father he says is just one solution – that's very interesting – in terms of the exit from the Oedipus, just one solution which will stabilize the fundamental fantasy. Just one version. This anticipates really almost his last seminar *The Sinthome* – there was one after that – where he is saying that one finds a way to live; it is not necessarily the traversal of the Oedipus complex. How does one find, what does one find that will be enough of a support to sustain your existence? And he leaves that question much more open in *The Sinthome* than he has, you know, in the seminar on the psychoses – it was absolutely clear then that there was only one thing that would do that for you and that was the Oedipus complex. But you know things change very much over the years.

CO: On that latter point are you talking about the section where he is saying that the ego ideal is just one version, is that what you mean?

He actually says the image of the father, on page 76. Identification to the image of the father.

MK: The ideal of the father …

The ideal of the father that's right, and yes he links that to the ego ideal absolutely.

CO: So that's just one version of the fantasy?
MK: And actually he says later that this does nothing to resolve for us the problematic of desire.

Absolutely, so you know if you consider that Seminar V hammered the Oedipus home, copperfastened it nearly, and then later he completely disses it. So what he is saying here is that something is produced at the level of the Imaginary which is called castration. And it has its impact at the level of the Imaginary. It is something that is utterly devastating, necessitating a defence. This is the fantasy that will sustain you, keep you going. Now you know one of the problems with the phallus is that as something that can vanish and that can fail, it is, – well, the penis is actually not a bad example of what he's talking about. It can not live up to expectation and all that kind of carry on, so it is *a* good signifier and *a* good symbol. I would take issue; I do not see it as *the* signifier of the subject. That's where I have a problem. So I certainly see that it fits the bill in several ways as a signifier and a very interesting one and a very provocative one shall we say. But I don't see it as the signifier of the subject. End of rant!

[laughs]

CO: Isn't that bit on castration, this moment that he arrives at now, castration has an impact at the level of the Imaginary, isn't that like the link back to Seminar IV on the object relation, you know

where he talks about castration as an imaginary … it's of the image, you don't physically lose a part of yourself, what you lose is something of the Imaginary, so there's the link there.

There is a link but it has a lot more affect in it here.

CO: Totally.

You know, there, it's on the graph …

CO: And it's mixed up with privation, frustration.

Yes, but he definitely did say it in IV and here, then in VII, and particularly in VIII and IX, you visit these points of absolute destitution of being. So it has taken on a huge amount of heat and light shall we say.

KM: Olga does he reference narcissism here?

Yes, very much.

KM: We tend to think of the formula for the fantasy as a standing support for the subject, but it's driven in a sense by narcissism?

Absolutely. In Seminar VI, and again I see this is where a kind of blurring of the boundary between the theorization of the phallus and the theorization of the narcissistic image happens, what will stand so to speak. So the o-object has everything to do with narcissistic passion in this seminar … Lacan will move away from that, but I think there's a degree of validity in it, if you think of that story I told you about the woman in the office. It was her narcissistic image that completely sustained her there. So yeah its very linked. Guy le Gaufey talks about it in his book on the o-object – and he talks about the term o-object giving the game away showing where it had its origins, it had its origins in the little other. And that's very obvious here. It's still very much the little other but with extra stuff added in, and sometimes he talks about it as narcissistic passion – in I think possibly the session on *Hamlet*. So the o-object is very linked to narcissism. By Seminar VII, he will be looking for some kind of concept that is outside of narcissism so this is of course the problem. He goes headlong into something and then proceeds to move away and by the time he gets to Seminars IX and X the o-object is non-narcissistic. But as I say I find this valuable clinically and I like it anyway. He's going to say other things … this is the problem, and it's the same with the phallus but what he says about the o-object here has a truth. What he says about the o-object in IX which is completely different also has a truth and so … what you're reading is true …

it's just that it would be nice or even useful, if you had – first phase o-object, followed by o-object phase 2 – This would be good for scholarship if it wasn't going to be too pedantic. And it's the same thing with the phallus ... you think oh yeah that's true but then at times why call it that? So that is a real problem. It doesn't invalidate what he's saying, but it's a big problem with Lacanian scholarship I think.

GC: You're talking about affects and I'm just curious how you and Lacanians define affects.

Well, I don't know how Lacanians would ... I think how one does oneself ... you know you have to remember, I think, the context in which he was fighting this war. Like what psychoanalysis was like in the 1950s. Affect was used in what seem now like extraordinary ways. Anecdotally it was said that you could go in to your session and lie down and before you say a word the analyst might say I feel a lot of hostility coming out of you today. So there were very different assumptions there – analysis was predicated on very different uses of affect. Or particular understandings of projective identification – one of the ways in which it was used, is to interpret something as, – you're putting all of your bad feelings into me – which is a very presumptive thing to say. For you know the analyst could be having all her own bad feelings and so there was a kind of invasive use of affect and a culture that supported it. I do think Lacan is fighting that madly in his early years, but he does defend affect in these early seminars and certainly he goes right down the road of profound and devastating feeling in this seminar. I think we as analysts have to recognize, affect is how people live. And also it is no guarantee of anything. It is how you react – you have a gut feeling and you are just as likely to be wrong as right. It's no indication of rightness although we like to see it as such ever since the nineteenth century – the holiness of the heart's affections, etc. It's an indication of the person's fantasy or even of your own fantasy. It is absolutely no guarantee of correctness but yeah we have to take ... people don't come in with ideas, they come in with feelings. So we have to take that fully into account. But I think it's important to take into account as an analyst that we keep our own affect out of the session. Lacan will talk about this in his seminar on transference. You recognize that such and such client is disturbing you because their stuff is too like your mother's or some such. That's for supervision, and it's for recognizing, so that you don't bring it into the session.

AB: They call it verbalized affect as opposed to just what we might think of as chained signifiers.

But the signifier isn't just verbal. Say in the session if somebody cries. Or laughs. I would mark it by saying, "that makes you laugh", or "that's upsetting you".

But Lacan talks about things that happen in the session that are too close to the narcissistic image and these you would not mention. I might not mention if somebody was shaking … it's too invasive.

AB: I think the British school give privilege to the verb of affect over other expression.

Oh, right, ok.

SM: But then crying is a signifier too?

Yes, he actually says, when he starts into the graph, he says man's reality is not coextensive with the signifying chain which allows you … you know, there's a whole heap of stuff that is not going to get into the signifying chain. So insofar as it doesn't you're not going to be able to say anything about it. Insofar as it does – say in the case of a phobia or crying or laughing – yes you might. One of the borderline things which I found interesting for myself in terms of an ethical, and a clinical question is when somebody is recounting a dream, and they do the actions to themselves, and they say, "and so and so kicked the ball down the beach" and they kick their foot up in the air. I'm kind of thinking should I say that? Should I comment? And what I actually did, I got them to go over that territory three times – the poor person must have thought I was deaf (laughs) and when there were three kicks I thought I could say yeah and you're doing the kicking yourself. Lacan would certainly think that Freud wasn't okay in commenting on Dora fidgeting with her bag. You know that you cannot invade the narcissistic space.

CO: But I guess the *geste à peau* moved him right across the room where he put his own hand on that client's face.

Say again.

CO: You remember the *geste à peau*, the woman who was in analysis with Lacan and she said you know every morning she would remember the Gestapo knocking hammering on the doors …

Oh yes, that's right …

CO: And the thing he did as an intervention was to get up and put his hand on her face the *geste à peau* as equivoque I think.

Wow. That's right.

CO: Well he was quite old at this stage maybe he ... I don't know; we don't know what else he did apart from these little glimpses we get via ...

SM: But drawing attention to the kicking, it's similar ...

CO: And it is brilliant because "you're kicking yourself" is in the vernacular. Or "I could kick myself".

Yeah, absolutely.

[Audio recording ends here]

Chapter 8

Lecture II
21 February 2017

CO: You're all very welcome to the second of our lectures by Olga Cox Cameron on Seminar VI and this session takes in lessons eight to twelve which we've been working on. Over to you Olga and thanks very much.

Thank you very much Carol and good morning. I was going to say that this was the easiest part of the seminar. But Susan [Cassidy] says she's been wading away in thick obscurity [laughs] and I don't think it is easy to come across a simple piece of Lacan. However, to me the most difficult lesson in this section of Seminar VI is lesson twelve, which is the first one we will look at today. I thought that maybe I would start with that while you're still energetic and fresh. I think it's also the most important in terms of theoretical innovation and it's also extremely dense and a very good example of "Lacanese", of how Lacan actually puts theoretical innovation together, and I'm very pleased to be working with this group on it, because you can't start at this level with people who've just begun to read Lacan, you know, you can't explore the mechanics of how he's putting things together. So you have to have a degree of experience in reading Lacan and as I was saying the last time, it can be like standing under an avalanche! So this lesson is a good one because it allows you to see various components twined in together to give you a new theoretical position. As I was saying the last day, I like this seminar because it is a big turning point from Seminar V even though Lacan doesn't always acknowledge this. You have this new emphasis on being whilst still not abandoning the matrix of the opposition of being and having. Nonetheless, while he puts forward that he's still within that matrix there is a very definite shift with an emphasis on being rather than having. He uses quite a bit of what he had said in Seminar V on the Oedipus complex here in this lesson. So there's a restatement of Freud but this time with a lot of different accents and he amplifies this rehash of the positions of Seminar V from two other sources. One, a reading of a very famous paper by Melanie Klein which is "Symbol Formation and the Development of the Ego" and the other one is the Saint Augustine story which had first been cited in 1948 in his paper on "Aggressivity and Psychoanalysis" but which now appears with a completely different accent, one that will be repeated over the next couple of years and amplified yet again in Seminar IX – *Identification*. So the Saint Augustine story is fore-grounded with a huge new intensity in this seminar and will remain in focus until Seminar IX.

Here in lesson twelve he starts by wanting to specify what he says are the characteristics of the signifier. Now by the time we get to page 10 and it's really the first ten pages I'm going to look at closely because they're the theoretical pages, our question will be, is this signifier simply the signifier phallus, or does he mean the signifier full-stop? So it's the signifier phallus which is *one* signifier or *the* signifier? By the way interrupt me any time you want with questions, that's absolutely fine.

He presses Klein into service for his own ends as he always does. Every theoretician he's using whether it's Saussure, Klein, or Benveniste, there will always be a little twist on it. So, Klein first. I know that not everyone reads Klein. I suppose if you look at Klein and Freud, Klein sees the psyche as developing and driven by anxiety, where Freud sees the psyche developing and evolving itself in the wish. Nothing but a wish can set our psyche in motion is Freud's conclusion in *The Interpretation of Dreams*. For Klein it's anxiety as is very evident in this paper, so for Klein the primary object which she names as the breast, but also the penis, and the vagina – they are also primary objects – really what she says about them is, they are too hot to handle. They are too anxiety-laden and as such, because they're too intense and too anxiety-laden the child is driven to find substitutes for them and turns to other things. So, a blankie, or a teddy, or a toy. The child is driven away by the intensity of the primary object, and so this too much of intensity is channelled in to lesser intensities and as Klein says in this paper, this is how we create our world. A world of things that interest us – by moving away, away, away from the primary objects, and becoming more and more interested in lesser but absorbing things. This is how the child creates his or her world. And I quote here: from page 220 in "Love, Guilt and Reparation",

> anxiety makes the child equate the organs in question with other things. Owing to this equation they in their turn become objects of anxiety and so he is impelled to make other and new equations which form the basis of his interest in the new objects.

So you can see what she's saying can't you, that there's this drive away from intensity with this propulsion towards things of lesser intensity and this gives the child his or her world. What she's talking about there, which Lacan of course likes, is the possibility of substitution which is also of course what metaphor means. So the impossibility of this substitution, if you cannot substitute, is quite likely to bring your world to a halt, and Klein in this paper goes straight into the case history of little Dick. Lacan's interest in Klein goes back many years, and this same case history – little Dick – had received extensive commentary in Seminar

I. It focussed on a child who was unable to engage in the process just described by Klein and remains stuck in a world of primary objects. What's interesting here is that next year in the *Ethics* seminar Lacan will pick up on the inability to substitute and will trope it as a heroic stance. Antigone cannot substitute, and in the text of the Greek play, Antigone actually says this: "if the one who had been murdered was a lover or a child I could have found another lover, another child, but a brother cannot be replaced". So it's interesting that Lacan a year later will trope this inability to substitute as heroism and as the primary example of the ethical position. Here in lesson twelve he says that the phallus has taken on a certain function of equivalence in proportion to a certain renunciation; the subject enters into possession of this sort of infinity, of plurality, of all-ness in the world of objects which characterizes the world of man. So you can see or hear how close his language is there to Klein's thought, a function of equivalence which gives the subject his all-ness, a world of plurality, that's very much a restatement of what Klein had said in "Symbol Formation". You see the Kleinian slant there in what he's saying about substitution. Klein's reference is the penis which morphs into the Lacanian phallus here, but very obviously what is being spoken of as the phallus by Lacan is here clearly the penis. So the question of the phallus never being the penis, once again as scholars of Lacan we have to mark the fact that that is truly a rubbishy statement to make. You know. It may not always be the penis but sure as hell, it quite often is. Especially in these early seminars.

Since he's been talking about metaphor since Seminar III, the question of substitution isn't new, but here he's going to insert it into a whole new drama. Let's start with the new emphasis on being. He begins by reasserting the Freudian opposition of being and having. He says on page 213, to be it, or to have it, that is the essential distinction. That's a pretty clear sentence. But then he will go on to undermine that essential distinction. Just in terms of watching how Lacan moves … Very often he plonks himself back into a Freudian orthodox position and then slithers out of it almost with the simple aid of grammar, almost via a grammatical move, so he manages his slither if you like by saying first that the phallus has primarily a relationship to being. Again that's on page 213 and then he goes on to repeat a number of times, the subject is, and is not the phallus. So first of all the opposition is between being or having, and then it's between is or is not. You can see that the slide is linguistic. This statement is not made about just about anybody, but it is specifically about the subject in so far as he assumes his identity. In other words the speaking subject, and this is an important distinction that is very easy to miss. But you remember the emphasis on this that I talked about the last time, the fact that he insists, and he will insist all through this seminar on this speaking subject; that we are not just in the world – we don't just *be*, but we think about our being, we reflect upon our being. As I was saying about the seminar on identification, we are caught between immanence and epos, or saga. We're caught between just being and the stories we tell ourselves about our being. And that's really absolutely essential for psychoanalysis – this realization that the speaking subject is caught between these two different levels. Now by the end of the page it's no longer a simple opposition between being and having so something that starts as one assertion is immediately undercut and the distinction now is – it isn't even a distinction – it's an inclusion. The subject is and is not. So it's not the subject is *or* is not the phallus, the subject is *and* is not the phallus, and in order to talk about this he insists that we now have to take into account the formula for fantasy the $0a. This is what complicates the new theory. So we take that into account and we try to recognize that it is insofar as this subject is a barred subject that it is possible in certain conditions to give him the phallus as signifier. Not a very clear statement because he doesn't say what the conditions are and why it would be possible in certain conditions to give him the phallus as signifier.

CO: Olga do you mind saying a bit more about ... he is and is not the phallus ... please. He says: "he is it because it is the signifier in which language designates him and he is not it insofar as language takes it away from him".

Yeah. I mean the whole bit here is about the prevalence of the subject as subject of language ... but all of this is about man as engaged in symbolic activity so if language gives it to you – "I am" – does language then support it? That's a very obscure sentence Carol that I don't get. I do get, the grammatical ... the only way that some things can be installed for the speaking subject is via the trickery of language. You know? Which I really didn't get myself until quite lately and when I was thinking about this – because he goes on here to say this is only possible via the slippage of the verb to be. Do you remember that ... where is it now ... where do I have it ... again its back on – just before the bit on Melanie Klein and equivalence. The paragraph before that "to grasp in a formula in which there is preserved the slippage that concerns the use of the verb to be" (p. 214). Now when I was reading that sentence this time around I suddenly remembered that in *Crucial Problems in Psychoanalysis* where he's talking about the move from the zero to the one – where instead of using language he's now shifted into mathematics and Miller, Jacques-Alain Miller, points out that the only way that zero can be moved into one is by linguistic trickery: that we say it and we make it be. And that is really, really, interesting I think in terms of the formulae of sexuation of which this is the matrix, this is the first inkling of this later major direction, this is the beginning of creating a position, two positions that are not really two, so I think it's interesting to see where all that started. It starts in this Seminar VI with all this undercutting of the earlier more stable positions ascribed to *being* and *having*, but I think it's also interesting to see in terms of symbolic and imaginary identities particularly around sexuality that if we are relying on the Symbolic and the Imaginary as in what we make with language, presumably that can't be hugely stable. Historically the positions of masculine and feminine, well we can see even now in 2017 even those two positions are not enough to talk about. There is a whole lot in between, so

Lacan's two positions have now become a multitude of positions. But also what creates a masculine and what creates a feminine for Lacan here in 1959? If you look again historically you can easily see that what created those positions in the 1950s – the hyper-masculine man and the hyper-feminine woman, particularly after World War II, now looks ludicrous. If you look at Donald Trump being *the man*, it's very interesting to hear on Ryan Turbidy the phone calls that come in … "Oh he's a real man" – people that are back in a certain era are thrilled with a certain hyper-masculinity, but other people are thinking – for fuck's sake who thinks this is a man? So it's actually interesting because Lacan remains to the end fairly masculinist, and fairly stuck in his own notions and yet what he's saying would be that we are in these positions because we say we are in them and if we say we're in them and we take what he says in *Identification* (Seminar IX), caught between immanence and the story we tell ourselves – the story you tell yourself is never good enough. You know? Like I'm great, but Jesus Christ am I really? Or even I'm hopeless. The story I tell myself subsists in a fragile space and can be undercut. So in that sense language can give it to me but it can also take it away from me.

MK: So we function on these different levels?

That's right, but because I suppose that *not being* is so alarming and potentially so devastating, we try very hard to believe that there is … that we cling to all sorts of things, and to paths that will give us the totality that we need. Non-being can be far more devastating … the fiction that I have managed to create about myself will have fragilization points and so … fragilization points which I probably don't know about. So, for example, I could be at a party and somebody could say something to me where the ground just drops from under my feet and for some obscure reason I'm devastated. I want to vanish. And if I'd been a nineteenth-century woman I'd have had the joy of being able to faint …

[laughter]

Alas, I can't! So the non-being can take many of those kinds of forms. It has something to do with the image and the fact that not all of the image is sufficiently supported by the Symbolic to see me through every situation. The difficult one being that I probably don't know where my being is going to fall from under me. It's unlikely that I will know that. So the push into non-being that exists in me lurks somewhere in the interval between being and non-being. There's a big insistence – if you take Trump who probably is suffering to some extent from not being loved, and probably suffers a lot from not being loved because he would be exactly the sort of person who would suffer very much from not being loved but presents himself as without chinks in his armour. So there is that need to present yourself there, but behind that the lack that you cannot get into focus.

AB: It's the analyst's role to adapt to this constant venting.

Totally, I think so and I always think that the best analyzed person I've ever seen function, at least on screen, is Žižek, because he doesn't give a fuck, you know. He's really quite happy to look like a complete eejit and to clown and he doesn't have to hold any kind of so-called phallic position, as in "the man has to be the man".

AB: His thesis is the stupid versus the enlightened; he loves that.

Well, maybe that's true. All of these things … I was giving a seminar last week on *Mulholland Drive*, and I was introducing it to the MPhil students at Trinity and one of the things I said which afterwards I thought yeah maybe I'm right … was that when Freud looked to where the unconscious is active, he looked at two places, one to the symptom which is the obscure suffering with which we weigh ourselves down and hold onto for dear life, and the other is in play, the dream, the joke, the laugh. They're the two places. And I was wondering if a psychoanalytic treatment might actually take you from one to the other, so instead of losing those essential parts of yourself that cause you to suffer it might be possible to hold onto them but shift them into the domain of play, and joke and dream, so they're there still, but you're left less riveted, less concentrated, and less imprisoned by them. You have an essential relationship with that which makes you *you*, but a more playful one … It's a notion of what a psychoanalytic treatment might be that's probably more realistic than say – do you remember poor old Freud with Emmy Von N.? He wanted to cure her via hypnosis by wiping from her memory all the events in her life that had made her suffer. And Emmy, who was a weapon, as my daughter would say, played the compliance game and said yes, yes, yes, and allowed Freud to think that she forgot that she was married, that she had children, forgot everything, and Freud was appalled, because this woman's whole life along with her symptom, everything about her is also gone. Well you know that's not what a psychoanalytic treatment should do, but it could be that move from one relationship to your unconscious underpinnings to another. A possibility.

So, this is only possible via the slippage of the verb to be. So now instead of the opposition between being and having, two positives, you have a double negative. As Lacan says: it is not that he does not. And so the man is not without having it. What we now have, Lacan seems to be saying, is a form of assertion or negation that is intermediary, more an inflexion than a clear cut position, while at the same time insisting still on two positions. And again I would have the same question as I do about the formulae (for sexuation): why are these positions necessarily called masculine or feminine? Are they not possible positions – I know he says in the formulae that everyone can pick them up – but would there not be the possibility that quite a lot of us just oscillate between the two? So that we don't necessarily choose one or the other, whether a man or a woman, but we sort of migrate, that these are two of the positions with regard to having and being that are available to us and that we just oscillate between the two. The other thing which is very interesting is his emphasis on the importance for the child not just of his/her position in "the mother's powers" but also that the child must become integrated with respect to the mother's culture. The child must become satisfactorily integrated into the world of insignias that are represented by all the mother's behaviours (p. 218). Now if you remember, he had said this in Seminar IV about object relationships that it isn't really possible for us to take up a sexual place or a place that is that of a sexual being while completely ignoring the cultural insignia. The big question then is: what does the culture offer you in terms of … like it wouldn't be possible – much as a man might like it – to walk down Grafton Street wearing the Elizabethan codpiece – you know, the penis in a different coloured cloth, tight leggings, silk, maybe say yellow silk leggings with a big blue codpiece in front. You would be stopped on Grafton Street probably by the Garda.

CO: But Olga there is the … if you think about the David Beckham posters for the Calvin Klein underwear … what you actually see on the billboard is his, you know, everything that fills his boxer pants.

But it's done in a twenty-first-century way … yeah … so the cultural insignia which … What's the woman who writes on sexual masquerade …

CO: Riviere?

No, she's modern … she's a modern feminist version.

LM: Orbach?

No, no she's American.

IM: Camille Paglia?

Yes!! Where she, for example, has written about how the cultural insignias in the nineteenth century, in particular, hugely underscored the difference between masculine and feminine identities through the handlebar moustache, the waistcoat, and for the woman the long hair and the long dress, where she says that for the seventeenth century, the opposite was true with everyone wearing lace, perfume and huge long-haired wigs. So historically we can move from unified sex to polarized sex. Today fashion even uses the term unisex. As Paglia says, these shifts are in part what fuels eroticism.

IM: **Historically speaking and now that you're mentioning the nineteenth century, the theory that every man being one quarter a woman and every woman being one quarter a man is somehow related to Camille Paglia's theory about the testosterone effect. I mean the idea that we, as women have testosterone which is a driving masculine force.**

We have what?

CO: **Testosterone.**

Oh, testosterone, ok.

IM: **Her theory is a lot, that women are never, well she is saying that you know you will never have a Hegel woman but that you will never have a Jack the Ripper woman either because the scale in women operates differently. I mean it's not psychoanalytic, but it does fit in this idea of cultural insignias.**

Hmm. And but, you'd have to ask what does culture do there? To inflect that. Say, for example, if you think of the average nineteenth-century woman who would give birth up to 14 or 15 times; think of the strength of that body, but these strong women would have been shocked at the idea of running like Sonia O'Sullivan [Irish Olympian runner] and yet you know – in a completely different way, you know, these were stunningly strong women having all these childbirths (as well as probably a few miscarriages), but the possibility of being Sonia O'Sullivan was altogether out of the question. So it can be extremely difficult for us to think in terms of certain possibilities because we are so caught within our own cultural mesh.

That said, Lacan emphasizes the importance for the child of being integrated into the cultural insignia of the mother. And the other thing that is interesting here is that he's beginning – which I don't agree with either – beginning the process of the privileging of women as a sex which he will end up with in the formulae for sexuation … "he is not without having, she is without having it … and that's where the woman's transcendence is …" Is he saying here that woman is in the more solid position because she can *be* without having it where the man is somehow caught between the being and having? But it seems to me that all human beings are probably caught between the having and the being.

CO: **Is it a contingency as well though Olga that you're trying to draw attention to, in other words, that he is not, unless he can have it?**

Well no, he's not saying unless, he's saying without …

CO: **But you know in the sense of … without an umbrella I will get wet, so I wonder if it's that without as …**

I don't know … there's a very simple song in French which… yeah … I've just seen the film "Unless" so I'm very conscious of that particular recognition …

CO: Because, you can see it there more clearly, he is not, in other words, it is an operation that cannot take place …

Well, you could also say, well the question then is that you can move it … so that either reading would seem to be possible. So one, that the man – and masculine masquerade exists just as much as feminine masquerade exists – so the man is not without having it and the woman is … I suppose both sexes make a strong shot at the "is". You want to *be*, so masquerade would be a huge part of life for both sexes inflecting the manner in which they "play" their part as sexed beings in the world. So I'm just pointing this out, it's very dense, but just I think it's useful to see that this is probably where the sexual formulae will be developed from, so early in his middle years, which is why I find the middle seminars so interesting. They allow me to get a grip on what he's on about, because I find the later ones so elliptic and so curt so for that reason among many others, the wordy middle ones are useful.

So again, and of course the question of being and having, remember the last time that I said that was a big deal in the mid-twentieth century, so you have Gabriel Marcel writing *Being and Having*, you had Heidegger's *Being and Time*, Sartre's, *Being and Nothingness*. So *being*, is a big topic philosophically. And in the arts you have Beckett stripping away all types of *having*, in order to give you just *being*. And of course advertising in its heyday overtly played with this, and even still this is a place where one can easily see how being is amplified by having. I am someone *if I have* a good car, I am someone *if I have* this whatever, these clothes. So Lacan is engaging in the same dialectic, so prevalent in these years, but from a different point of view. Looking again at the density of these ten pages, first of all we note the Kleinian substratum recognizing that he quotes from Klein for his own purposes, appropriating and modifying Kleinian positions, second you have this play with negation, is and is not, and the intermediate place – he's always been fascinated by the intermediate places marked by negation. Do you remember the last time he was talking about the *ne* – he talks constantly about the *ne* which in certain usages is something that undermines the positive statement, so this reference is not completely new, but here given a different accent, and the third thing that he uses is the four positions of the Z schema he's been using since forever. Certainly since the seminar on the psychoses and in the *Écrits* chapter on the psychoses "On a Question Preliminary …". You remember the Z Schema, over and over, the mother, the child, the little other, and down here you have all sorts of things, you have the father, the big Other, the phallus in that fourth term. So he uses that again here in conjunction with the Saint Augustine story on page 218. Here at this point he's going to talk about the relationship of the child to the body of the mother which is primordial, and is the framework in which there can come to be inscribed these relationships of the child to his own body which will include the specular, to the degree that narcissism intervenes. For Lacan always, unlike Freud, and certainly unlike Klein, when he talks about the body particularly at this stage – whatever he means by the body in his later work – the body here is always the narcissistic body, the specular, the image. So he talks here of the narcissistic affect, and he says it is insofar as it is from a certain moment that the subject recognizes himself as separated from his proper image as having a certain elective relationship with the image of his own body. So it's always the image at this stage in Lacan, the narcissistic or specular body, which then very easily becomes the counterpart, the other little child. This allows him, because he's talking about the specular, in other words what you can see in the mirror as well as the counterpart, this allows him to segue into the Saint Augustine story. And he will use the Saint Augustine story now, in a whole new reading unlike that of 1948 – here he will use it to underpin in the first place the new focus on being, then second, the formula for fantasy, and then the profoundly alienated relationship we have with our own drives. Which he says again a couple of pages on from there: that what I think of as most authentically mine is profoundly deviated from the beginning, more or less deviated and it's deviated in function of the other, the relationship with the mother. Now with the Saint Augustine story, he gives you the story which he's given you before, and before it has to do with the intrusion complex and the pallor of the onlooking child, and here he gives it to you as something absolutely devastating. The onlooking child, the child who's looking at this image, sees for the first time the image of paradisal totality which is the baby in its mother's arms. And culturally you know if you look at the history of Western art, and the prevalence of paintings of the Madonna and child, and if you look at how it's painted, it's very often in that unifying sweep that creates an image of oneness. So an image that encapsulates what which is most longed for. But an image of impossibility. Lacan is explicit: it is impossible for human beings to accede to an experience of totality. That thing we most long for is forever out of the question for human beings. Because we are "divided and ripped apart". No ambiguity here. It is forever out of the question and it is seen simultaneously at the moment it is lost. You have never given a thought to the world that sustains you – it is simply the ground of your being. But of course this is what it is – this being held in the mother's arms. And suddenly you see it, but the other baby is there in your place. You look at this image and you take in for the first time all that you have ever wanted and you see it at the exact moment that you have lost it. So that ties in this anecdote very well with Freud's insistence always on the object as lost object. At the second that you see it, you know – never again … so this story now, in this new telling is weighted with a huge intensity and you can see how this operates in real life – for example, with crimes of passion, and in so many great ballads. For example, Little Musgrave where the lord comes back and he finds his lady in bed with the young page and without transition he murders them both. Or in that great play *The Duchess of Malfi* where the jealous brother murders her children. Or you find, without transition, the person kills him/herself, that they – something there is abolished at that point; it's not a sustainable, a liveable position to be faced with the image of your own destitution and the other's absolute enjoyment, and the most usual response in the stories recounted in the newspapers or the news is either a murder or a suicide. You either murder them both or in the ballads – Christy Moore sings a great ballad – the murder is a kind of *passage à l'acte*; it happens without your own subjectivity being involved and very often the person turns to his attendants immediately afterwards and says, "why stayed you not my hand?" Why did you not stop me? So it is a rush of non-subjectivity if you like. The subject as Lacan will say over and over – in this seminar – when the subject is faced with the o-object unmediated, the subject is abolished. So ... and Lacan likes that. There is a dramatic intensity in Lacan in these years. These are his tragic years so this is what he kind of favours and he will go back over this further on in Seminar VI and again in Seminars VIII and IX. So there is something – even if he is, if you like, teaching us about the necessity of substitution here – there is a part of him that is very attracted to the drama of non-substitution; the subject's abolishing himself or the other in this type of tragic confrontation. So for this not to happen and again you know the seminar to read with this is *Identification* (Seminar IX), for this not to happen, for the subject not to be abolished, some kind of subjective presence has to be possible here. Continuity has somehow to be established. And what he's going to say is that at this point the abolished subject has to become something else and this has to be somehow (pointing to formula) less intense. The mortal pallor of the child in the Saint Augustine account marks the eclipse of this onlooking baby, and here Lacan suggests that the situation is made liveable by means of substitution. The image of the other child is substituted for this "fundamentally pallid, and anguished" being which is the devastated onlooking child (p. 221). Lacan names this image of the other ego $i(o)$. We will have to wait until the seminar on identification for a much fuller exposition of how this comes about. For now, if the fundamental fantasy is a substitute formation with something like the Saint Augustine story as its underlay, we can certainly see why the subject is an evanescent subject when confronted too directly with the object of desire.

So that's what he's saying in these ten pages. This is a process necessary as he says for the subject to become a speaking subject, in other words, what Klein calls, and what Lacan himself calls some kind of symbolic activity, has to be possible.

So he talks again about the four-fold relation: the mother, in the position of Other, the child, and the counterpart, and as he seems to be saying here, and using Klein as dubious back-up, this o-object has to have a signifier which he's more or less suggesting will be the phallus, some process of substitution has to happen here. At this point he emphasizes very much Saint Augustine's insistence on the pallor of the child. The pallor of the child, he says, "in his destructive passion", is in fact the abolished subject. So here he suggests that what you do there, is you pretend you're the counterpart, you pretend that you're the one that's in the good place, the one that has it … So instead of the abolished subject that you are, you identify as the image of the other. You're not required to believe this, but this is what he's actually saying. But it is interesting, and he says later on in the seminar on identification, he comes back over this again, and he's intensely seduced by that dramatic moment, by the moment of the abolished subject, and he says it's actually not easy to see what might rescue you from that devastation. And indeed it is fair to ask: what can modify such disaster, is there anything that modifies that? By Seminar IX in asking that question again he answers it by recognizing that it is indeed not easy to see how this modification could happen and that in fact it is only because the Symbolic exists, and pre-exists the subject that that rush to destruction can be modified and turn into something else. So you can hear first of all his seduction at the drama and secondly his seeing that it's really not easy to see how you would be stopped from the extreme response of murder/suicide. And of course the only way you could be stopped from doing that would presumably entail immense suffering. So just if you take that scene of coming upon your lover in the arms of someone else. Either you commit suicide, or you murder them both, or you suffer. You suffer and you endure over time. And he's saying, what makes that possible? And in [the seminar on] identification, he says it is the law, the imposition of the law via the Oedipus complex.

NA: … **and in these crimes of passion usually after the crime has been carried out is when the suffering begins so is it that the subject becomes the lost object having murdered the object?**

Absolutely but very often they can't even remember doing it; it's very common not to remember, to find yourself with the knife in your hand but with no idea why it's dripping with blood. So there is something a-subjective that occurs if you act in that space – that's what the *passage à l'acte* is. Lacan will expand on this elsewhere. It is a hugely interesting phenomenon, and a potentially tragic one where you act in the space of no subjectivity. And then you realize afterwards that you have lost everything.

MK: **I'm just thinking that there's also some link there with childhood depression – identification with the lost object leading to a vanishing of subjectivity.**

Right. Really it's a huge … one of the things Lacan is fighting about in this seminar and fighting really successfully is that he's fighting his critics who say he's too intellectual. He takes you right to the searing heart of suffering and to the searing heart of experience in this seminar. So in terms of an answer to his critics, even though it's couched in difficult language this is really, really not an intellectual exploration.

MK: It's really clinical.

Absolutely, it has huge clinical relevance absolutely.

CO: Olga could I ask a tiny thing.

Please.

CO: So this bit you've just been drawing our attention to ... so he says ... the object's totality to the extent that the image of the other can be substituted for by the subject that we enter properly speaking into symbolic activity.

That's right.

CO: So there's a funny kind of operation because on page 154 we have "the image of the other which substitutes for the barred subject", but it's ... very bizarre.

Yes, it's very bizarre.

CO: And kind of annoying because he seems to contradict what he's actually saying here.

Very annoying, I know, I agree.

CO: So that bit was one we had a bit of a tortured discussion about before.

I can imagine.

[laughs]

CO: What the hell like Lacan?

Yeah, I know.

CO: Okay, but if we leave aside that you know annoying thing there for the moment I suppose in a way what we're also saying ... picking up on Nadezhda's point that it's only possible for the image of the other to be substituted for by the subject via identi-fication, isn't that what ...

Yes, that's what he's saying.

CO: In Seminar IX, I mean you can only, by virtue of your ability ...

That's me!

CO: That's me ... or I want that to be me? Or it was me? Or I recognize me?

Well, that's me and I want it to be me are very you know, that's absolutely how we are ...

CO: That frames the fantasy doesn't it? It furnishes ultimately the fundamental fantasy because the hysteric is the one living to be in that position where somebody else is always.

Always, always. Yeah, and of course it's not stable that's the problem ...

CO: Of course not.

You know there's no stability. You can fall out of that. But you know you hear it with children when you're setting up a game, who will I be? I want to be the Prince or I want to be Cinderella. I'm not going to be the ugly sister, so who will I be is the question we ask ourselves all through life really in a sense and I suppose women are probably more ironic and more aware of it ... you stand in front of the mirror and you say ... fuck it, you know, who will I be today kind of thing. But the notion of masquerade is more easily accepted by women than by men or perhaps up to now we could say. Up to now.

So like I say, this is far more intense fare, more existential as a drama than Freud's Oedipus, you know this really is the edge of annihilation. At the edge of annihilation I choose to be. To be the one who has it shall we say. So it's much more ... it's a whole different tonality than Freud ever had. And at the same time really interestingly, he stays within the Freudian matrix, as in, it is a narcissistic drama. Do you remember Freud says narcissism wins in the end, because the guy won't accept to lose his penis so he will renounce the mother rather than lose the ... so he stays interestingly within the Freudian framework because his is a narcissistic identity. So the phallus he would seem to say here, he will not keep to this of course, he will say all sorts of other things about the phallus, but it would seem that in this reading the phallus is a substitute for the o-object ... he is certainly not going to stay with that, but just for the moment that's the way it looks. So the phallus becomes a signifying element of something that has been substituted for what's too hot to handle. Now whether of course ... I'm back to my eternal question is it the only signifier? Should there not be many other contenders for that signifier including using his own language ... you could say ... the fading of the subject, that would do it very, very, well ... aphanisis as he explains gives you that drama very well, the formula for fantasy, the abolished subject gives you that very well. So, and also just before I move away from that, Klein's take on the concept of totality is very different. This is not what Klein was saying at all. Klein is actually saying that the depressive position is where the child begins to realize that you can't push bad out and keep good in, that the child, the baby is himself both the bad and the good; the mother has both the bad and the good, and the baby then begins to realize that in trying to destroy the bad mother he or she is also destroying the person he/she needs most. Because they're not separable. The concept of totality for Klein is a whole other drama and I just point it out again in terms of Lacanian scholarship, he's using the concept of Kleinian totality but in his own framework. So as I say the theoretical position has been altered but within a complex repetition of earlier stuff meshed in together with several different lines of thinking; the Kleinian, the negation, the Freudian being and having, so all of those are somehow mingled together. I did it in detail just for you to see with other stuff that you're finding hard, just to try and see what are the lines of thought that are intersecting – not clearly and not necessarily even accurately – but it will help your reading to see what's happening.

CO: Totally.

It doesn't invalidate what he's saying. But it does make it very hard to follow what he's saying sometimes.

AB: I was thinking – talking about Lacan's use of Klein about parental separation where a boy is entering puberty … often the custody is with the mother where the boy has to negotiate allegiance to the mother versus the whole aspect of emerging masculinity and identification with the father and oftentimes not being able to.

Absolutely, yeah, yeah. It's actually amazing that people – given the enormity of what you're faced with at puberty – that you manage to grow up at all … and you have as you say the parental inadequacy or difficulty and then you have all the cultural icons and very little leeway given to you at school. You can be a really bizarre adult without too much bother, but you can't be a bizarre teenager without loads of bother. So it's an absolute minefield to make your way through

AB: Yes and with often the mother reinforcing – the idea that the child exclusively belongs to her and the father is just an appendage and it makes for the idea of a horrifying betrayal, the sense of betraying the mother.

Indeed.
So, okay, are you ok with that intense reading of lesson twelve. Will we have a quick scoot through the dream?

So in this second section then, we find the same coordinates as the first one: you have a father, son, death, and the relation to desire, and in each of the three sections, the same drama impacting on the subject at different levels. The first one was very much the dream. This one which is also the dream is also largely the symptom of an obsessional neurosis, and the third one then will be the collapse of subjectivity, the abolition of the subject which is Hamlet, and the refinding of subjectivity. So the same thing taken through three different modalities. Now the first one that we looked at the last day, the dream of the dead father wasn't that far from being a typical dream. "He did not know that he had died", dreamed by many people as we know, about a death which is not possible to encompass. You don't have that about every death but about the impossible death. And I quoted Mallarmé's beautiful poem about the death of his eight-year-old son, Anatole. So how does the dream think about the unthinkable – that was very much what we saw in the first one and one of the ways is via that switch by virtue of which it is the other who mustn't know what cannot be known. Now, this second dream is much more the revelation of a subject position which is singular, where and how this subject positions himself in the world. So it's a kind of clinical masterclass, and as I say Lacan's reading is as much about the subject's position in the world, which is his symptom, as it is about the dream which bodies forth this symptomatic stance. So in one way the seminar takes us successively through dream, symptom, and subjective collapse. Now Freud made of the dream (in *The Interpretation of Dreams*) as we know, the royal road to the unconscious, and I also think it was precisely for that reason that no one reads it, no analyst reads it. It would be an interesting thing to ask in any group of analysts: how many of them had read it more than once. It's a canonic and unread text you know like Proust and like *Finnegans Wake*; everybody says it's great, but nobody actually reads it.

[laughter]

Yeah, isn't it really interesting? I've been so lucky, I've had to teach it 20 times which has been a great help to me, but I don't know that I would have voluntarily gone back to reread it, but every time I read it, my practice improved so very much. And you know as Lacan says about *The Interpretation of Dreams*, it mimics the condition of the unconscious in that it slides towards oblivion and being repressed, and ignored, and neglected. It's what … it's also what we don't want to know.

So you have here two different analyses of the same dream and two different theoretical paradigms. Lacan is insisting, although he does a little bit of this himself – on the danger of importing preconceived ideas into the session. There was an interesting little bit – I don't know if any of you saw the Ivor Browne documentary and the conversation between Tommy Tiernan and Ivor Browne precisely about that – you know coming in with a truly open mind rather than with your own preconceived ideas. Very important, and clearly very difficult, as we see Lacan having a few slippages here himself.

So what the analyst can hear in the dream narrative as well … obviously only the analysand can talk about her dream, what the analyst can hear nonetheless in the telling of the dream, not always but sometimes before you even begin working with the client on the dream you can hear the places where the surface of the narrative is interrupted by the breakthrough of unconscious activity. You can often hear that. Freud distinguishes between the manifest and the latent content, but in a very important footnote in Chapter 6 he insists that the unconscious is to be found between the two. In the actually breaking through, the disruptiveness, in the insistence, that turns the latent into the manifest which Freud calls the dream-work that's where the unconscious is. So our question then, and Freud was hugely conflicted about this, is not what does the dream mean which Freud would have liked to have asked, and as a nineteenth-century man would have liked to answer very exhaustively, but *how* does the dream mean, that really is the question. And Freud struggles with that, the conflict between those two questions, throughout *The Interpretation of Dreams.* Now Lacan introduces Ella Sharpe's dream by linking what he's just been saying to what Freud says in *The Interpretation of Dreams.* The important thing, Lacan says, is to spot where the enunciating happens in the enunciation. Do you remember we talked about that the last time and we … so when Freud talks about doubt: "I'm not sure if this happened […]", you latch onto that, everything that is part of the text of the dream and also the "not sure" can also be an enunciating, remember last time we talked about Benveniste talking about the different places indicating where and how the subject owns what he or she is saying. The enunciation and the enunciating and how they connect; phrases like "I believe, I think, and as far as I know", these are all phrases that lock what you are saying to your own subjectivity. Of course, the major one is I, you know, and we were saying that if the newsreader Eileen Dunne instead of saying, "This is the news" if she said, "would you believe what I fucking heard today on the radio?" you know? She wouldn't say that, so you know in many cases the enunciation has to be shorn of the enunciating. But in the dream, everything is in the telling; you have to listen for that. And Lacan talks about the different forms, the different modes of assumption, which would be − "I don't really believe this happened" − so how does the teller tell the dream and in what way does he take on the dream? One of the things that really struck me and what I like about doing this sort of work with say Ella Sharpe's dream or with the Irma dream is that it allows us to play with it. We don't really know because we don't have the client in front of us, but there's nothing wrong with looking at the stylistics and seeing what we see for ourselves, so, for example, if we read the Irma dream Freud gives two different accounts of it. You know, he gives the dream and then he gives the associations but there are a number of omissions and a number of changes of emphases, particularly around the verb "to look" in the Irma dream as text and the same dream as commented by Freud − differences that we can see are worth closely examining. Here, for example, in the Ella Sharpe dream the thing that struck me hugely was the way the client passes over a significant event or a significant thought to the other. When he talks about the motor hood and the hood, eight times he mentions the hood, and he says … "I'm thinking of the hood again", "there's the hood again", or "it's strange I think of the hood", all of these little sentences which are kind of like – pay attention! They are precisely not an assumption by the subject but an attempt by the subject to pass this over to see what the other will do with it. And if you remember, this is his whole pathology, that he wants the other to take responsibility, and Ella Sharpe for the most part is fantastic about it – she doesn't say half of what she says in the case history to him because she knows that that's what he wants. So I found that, the telling of the dream, that kind of constant calling of the analyst's attention to these little clearly useful details reveals something immediately, puts us on the path of what Lacan discovers, and indeed Ella Sharpe knows and points out early on; this client has to pass the initiative over to the other person … so again to some extent we would say, classic obsessional carry-on. Okay, so Lacan is looking at this stage to where the unconscious can be tracked down and at this point he is talking about two signifying chains. These feature largely at this point in his teaching: he indicates two different signifying chains one the coherent, holophrastic, as he says, chain of our conscious ego, and the other evident in our free association and our dreams. This is the fragmented signifying chain that is the unconscious. Now Soler would say that *lalangue*, the content of *lalangue* radically changes this idea and that there are really two unconsciouses. I don't think that that's true. I think Freud from the very beginning speaks of a knowledge that is impregnable, a knowledge that is impossible. He talks about a tangle of unknowingness that runs down like mushroom roots, runs down into an unplumbable tangle, and he also talks about the navel of the dream. So Freud never thought that there would be an unconscious that would be entirely decipherable, and he says this two or three times throughout *The Interpretation of Dreams*. This emphasis on the unknowability which is the navel of the dream to me sounds very similar to what Soler says when she says of the late Lacan "from now on *lalangue* appears as the vast reserve from which deciphering extracts only some fragments … the *lalangue*-unconscious remains as an impregnable knowledge whose effects exceed us". Now to me, that's just straight Freud – the impossible tangle that there's no deciphering. Also I don't see that definition of *lalangue*, shall we say, as innovative. So then what would dream interpretation imply? Not at all something intellectual, as I say but what Lacan specifically spells out (I think it's on page 141) "to interpret desire is to restore something to which the subject cannot gain access by himself – namely the affect that designates his being". Being again. Specifically, what Lacan calls the positional affects with respect to being. So what are my positional affects with respect to being? Lacan names them: how I love, how I hate, how I insist on not knowing. So the dream is going to reveal not any intellectual discovery about the unconscious, but it will tell me something of how I love, how I hate, what do I refuse to know. And so affect, Lacan spells it out, is always involved. Now these positional affects are tangled up – at this point – in repressed signifiers, Lacan will say behind these repressed signifiers are the affects and behind these, he says, we will discover what he calls the essential thing which has happened to the subject which keeps certain signifiers in repression. That's very much straight Freud, isn't it? So the essential thing that has happened which makes certain signifiers impossible. Now at this stage the goal will be the restoration of these signifiers, to discover not simply the primal demand or the primordial demand that you experienced, but more importantly, who did you become in function of this primordial demand, who did you become in function of the demand unexpressed possibly – of your mother. Did you become the good child, the bold child, the funny child, the rebellious child? So, who you became is what needs to be revealed. Which is a very interesting question and here he says Ella Sharpe's client has become dead. He has no access to his own potency in function of the father's words: Robert must take my place. The child Robert hears this as: Robert must be dead. One of the first things we see is the place of the dream at the point in the analysis, this point being where the analysis has worked well enough to effect a disturbance in this positional affect. The client's position is to be dead and something or other has worked sufficiently in the analysis to disturb that. So without wanting to, he coughs. An involuntary sign of life that annoys him and this is followed by a chain of associations in the session which Lacan will see signals his presence as always "not there". So whatever is in the room, is not there, or must not be there. It must be made to disappear if it's the brother kissing the girlfriend; it must be rather ludicrously not there if the client signals "no person here" by barking like a dog – you know, it's so mad that particular association. And it must be not seen by the Other, the big other, it would be very embarrassing, if somebody came in and saw me letting the dog masturbate against my leg. So all of these associations allow Lacan to see immediately that here there is no person, but the question is, in what way, is there no person, and *for* who is there no person. And, *with* whom is there no person? The dream seems to say, sexually, and with a woman, there is no person. So although Ella Sharpe is very astute and Lacan says this over and over, he will criticize her for being over-invested in the Kleinian paradigm, to the notion of omnipotence, it's a very Kleinian … actually it's much more Klein's followers than Klein herself. But the notion that the baby feels omnipotent is one that Lacan always disses; he will say the baby thinks the mother is omnipotent, the mother has all the power. The baby himself or herself rarely for any prolonged period can imagine themselves as omnipotent. So the notion of the baby's omnipotence is one that Lacan will frequently quarrel with, and he will too with respect to Klein's notion of the proximity of the life drive to aggression, Lacan will say correctly that some of what Ella Sharpe develops is based on *a priori* positions and is therefore a bit off the mark. So nonetheless the client is dead to his own aggression, to his own life drive that certainly is true; he has to play dead.

[Audio recording ends]

Chapter 9

Lecture IV
24 June 2017

CO: So without further ado, we'll crack on with the last seven lessons, thank you Olga.

You know it's actually useful for me to go through these lessons because they are so enormous and so unwieldy and it's extremely difficult to get an overview – anything like a coherent overview – so it's always a very useful exercise for me. So thank you for having me. This last section for me certainly is almost the opposite of what he does in the seminar on identification. Which is endlessly, endlessly abstract and dry and topological all the way through and then bursts into poetry in the last few sessions, in those wonderful last few sessions. This is the opposite. Wonderfully powerful, wonderfully organized around three … almost one might say, three set-pieces: the dream of the dead father, the Ella Sharpe dream, and *Hamlet* and then it sort of mish-mashes into an all over the place summary. And it's interesting because in the last bit he's focussing to some extent on the clinical relationship, and bizarrely the focus is actually less clinically useful say than when he's not focussed on the clinic. As in *Hamlet*. So here even though what he says is, of course, accurate and some of it incontestable, it actually looks like he's simply trying to fit what he's newly said about the formula for fantasy and make it applicable to old, more established theory. So, for example, when he takes the formula – and I've put the formula up on the board just to refer to it for you – $\$\lozenge a$ – he takes that and relates it to the hysteric's position as having an unsatisfiable desire in the dream of the beautiful butcher's wife, and the obsessional keeping himself and his desire out of the picture – all very accurate but sure they are theories that have been well established in psychoanalysis, so you kind of wonder is he legitimating himself by locking back onto Freudian positions. So much of these are – they're fine, less exciting, nothing new. More interesting I think is his discussion on perversion and his distinction between perverse fantasy and perverse structure. So what he has to say about perverse fantasy is something he will come back to further on. A very interesting emphasis on the need for a substitute, for somebody to take on the form of desirer, somebody else to be the desirer, to hold the place of desirer, so that the perverse subject can gain enjoyment without actually standing in the hot seat themselves. That's quite interesting and it's much more widely applicable I would say than just to perversion. It's much closer to the structure of subjectivity itself.

So where would one start? If you look at the very last lesson he asks: is desire subjectivity? That's on page 474. So how does the last section then address this question? I would say incoherently, is how he addresses it. He's breaking new ground here, but the fermentation of new ideas often results in long complicated tautologies where you battle your way through impossible syntax to end up with, where you started, like desire … blah blah blah blah blah … is desire. The advent of the cut is … blah blah blah blah blah … the cut. You're going to see that several times in this lesson which in fairness is excusable because he's thinking mostly as he's speaking, but in terms of us trying to be Lacanian scholars we have to isolate those moments and see that instead of this being the last word in wisdom it is a tautology which may contain … little nuggets of interesting stuff but which are actually fetching up on impossible and senseless shores. And I think myself – not knowing well enough to be sure – but I think it's when he has actually not thought it out. This incoherence, it's a bit like what Freud was saying about *The Interpretation of Dreams*: he felt it was incoherent and badly thought out, that's how Freud viewed it in some of his letters (as well as thinking it was his greatest achievement). I think when you're pushing out into new waters that's when this can happen to you – your first draft doesn't satisfy you precisely because you're not quite able to escape the mesh of your previous thinking into something new. So, as I say, venturing out into newness and trying to find the words for this venture is going to be almost by definition at least in part disappointing. "Desire is" … you think hurray! But you're disappointed. So what he does in this section – we're going to get further elaborations of what he's said in earlier lessons, so that's one thing you're going to get, you're then going to get a development of some of the new metaphors he's using, especially the cut, then at the end, for the last few lessons he will set out a few markers which sketch out the ground that's going to be covered in *The Ethics*. Ok. So first of all the most notable shift obviously concerns the structure of subjectivity itself. It's no longer just the $, although he'll continue to use the $, but this new notation. The notation for the subject is now $◊a. And it's very difficult to hold onto that; we all go back, including Lacan, to the $, but what he's saying now is that the barred subject is sustained by something from the imaginary register, something that isn't just an outcome of the symbolic order, which was the Oedipus complex up to now, but something much more, much more existentially dramatic. Lacan says "sustained by something that the subject draws from his own substance" so something much closer to the bone, and closer to elimination or annihilation. Nothing like the tranquil possession of the penis which fetched up in Seminar V, in lesson eleven when he put the coping stone on the Oedipus complex. Now at this point in his thinking he calls the paternal metaphor a fiction (p. 458). A fiction. So that's a huge jump from "this is where it's at" to "this is just a fiction". He says here it is the fiction, real or not, of the one who enjoys the object in peace, and he says that this metaphor actually masks the metonymy for castration. So even though he will continue to use the language of Seminar V, it may also be opined that in that sentence the paternal metaphor has been shot to bits. Of course, he will use it again but it's not the lynchpin that it was in Seminar V. This metaphor is now only a metonymy for castration. So it looks as though he has absolutely undercut it. But the difficulty with Lacan is that serpentine way he has of navigating theory: where it appears to be gone, and lo and behold it's back again, then it's undercut again, but it's undercut in a different way. Like I say part of what I'm doing here, is I suppose to alert you as scholars to look at what's happening, to recognize these shifts, and then you know, your assessment is a different matter. So this is a very big statement. The outcome of the Oedipus now, just one year after the positivities of Seminar V is something fictional but necessary. Later on – on the same page in fact – he calls it a mythical guarantee, and he says we need those fictions because the alternative would be to live in a state of vertigo. And a year after this again, he actually describes the symbolic order as fictional in *The Ethics* as we'll see next year. So the installation of the fundamental fantasy which is the focus of this seminar is something crucial, is prior to the Oedipus complex; so that's the first thing, the shift to something prior and much more fundamental, and the second which is related to it is that this has to do with being. The question of *being*, he says himself on the first page of lesson twenty-three is massively foregrounded in this seminar. So the opposition and the mutual exclusivity if you like, of being and having, which he's been operating with all through Seminars IV and V is both – typical Lacan – is both kept in place and again totally undermined. Totally undercut. Also since the structure of fantasy emerges directly from a crisis which involved being and involves the absence of guarantee, the role of the big Other has also massively changed. This change is first mooted a year earlier. The big Other, if you remember in Seminar V at a certain point I think it's lesson seventeen, where the big Other now appears with a stroke through it, the big Other is now presented as faulty, as helpless, as unable to hold the fort so to speak. So the subject now is confronted with something which threatens to cancel him out and Lacan's new use of the Saint Augustine story is the best example of that. The child who didn't think at all, lived in paradisal oneness with the mother suddenly sees that paradisal oneness imaged in the mother's embrace of the new baby, and both realizes in the same instant – this is where I was happy – and this is now gone – it's not as if he or she had been thinking this is where I'm happy, and it's gone, it's that both realizations collide together, that he had never even thought of being happy or unhappy until that moment so the mortal pallor that he talks about – Saint Augustine talks about – Lacan tropes as subjective elision, the being wiped out completely by this image. This imaginary point is evoked over and over in this seminar. Lacan will say that something at this point is brought in from the imaginary register to keep the subject from being completely cancelled out. The imaginary point in which the being of the subject resides with the greatest density. Note again the repeated privileging here of that imaginary point. If you remember how he disses the Imaginary in Seminar V, and he says at one point – which is extraordinary – that the Imaginary is the bond with the mother that needs to be overwritten by the Symbolic, so in Seminar V the Imaginary is very inferior. Here it's pushed to the foreground. What's extraordinary is the small time-lapse in which so much will have changed. At this stage you've got several different angles of insight into this new formation, not all of them necessarily adding up, some of them more productive than others. So for example for myself I find very compelling that notion of the brink – that on the brink of extinction something is brought in that sustains the subject and this something which will be the o-object is electrified by the possibility of loss. It's not just a comfort blanket by any manner of means it takes its power from the possibility of non-being. So on the cusp of being and non-being, something is preserved there, that keeps me, that allows me to be. And the best example of that, for me anyway, I think is where in *Henry V* we mentioned the last day, do you remember, where the British army is vastly outnumbered and they're definitely going to be annihilated, and then that speech: "we few, we happy few […]" and the listening men are being named as the future heroes of a historic day, but that speech is only electric because … it wouldn't count at all … if the French were numerically insignificant, it's the fact that Henry's army will be massively defeated, it's the proximity of their annihilation that gives the o-object it's electric power. So as I say that's one that I find very compelling. There are several different angles of insight in this section of the seminar – they don't always converge and they don't all add up to a coherent whole. The other one then that he talks about is the flash, something, that can for a moment exist but perhaps is not sustainable in everyday life. So the moment of heroism is perhaps one such, and you have that moment, "it is I, Hamlet the Dane", that moment when fury allows him to be, with maximal density, these moments encapsulate something that you cannot ever bring over into your everyday life.

GC: It's a moment of stability?

It's not so much a moment of stability Geraldine I think it's more a moment of almost blind assertion, of heroism it could be, but it's not something that you're going to be able to get up in the morning, have breakfast, and then lapse back into. It's going to happen and it's again … even though he says, "it is I", very often those moments almost seem a-subjective, not typical of who you are in your everyday life.

CO: And yet, they're often taken, perhaps wrongfully, as moments of ethical heroism.

Absolutely, and also perhaps rightly I think.

CO: **I suppose that's where we disagree about Antigone, yeah?**

[laughs]

Yeah absolutely, I think Žižek somewhere ... it's in some journal ... talks about those moments where you do something completely unexpected in relation to yourself, and he says of these moments that at these points you are not in any way sheltered by the big Other, by what should be, and you stand out unprotected, and that afterwards you think – how did I do that? What happened that I was able to do that? I think here of Martin Luther's stance: "here I stand I can do no other". But there's always a big question here – can one stand there and if you do will you be allowed to stand there?

SM: **There's a lack of anxiety at those moments.**

Yeah, a lack of anxiety, of inhibitions, of anxiety, and it's something where in a way you don't have a choice. You can't not do it. That's what Martin Luther is saying. It's a huge and very interesting area.

MK: **Something very peculiar going on in relation to the other at this moment isn't there? I mean the other on the one hand to whom the stand is being made and at the same time it is often about the other the stand is being made.**

Yeah, give an example.

MK: **Like the example you gave about Martin Luther King.**

No, this was the original Martin Luther – the protestant!

MK: **That's interesting!**

He wrote all the edicts on the church door, the edicts of Protestantism and he stood, he stayed standing, "here I stand I can do no other", pushed into an ethical position. What we were saying the last day, sometimes one can do that when all is lost.

SM: **That you're no longer anxious about losing it.**

Yes ... like that book, I think it's a film now "Alone in Berlin", you know this really ... conformist, office worker ... obeying all the rules and then their only child is killed in the war and he starts dropping seditious stuff about Hitler all around Berlin because you know ... he doesn't care. And of course he is caught but in that moment where you stand outside the edicts of the big Other ...

and I suppose the question is do you … the flash is one way … and the flash is not the only way, there is also something that will sustain, that sustained Martin Luther, sustained this man in "Alone in Berlin". So the flash is one way and Lacan loves the flash. Lacan emphasizes the flash but as I say, it's not the only way. The other thing that he talks about in these lessons then is that the subject is to be found in the interval, and in the cut. Now the interval – in one way, Freud will say exactly the same thing, so it's not a departure from established theory. Freud in *The Interpretation of Dreams* in a footnote towards the end said that he'd huge trouble getting people to move from the manifest content of the dream to the latent and now they're all fixated on the latent, but the unconscious isn't there, the unconscious is in the energy between what turns one into the other which of course is a much more difficult question to ask, and it's even the question one would ask about say artistic creation. How does this scene in my life turn into its fictional version? That jump, you know because they're not identical by a long shot, but something has to happen to transmute one into the other. So there, in that interval is where Freud sees the subject of the unconscious. And again he does exactly the same thing in *Screen Memories* where he is saying that the screen memory has already undergone modification. The value of the screen memory is not in its own subject matter but in the relation existing between that subject matter and some other repressed psychical material, so it's the same thing. It's not the memory but the relation between the memory and whatever cannot be remembered. Lacan himself will talk in the seminar on identification about how we're caught between the vital functions of our being – our vital existence – and the epos, the story we tell ourselves about it. We're not in either of these places but in the tension between the two, and here he talks about the close relationship to the vital drive insofar as it is separated from us, so again the focus is on that between bit, the intermediate zone. Lacan uses a very thought-provoking pun in lesson twenty-one which is what we were talking about the last day – I don't know if you remember it because he doesn't really develop it – but I find it very interesting. He's focussing on the verb "*esse*" to be, – and a between – literally "*inter-esse*", – that's where the subject is and what I hear in that, is also of course "interested". That as subjects we are interested and one of the places I see that breaking down is in both mourning and melancholia, particularly in melancholia. Instead of being caught and somehow intricated between the three terms of the formula for fantasy, the subject is to be found at one or other end, the subject as attacking herself or as an object beating herself up. So the subject is caught in this battle with herself. And is no longer interested – the subject of melancholia is entirely self-absorbed, caught up in this battle against herself and of course in mourning the subject is suctioned into the lost o-object. Normally we are in the space of "*inter-esse*" we're interested in this and that, and our lives are in some sort of fragile equilibrium, so here in these last lessons we have the interval, the cut, the flash foregrounded. Next year you'll have the *éclat*, the radiance of Antigone.

The year after that you'll have the agalma in Sophocles, so he's moving away from what can be caught in the folds of representation to something that is less easily catchable in representation and we find this too in the Freudian text that he uses in most of these last lessons. Freud too is focussing on something that falls between the folds of representation in "A Child is Being Beaten". Do you remember that? There's the first fantasy and the third fantasy and the middle one that is not capturable, which is where the unconscious is. So again, Lacan is moving away from Freud, to a degree but he's also staying with some of Freud's most interesting papers.

Now of those different metaphors that he's talking about, the one that he develops at length in this last lesson is the cut. He will go on about that more in the seminar on identification. But it can be hard to grasp what he has to say, especially since it's wrapped up in those topologies, and he comes at it from a number of different angles. He had talked for years about units of meaning in language; about probably the smallest semantic unit, what is not divisible and in the later Lacan he will hit upon the letter as the most indivisible possible unit of meaning. He is also interested in the discourse that develops in non-sense, which is the splintering of meanings, the crash of micro meanings creating the flash of wit, something that can't be elaborated on or else the joke is lost. The joke is actually one of the very best examples that can give access to the cut as Freud saw in *Jokes and Their Relationship to the Unconscious*, a place where the signifying chain is cut into by laughter and cannot be continued. If you try to explain the joke it dies on the floor. So the signifying chain is cut and the cut is the point. Go on from there and you know you have everybody fainting with boredom. I really would like to see a lot more conferences around the joke because I think it is really the place where we can get a sense of the unconscious, because the cut – you erupt in a body event in laughter – but you're not laughing at nothing, you're laughing at something or other. So the joke in my view is a very good example of the cut.

SM: Olga, did Freud believe in cutting the session?

No.

SM: No?

No, six days a week 50-minute hours. No, I don't think so. That was purely Lacan, the cutting of the session.

CO: Olga, this bit about the cut interrupting the signifying chain … you seem to be pretty smitten with this …

I'm smitten with a number of the analogies that allow us access to think about the unconscious.

CO: I suppose what I wanted to ask about is, you know how a lot is made of the preface to Seminar XI, the 1975 preface where in the wake of the lapsus, where there is nothing left to say, there is no more meaning there, is where, Soler would call the Real unconscious, but I know that that is something you've not been too keen on or too fond of I suppose, that you would say the dream is a much better place to look for the unconscious at work …

And the joke.

CO: And the joke. Would you see the joke as, in terms of this, you know, in terms of what you're developing here, the interrupting of the signifying chain, where "there is no longer meaning" …

I take issue with the "no longer any meaning" …

CO: Yeah I'm not saying I agree with that, I'm paraphrasing …

Yes, I know, but if somebody tells me a story or a joke or an incident in Chinese, for me there is zero meaning, so that's no meaning. What I'm saying here is that micro meanings … that is what the joke is about. But you tell me that joke in Chinese and I'm not going to laugh. Tell it to me in English or Irish, or French and I get it, and I will laugh. So it's not no meaning, it's the break-up of the chain of meaning and he will move in fact – the seminar on ethics is the first place where he leaves this paradigm – here you remember there are the two signifying chains the conscious and the unconscious; in the seminar on ethics, the lower one stops being a chain. It becomes what he calls a flocculation which is like snowflakes, things that just you know drop. But the whole reason that we latch onto them at all is because they have a sort of unelaborated meaning. Something touches my funny bone, or something grips my attention. So it's meaning that is not elaborated, not cumulative and not coherent; that doesn't mean it's not meaning. So again he will be spot on in isolating *Finnegans Wake* because *Finnegans Wake* by and large is not access-ible to the coherent imaginary, you cannot imagine a page in *Finnegans Wake* the way that you can imagine a page of *Jane Eyre* but what you encounter is a whole load of micro meanings clashing together. I was thinking there to myself about the letter as indivisible and the pun. *Finnegans Wake* puns on the couple in the sidecar versus the *capall* – *capall* being the Irish for horse – between the shafts, drawing the couple along, so it's all about – well you see that joke means nothing if you don't know that *capall* is the Irish for horse. So it's all about micro meanings that flash, that flash, that flash, as opposed to the build-up of meaning, and in some ways it's about a twentieth-century reversal of a movement dating perhaps from the sixteenth century through the seventeenth with the development of, you know of narrative forms and the rise of the novel, where meanings cohere and cumulate into happy or non-happy endings. And you get that very strongly in seventeenth, eighteenth, nineteenth centuries, and then the twentieth starts to move towards the theatre of the absurd, towards Beckett and non-meaning. So Lacan is part of that movement. But the thing that I object to is the focus — there's a kind of focus on non-sense — as if nonsense didn't depend on a lot of little meanings and why children love little nonsense rhymes and all the ridiculous meanings that are caught in it — even I was thinking when my daughter was two years old — you know and singing "and pretty maids all in a row"? she used to sing "and pretty maids all in a roll" (pronounced ro-ill). So meaning is not something that has to trap you. "This is what it means". A lot of classic psychoanalysis is like that … you know… "this means that" which is very oppressive, yeah very oppressive — so it's the breaking out of that, but like I say it's not complete non-sense. That idea is also very useful in terms of working with psychotic people. Because a psychotic tends to be over-invested in meaning. The fact that some-body is wearing a red dress means that they want to attack me. And it can't mean anything else. So the non-meaning and the overflow of meaning — there is an overflow of meaning in the world and only so many signifiers. And if the psychotic could realize … meaning might indeed be there in everything … but we would be snowed under if we addressed all these meanings or bothered trying to decipher them. I don't know if I've gotten away from the question …

CO: No not at all you've brought out very well that nonsense isn't non-sense, that it doesn't mean "no meaning"; it might be silly, ridiculous, mad, but not "no meaning".

No, not at all. And one of the plays I was looking at when thinking about the cut — Beckett's *Not-I*, where there's just a mouth on the stage and she keeps talking about the usual stream of non-sense but every so often she says "tiny little thing out before her time", "No, No, She" "Not I", there's this constant coming to the edge of the unspeakable so the hearer can hear what is not spoken and sometimes in the session there's an "impossible to hear", so it's not that it's absent — it can be in the joke — there is something but if you start saying it, it's gone, and in that play, you can think it, she even, can come to the edge of knowing. So the unspoken and the unspeakable are somewhere but they're not spoken and they're not speakable.

GC: It's like constantly moving toward something but never finally realizing it?

Yes. And if you do realize it, if you have a narrative that ties up all the ends — Dickens did that brilliantly, you know, the nineteenth century liked that — and you can see it very clearly in Freud, early Freud, he wanted every last fucking detail and symptom accounted for. Do you remember the butcher's wife? He leaves nothing un-interpreted. You know. There was one bit missing, he says, I can't remember now if it was the caviar or what it was, but he goes after every little bit so there's that sense in the nineteenth century of gathering everything into a satisfying meaning which can work as long as it's broken up again. It can work in a piece of music – the development of the theme happens, pushing away from the initium and then there's a wonderful final chord. Then you go out into everydayness again, and that unifying moment is all smashed up. So too much meaning can be I think, oppressive, and theoretically, it can be used oppressively. There's a lot of dreadful theory about.

SM: And totalitarian ...

Absolutely, and totalitarian. So this was an interesting direction for Lacan to take in these lessons, a direction he will pursue and elaborate on later. Right now he looks along the path of Freudian theory in terms of objects in order to ask: what objects could be cut? So he comes up with the relation to the breast that can be cut, the relation to shit that can be cut, and the relation to the penis or phallus and the whole notion of castration is about cut. And he recognizes that this is not a complete list but what he's saying is that there are intensities which accrue around these objects precisely because they lend themselves to dramas of cut or of separation. And he's not at all wrong there, the weaning, the toilet training, all of that kind of thing. It's established theory, but it's an ok way to think. And as well as that, there is a solid foundation in Freudian theory about the object only becoming an object once it is a lost object. You have Freud's paper on negation where Freud very clearly states that an essential precondition for the institution of the function of testing reality is that objects shall have been lost which have formerly afforded real satisfaction. So the object of enjoyment etc. has to be lost. Lacan then is on safe ground when he's saying this. It's also of course brilliantly and very poignantly illustrated in the Saint Augustine story: in the moment of realizing this is my most precious possession, I have already lost it. So there is that moment of instantaneity where you recognize the object as the lost object. Here he offers another list which is the pre-genital, the breast, and the shit, the phallus, and there's already the delusion. Now he's really thinking here about the delusion he knows best, which is Schreber's delusion, and if you remember in Schreber's delusion, the cut was conveniently located – and he was right about this – between the enunciation and the enunciating so ... it will rain today – enunciation. I think it will rain today – enunciating. If you go back through Schreber, you'll see it yourself, the sentence is generally cut at the moment when the subject is going to enter the picture. So, Lacan is interested in that. But I was thinking afterwards, if the cut interests you, there are all kinds of really pertinent ways to look at it, especially in terms of language. In the very last session of the seminar Lacan talks about "this radically new thing": that every cut introduces the opening onto something new – that's in lesson twenty-seven – and we know he's read Eliot and if you remember in *Four Quartets* Eliot says, "each venture is a new beginning, a raid on the inarticulate". So each time you go to write you have to cut into the huge web of language to begin. And if you think say, for example, say you're writing a novel or a short story, where do you cut in to make a start … if you take *Jane Eyre* … "there was no possibility of taking a walk that day": into the continuum of 11 years of her life, the heroine starts here: the beginning of *The Snapper* … "You're Wha'?" [laughs] and it's the father, and of course, she's pregnant. Where do you cut in to make a beginning? So you can really see the cut happening in literature, you can see what he talks about happening in cinema, where, as he says, the trailer functions as a little piece taken out of the narrative sequence and offered as a self-sustaining little unit, cinema is a great place to see the cut in action. In Beckett's work, as I say, in *Not-I* where it's all cut, cut, cut, and in *The Unnamable*, where there is the non-cut, as in say [*Waiting for*] *Godot* you know, where yesterday was exactly the same as tomorrow is going to be, so there's no cut, no cut, no cut. In *The Unnameable* you know, the third book of the trilogy, the last four pages have no paragraph, no full-stops. A few years ago, I don't know if any of you came across the wonderful novel by W.G. Sebald called *Austerlitz*, it's a novel of trauma and in the piece where he describes Theresienstadt the concentration camp, that piece that describes Theresienstadt is seven and a half pages, no paragraph, no full-stop. The experience of reading it is just unbelievably oppressive; it exactly conveys the oppressive sameness and non-hope of the concentration camp. So experimenting with these things in terms of literature and cinema is worth your while. You get a little sense of what he means as opposed to just mulling over these complicated sentences. I don't know if what I am referring to is exactly what he did mean or if he knew what he meant at this point, but he was onto something and as I say it's worth your while to explore this idea. He talks about cutting into the Real and cutting into language in this section. There are very many other angles on the cut – the joke, the narrative and almost all literary creations offer interesting angles on it – this is why I think these lessons can be so difficult to read; there's a whole load of angles which are not necessarily congruent with each other and they're coming at you in a kind of unstructured way. But a lot of the time, the cut is, he says, seems to be, the cut which inaugurates the unconscious. He talks about the advent of the cut in so far as there is manifested in it the Real of the subject beyond what he says. So this bit from *Not-I* is a good example, she stops at what can't be said, the Real of the subject beyond what she says. So that's the inauguration of the unconscious. The advent of being, he says again, beyond any subjective realization which for Freud is *it* speaks, not *I* speak. *It* speaks, Freud says, but Lacan will take this further and by the time he gets to the seminar on anxiety he will be saying that anxiety is the only subjective expression of the o-object which is identified to the cut albeit it in an unelaborated way here. Something, where literally the not-I functions, where the I cannot speak. But it is not really a move away from Freud. In fact one might say that's pure Freud, – that's Freud from *Studies on Hysteria* where he says that if you go back far enough you will come upon memories of which the subject will say, "this is what didn't happen", so there is no possibility of occupying the first person singular when encountering the unconscious, which is an amazing statement and it's also implicit in Freud's "it speaks" as well … very interesting. So all of what Freud says about negation comes in, and applies here …

SM: You can never recount an event …

The event you recount – and this is say the difference between the dream and its unconscious substructure – the derivatives that the Imaginary offers to you are very valuable. If what you have is a stoppage beyond what can't be said, then how can you conduct any kind of analysis? You know if you're completely at the point of the Real unconscious where there is a nothing … but what we work with largely are the derivatives, and that's where the dream functions so well. It offers me a fictionalized version of what I cannot say, one that I can live with, I can talk about, precisely because I don't recognize what it's about.

MK: So it's between …

Exactly. Somewhere in between and also essentially, crucially, in a form that I don't recognize as I. In this seminar particularly when he is talking about *Hamlet*, he says the most amazing thing about the o-object when he calls it as the analogue of the I –and it's interesting I think it's on the 20 May – that's not a word he usually uses, analogue, he uses homologue, not analogue – so the o-object is in a position analogous to the I. Remember I was saying he'd been studying with Benveniste during these years and Benveniste had talked about the crucial question which is: how you, how do you take hold of language? So the whole of the world of language is there and you have to cut in and you do this by means of the I. This is the means by which you appropriate language and presumably turn it into discourse. But the I, as Benveniste says, is an unsupported position it's only supported by your active speech, because I can say I, and Carol can say I, and Susan, and you know each of us … it's not like this table, it's not supported by anything solid, it's simply what is called a shifter. So I think he's trying to say that the o-object is similarly unsupported and fragile but nonetheless exists. Yeah. I find that certain things he says but doesn't go on with … interest me greatly because I'd be really interested to hear what he'd say about that. But then on the other hand it allows you to go on with it yourself, and that's certainly no harm.

SM: So sorry to come in again, so you can meditate on an event that's recounted literally?

Absolutely. Well, yeah, that's true, we are always in excess of ourselves and so when people say "what you see is what you get" you think hahaha [laughs] …

[laughter]

SM: "I say it like it is".

Exactly. "You can tell with me" [laughs] …

CO: **But that's to say that the I is non-identical with itself. And the I that you're drawing attention to …**

Yeah …

CO: **I think without ever realizing the full potential of this, that the I is analogous to the o-object … then as you are bringing out … no more than the I is supported by anything solid, neither is the o-object, that no more than the I is identical to yourself, then we can say the o-object fails in the same way. But he brings that out so much better in … let's say from Seminar XI onwards … emphasizing how the o-object doesn't have an image.**

That's right.

CO: **And actually though that's what we're saying about the I, it doesn't have an image, not the ego …**

Well here, the o-object is tied to the Imaginary.

CO: **Yes it is, but …**

We're gradually moving away.

CO: **Absolutely.**
SM: **It's tied to the body though …**

Yes absolutely, where the body goes it goes.

MK: **Where I go you go.**

[laughter]

IM: **It's also, when I think of it, it's very … the body and the not-body because there were these various studies in parallax, parallactic views, where actually whatever you can say about the objective reality is by excluding your blind spot, because you are that I that is actually the blind spot of what you see. The spot that you can never observe. There's a part of the world and you speak about that world from the point of view of that blind spot.**

Dizzying, dizzying when you actually think about it.

GC: It's like Saint Augustine once said: I become a question to myself.

Yes. Absolutely. And ... and better not to answer! Or better not to answer too fully. The other thing about the cut I want to say is that he says things about it that will actually be somewhat analogous to what he will later on say about the vanishing point in perspectivist painting in *The Object of Psychoanalysis* (Seminar XIII) and also about the −1 and the zero in *Crucial Problems* (Seminar XII). So there is the notion of something that is both constitutive − that creates the subject and is at the same time irremediably external to it or you know simply one of its ingredients. So he's thinking that out. Some of what he says slightly foreshadows that. And another thing, yet another thing he says, he uses Klein to talk about the cut, which he says − it's in the last lesson − creates a rejected core, on page 474. So you see several different angles of approach, but all targeting the unconscious which he calls the deepest part of our truth. We're located between the two end terms of the fantasy, and as we saw, that keeps us interested but also that structure is maintained under certain conditions, and the conditions he says are specific. At what point, where's the point at which the subject can indicate herself without vanishing? There are specific conditions under which you can live within the structure of your fantasy even at a relatively unconscious but also partially conscious level. So he says the hysteric can live it as long as her desire is not satisfied, the obsessional can live it so long as he stays out of the game, many people can live it in lives of devotion to the desire of the other. I am not the desirer, somebody else is and this is how I fill my life. So, and he's getting towards the fact that we need a substitute when we desire. We find it hard to stand in the glare of desiringness, to be the desirer, and so we reach for some kind of substitute in fantasy or in real life.

Now when Lacan talks about ... he uses "A Child is Being Beaten" to talk about this. About a substitute. But if you'll indulge me, I think that there's a terrific example of this in *Ulysses* − of the fantasy which supports the happening of a full sexual event. A full orgasm happens, but the person who's having the fantasy is fantasmatically not the desirer and the orgasm is not happening to her body (although of course it is). This is the "Nausicaa" episode from *Ulysses*. It happens on Sandymount strand and the voice, the narrator is a girl Gerty MacDowell. Gerty's voice is that of someone who is completely immersed in the language of women's magazines − how to make myself beautiful, what creams to use etc. and also suffused with a kind of soft porn sexuality. How to be the object of desire of the dark passionate enigmatic man of pulp romance. The stand-in for the dark passionate man here is Leopold Bloom having a wank on Sandymount strand! So you know there's a big gap between the fantasy and what's actually happening. There's a benediction going on in Sandymount church behind Gerty and there's a fireworks display going on on the strand itself. So Gerty is there with two friends and two children and I'm going to read excerpts from it ... the kids are playing ball and the ball rolls towards her and she gives it a kick back towards the kid and notices for the first time the gentleman who is Leopold Bloom opposite, looking:

[Olga reads aloud excerpts of the passage from Ulysses, pp. 473–479]

[Applause]

Can't you hear it? Who is the desirer? Not her. Where is the orgasm? Not in her. It's in the fireworks. So it's a wonderful instance of what Lacan is saying about the need for a substitute desirer – the whole event can happen as long as I am not necessarily in the hot seat, and then it swings back to Bloom who is anything but the enigmatic intellectual hero now buttoning up his wet shirt saying "that was a hot little devil". Not at all the romantic fictional hero! Lacan then talks about the voyeur imagining and getting off on the complicity of the one watched. That notion of who is desiring again and here, of course, it's the opposite. Gerty is the exhibitionist. I think it's important to realize, I was saying this earlier, that there are all kinds of possibilities here. You know the formula for fantasy is far richer than any of our theories. We would like to say the perverse fantasy is this or that or the other, but honestly we're doing ourselves a disservice. What is in each of those components, the barred subject, the diamond, the o, is infinite, as infinite as human life and human desire is infinite. And so it's extremely important for us not to harden into theories about it. That tendency is irrelevant and it's suffocating. So I just want to look at maybe the last third to see how Seminar VI connects back to Seminar V and briefly forward to Seminar VII and later.

The most obvious break with Seminar V is the absence of guarantee – the assertion that there is nothing in the big Other – no guarantee of the truth of the signifier. This will be much further developed in Seminar IX – *Identification*. Here though he distinguishes between two different levels of this realization: the absence of guarantee on the one hand and the absolute cancelling out of all possibilities of trust on the other. He's saying they're not the same and we saw that the last day do you remember … Hamlet at the beginning of the film when he was in mourning, where he was devastated but hadn't lost his bearings completely. So he's in mourning at the start, but then when the whole truth of his existence is smashed by the revelation of the ghost he's in another space. In one way that will kind of correspond to the fairly solid theory distinguishing between neurosis and psychosis. And Lacan will talk in *Identification* (Seminar IX) about the lack of guarantee creating the uncertainty that allows us to live, versus something much more catastrophic, which is the smashing of all possibilities something that renders ongoing life impossible. We can see these two events in Hamlet – at the beginning of the play, he is mourning and resentful; after the ghost's revelation he is completely undone, realizing that the entire world he inhabits rests upon crime and falseness. All of us have to live with the very real possibility that there is nothing there, but without the absolute certitude that there is indeed nothing, life is possible. In Seminar IX he will play with these two scenarios around what he calls a message or a question. The message being "nothing perhaps", no sorry ... "nothing perhaps?" is the question, and "perhaps nothing", is the answer. So if you come down on the nothing you have no space to live, but with the nothing perhaps? You could come down on the "perhaps" and that gives you a little bit of space. He goes on with that at much greater length in Seminar IX.

A huge move away from Seminar V is the changed status of the opposition between being and having. And the question then is why did he set them up before as mutually exclusive. Why would being and having be *either/or*? They don't have to be. If you think about advertising, it's all about "and". If I have a car I am a cool person. So being and having and indeed Beckett as well ... the stripping of having back to pure being ... you know, all advertising is, you know, if I have this amazing house I am somebody, if I have these clothes I am somebody else, so being and having are normally actively supportive of each other. You know Stan Kennedy working with the homeless will say it's very difficult to continue to be who you are when you lose progressively you know ... your house, your children, your wife, your car, your everything and you are stripped back to being this hobo on the street.

MK: So can having become being?

Yes, having can completely become being in an alienated existence. But I would question the need to make them mutually exclusive as Lacan does very much in Seminar V, you either have it or you are it. Now that has had to break down here.

CO: I was thinking it might have to do with French philosophy and grammar ... that we don't have the same relation in the English speaking world to the verb "to have" and the verb "to be" and you can't speak French without this complete saturation in the verbs *être* and *avoir*. You can't speak at all about anything without deciding do I use *être* or *avoir* to describe an experience ...

Absolutely.

CO: So they are knitted into the spoken existence of the French.

Yes, it could be ... and they are the first verbs when you learn French grammar, *être et avoir* ...

CO: Because you have to decide ...

Yes, and they also conjugate differently to any other verb ...

CO: I really feel it must be rooted there somehow.

It could be, and of course it's also rooted in a very slightly Cartesian way to Freud's having or being. Freud of course gave us "having the woman" or "being the homosexual", the having or being in *The Ego and the Id*, you "have" your mother or you "be" her, so it's very likely that Lacan was just adopting Freud's distinction.

GC: And there's a being in having and a having in being?

Yes, they can and then at one end as Magda was saying you can only be what you have unless you opt to be the stripped-down Beckett character.

SM: There might be more of a pre-dominance in having?

That's right, that's right, people finding it very hard to be unless they have the appurtenances of being, which could be children, for example, or something like that.

IM: It's also I think interesting about language – now that you mention this difference between English and French – for the child who sees herself for the first time in the mirror and she can say oh look my eyes are blue, but more likely the child or adult will say I have blue eyes or I have blonde hair or I have big feet.

Really interesting how that works in Irish "*Tá sé agam*" the Irish for "have" is "to be to me", it's the verb "to be" for "to have". What you're saying is interesting, but we could deviate greatly and go down that road. In the example, "I have blue eyes; I have big feet", it's the relation to the body, we both "are", and "have" it and we can't seem to escape that doubleness. You know people say you are your body, and we are, but we can't seem to escape saying "I have" blue eyes. So there is that impossible intrication of having and being.

What's interesting then is that Seminar V was the high point of the pre-eminence of, and one might almost say, the celebration of – the symbolic order, and immediately afterwards, not five years afterwards, he resets the dials for the Imaginary. People think that Lacan's thought is divided between privileging the Symbolic first, then the Real but you have this huge swathe which privileges the Imaginary which I would see as running roughly from Seminar VI to Seminar XIV *The Logic of Phantasy*. The question in Seminar VI is not going to be: to be or to have, but to be or not to be. That's the central question, and as he says in the first section, desire is an existentially acute question, desire poses for man the question of his possible elision, the question of his not being. So you're on the cusp of non-being. And he says, again he takes it back to what he will develop further in the seminar on anxiety, he will talk about imaginary castration which long precedes symbolic castration and is perhaps its underlay. He says here that something is produced at the level of the Imaginary which is called castration and has its incidence at the level of the Imaginary and what he will actually end up saying in *Anxiety* (Seminar X) is that what everything starts from is imaginary castration. Now what he's talking about is something, a specimen story, different for everybody which will be like the Saint Augustine story – something that brings you to a complete halt, whatever the story might be in your particular life, and where you have to bring something in from the Imaginary. And in *Identification* (Seminar IX) he even asks how does the Oedipus complex sit on and somehow complete that earlier event, and he says, honestly, we don't know. We only know that the Symbolic can offer a solution, but can only come in because it's already there. Which again is a slight tautology but you know having been so sure of the Symbolic in Seminar V there is a massive leaching away from it starting in this seminar.

The other thing then that's extraordinary is the fact that in this seminar he has undercut one of the major binaries of all Western thinking – as in the distinction between subject and object essential to Western thinking, especially since the seventeenth century. He blasts that into the water with the formula for fantasy. It is no longer a question of the subject versus the object, but of the subject and the object as a correlate of each other. So you know he has managed to blast that particular binary which is huge – especially as the rest of his work will focus on dissolving binaries to a fair extent. But having done that he is then not able to completely extricate himself from the binary around the phallus … although now it's going to be shunted far more towards being than having. After the very definite opposition between having or being in Seminar V he now he stresses, and I'm actually going to look at this and if you have the seminar with you to see how he does this. He stresses the cultural reasons. First he says, that the phallus is a signifier in lesson twenty-four, he then, he says the most extraordinary sentence on page 419, he talks about the exhibitionist opening his trousers, he talks about what is symbolically the most intolerable thing in our experience "namely the form that corresponds to it in the place of a woman's sexual organ" (p. 419), an astonishingly misogynistic, and masculinist statement. Why would that be intolerable – the feminine sexual organs, – that's an exact quote. I don't know if any of you heard Mark Hederman on the radio on Marian Finnucane a few weeks ago, he talked about emerging now from 4,000 years of patriarchy which was you know, probably unthinkable in the 1950s for Lacan or for anybody else (who was not a woman!). The idea that we would emerge from patriarchy … Well, certainly there were women thinking about this. This is a bizarre little section even though it is doing the usual thing – thrusting the phallus into the limelight! Interesting to see just how the case builds, by way first of all of an interweave of a number of approaches which are not necessarily congruent in relation to each other. The first three things he says are completely standard theory, and in the context of patriarchy there's nothing really to argue about them. So the first thing he says is that the phallus is a signifier, and he specifically says it's not the penis which would just be an instrument of jouissance. Fair enough. So it's a sign. And he says it is a signifier because of cultural relationships, and he specifically mentions the murder of the father, the Levi-Straussian law of exchange: women are exchanged in patriarchal marriages, so that's why the phallus is pre-eminent – and within that context everything that he says is completely normal and completely to be expected. If this is the way that desire is regulated by the law then it would make sense, that the function of the father would be central. But then he starts going down some strange roads and this phallus which he has just described as the signifier of the law of fertility is now the marker of a crisis, where "the subject can no longer get his bearings in desire, starting from a certain moment; he is no longer, he fails to be" (p. 430). A twist that would certainly have surprised Levi-Strauss, since it is here that the highly charged subjective drama of "to be or not to be" will be played out. This passage is a good example of the different registers which frequently are simultaneously in play in Lacan's expositions – a certain sleight of concept thanks to which ideas become legitimated and it can be difficult to see how exactly this happened. Let's try to see what happens.

The phallus in Seminar V was the signifier which held all meaning in place – it was the signifier of signifiers. As it was also in "The Signification of the Phallus." Now a year later the subject presents himself as phallus (p. 430). "But desire comes in along the trajectory of the functionalization of the subject qua phallus" at the point where "he is no longer, he fails to be". The phallus now has to operate in desire and desire entails an encounter with that point where the subject is lost. What interposes itself here is not the phallus *per se* but the phallic function. So the phallic function interposes itself at this point, at this point of loss. Which makes it sound very like the fundamental fantasy doesn't it, like, as the imaginary support? Anyway it's interesting to see how it interposes itself. And where it interposes itself. This is one of the places where in the midst of dense theorization we encounter – tautology!! "The phallus interposes itself on the trajectory of this functionalization of the subject qua phallus" (p. 430). So a running aground in apparent tautology. The same with the cut, on occasion a definition running aground as with the phallus – on tautology. But then he does – manfully shall we say – go on from there in fairness to him. He seems to be saying that the phallus has to interpose itself there at the point where the subject must present himself in the Symbolic order. So this is where the subject has to appear. But: "it is in the measure that the subject is, insofar as from a certain moment he no longer is, he wants to be, he can no longer grasp himself". So there's a problem with presenting himself there, because not only *is he*, but also, *he is not*. And Lacan says it is from the encounter with this, with this phallic function – and I'd be interested to see, I think this is the first time that phrase is used, if you recall, le Gaufey says that the phallus starts to vanish and be replaced by the phallic function – so it is from the encounter with this, the phallic function, that there is produced the necessary point of equilibrium. Very hard to understand. Myself, I tend to think that he's trying to insert the new insights of Seminar VI — which is this subjective fragility and this imaginary drama back into the earlier theory which is predicated on the need of course to enter into the Symbolic order. But I find it unsatisfying, I have to say. And I think that the question of … to be or not to be, which is the question of this seminar, has deviated into — he says, on the same page, to be or not to be the phallus. Ok? But the problem here is that he suggests that you can be the mother's desire or the phallus, which is a definite slippage because before in Seminar IV the mother's desire was the phallus! So you can be one phallus or another it would seem. And at the end of this rather turgid passage then he fetches up on a terrific point which is the point he could have made without all this stuff — which is that ultimately we have no choice either as men or as women but to be in an inadequate position and that's exactly where we all actually live. As he has mentioned already in Seminar IV we all have to bear a lived incompleteness; this is the human condition. So whether you have to theorize this as he does via the phallus, which is one way of theorizing it, and as such not invalidated. It is invalidated, however, if it is the only way, there must be other ways of experiencing and engaging with lived incompleteness. So ultimately neither men nor women have a choice except as he says to live in an inadequate position which is radically different from the tranquil possession of the phallus in Seminar V. Something much less safe is afoot in Seminar VI and again in that same section, he links all of this to narcissism when he links the phallus very much to the specular image. Now Seminar VII then to finish up with will herald the search for a kind of non-narcissistic kernel in the structure of subjectivity, as Carol was saying earlier. We can hear it coming somewhat in these last lessons. Something less substantive is being reached for. You have the cut, the radiance in Antigone, the agalma in Seminar VIII. Also the major themes of *The Ethics* seminar are referenced in passing in these last lessons. So you have the question of the good — what is the good, the dissing of moralizing philosophies, the limitations of conformism. The rehabilitation — which is a great one — of sublimation as a full expression of a drive and not just a pallid substitute, and an extraordinary moment on the second last page when he invokes a literary metaphor that would have worked perfectly for what will preoccupy him in the coming years, preoccupations which he will engage in via topology, but he doesn't make use of this literary metaphor ever again. He says of analysis: "if I were to compare analysis to something", he says, "it would be to a narrative that would itself be the locus of the encounter at stake in the narrative" (p. 485), and of course that's always true in literature, the form is the content. Remember Beckett's very haughty article on *Finnegans Wake*, when he says, "Gentlemen, it is not *about* something, it *is* that something". So the narrative in analysis of course is the enactment of the drama being narrated, as well as the enactment of the transference. Concluding then, Seminar VI in my view is the great seminar of the Imaginary, and I would also say it's not invalidated by later developments, since the Imaginary is what gives colour and texture to all of our lives, it's where we, to a large extent live. Clinically the Imaginary is, as Lacan says, the arena which permits us to see something of those scenarios where for the subject, something perpetuates the happiness of the initial situation in a hidden, latent, unconscious situation of unhappiness. We may very, very, seldom be privileged to see exactly how this happens, or how also the following happens, quoting from lesson twenty-one … "the subject slides from a short-lived incident in his life story to a structure in which he appears as an actual being", but I think the most wonderful thing is that that is where our work as analysts can take us.

I'll leave it there and thank you.

[Audio recording ends]

Part III

The essays

Chapter 10

Seminar VI

Anamorphosis or palimpsest?

What Dali, Lacan's contemporary, liked about anamorphosis was its potential for proliferation, its ability to infuse the calm stability of a given perspective with unforeseen but incontrovertible otherness. To open *Seminar 6, Desire and Its Interpretation* (1958–1959), gateway to the great middle seminars, is to be immediately immersed in a very striking anamorphosis, a reading of Freud that is exact and faithful but angled to reveal an altogether new dimension to psychoanalytic theory.

This dimension is tragedy. Over the next two years and to a lesser extent in *Seminar 8, Transference* (1960–1961), this dimension will be deepened and made explicit to the point that the final section of *Seminar 7, The Ethics of Psychoanalysis* (1959–1960), will bear the title "The Tragic Dimension of Psychoanalytic Experience" (Lacan, 2008, p. 355). In *Seminar 6* the opening up of this new dimension will be tightly and repeatedly corralled within the coordinates of Freudian doctrine. But, by the end of *Seminar 7*, in the manner of all effective anamorphoses, the hidden otherness begins to impose itself more insistently on the viewer. Lacan, although still referencing this foregrounding of tragedy to Freud's appropriation of *Oedipus Rex* in the Oedipus complex, acknowledges its inadequacy, and suggests that "if tragedy is at the root of our experience this is so in an even more fundamental way than through the connection to the Oedipus complex" (Lacan, 1992, p. 244).

This cautious, unelaborated remark by Lacan during his impressively brilliant exploration of tragic form at the end of *Seminar 7* is important. It is not often acknowledged that Freud's reconfiguration of one of the seminal works of Western literature, *Oedipus Rex*, into the Oedipus complex represented a seismic shift from tragic stasis to narrative possibility, an exit from the domain of the impossible into that of the feasible.

This shift, marked in European literary history by the decline of tragedy and the rise of the novel, had been part of the zeitgeist which immediately preceded Freud and in which he grew up. As Terry Eagleton puts it, "with this development the accent was displaced from destiny to domesticity, a displacement visible in how the novel privileges chronos, the gradual passage of historical time, while tragedy is a matter of kairos, time charged, crisis-racked, electric with momentous truth" (Eagleton, 2003, p. 181). *Oedipus Rex* and still more *Oedipus at Colonus* are instances of such charged stoppage. The Oedipus complex by contrast, while menacing the small subject with crucial loss, offers the possibility of compromise and makes of this crisis itself the springboard into a wider, more expansive existence.

In contrast with Sophoclean stasis, Freud's Oedipus opens rather than forecloses narrative possibility, and does so in a manner not entirely dissimilar to the nineteenth century Bildungsroman. Classically, the narrative arc of the Bildungsroman not only shunts over-arching individuality into the safe harbour of socially-acceptable forms of fulfilment (usually marriage), but manages to trope this shunt as the truest realisation of singular desire. I am aware that these broad brushstrokes do not do justice to the complexity of Freud's theorisation but the recuperative curve of the Freudian Oedipus from prohibition to promise, its reinsertion of apparent impossibility into the flow and counterflow of everyday living, does suggest this comparison. With *Seminar 6*, Lacan dramatically relocates this event in the domain of tragedy and does so via an anamorphic reading of what for Freud had been an oedipal dream.

The timing of this anamorphic reading is very striking indeed. During the previous year, in *Seminar 5*, on the formations of the unconscious (1957–1958), Lacan had somewhat tilted the axis of castration by making the success of the Oedipus contingent on the castration of the mother. But it is also true that nowhere in the Lacanian canon is there a theorisation of the Oedipus complex closer to the Bildungsroman narrative arc than the solidly-secure outcomes envisaged in this seminar, where the subject (masculine) will emerge, having in his pocket the title deeds for him to make use of in the future (Lacan, 2010a, p. 147). At the end of the Oedipus complex "our castrated little man" Lacan says, will have this fine letter on which will rest the fact that he can assume in all tranquillity "the fact of having a penis" (Lacan, 2010a, p. 134). All of this is swept away in the first section of *Seminar 6*. More accurately, because it is a huge seminar, and Lacan is a somewhat serpentine thinker, it makes its reappearance here and there throughout the text but, for this reader at least, it has been fatally shafted in the opening lessons.

Nothing of Freud's delineation of the phases of the Oedipus complex is lost here. To paraphrase his drily matter of fact summary: "The Oedipus complex succumbs to the threat of castration" with what he terms "narcissistic interest, deciding the issue" (Freud, 1895, p. 273). One of the formidable achievements of *Seminar 6* is that it takes these bleached-out facts in Freud's formulation and recasts them in tragic mode.

However, if this seminar can be aptly described as anamorphosis it is also explicitly and implicitly palimpsest. Unusually, right from the start, Lacan announces it as such. Speaking of a stage in the specular experience he tells his listeners that "we are going to rediscover a way of using it in a context which will give it a completely different resonance […] at the end of our first year about the relationships between the ideal ego and the ego ideal [...]" (Lacan, 2010a, p. 11). And towards the end of the year he punctures the tranquil possessiveness of the successfully assumed paternal metaphor referenced above, by pointing out its status as fiction, the fact that this metaphor is just a mask for the metonymy of castration.

The entire seminar is also a rewriting of the object as it had appeared in *Seminar 4, Object Relations* (1956–1957) which by the end of *Seminar 6* is no longer an object at all in the strict sense of the word, but an index of impossibility (Lacan, n.d.). In lesson twenty-four he signals this palimpsestic re-write of the object which is he says "no longer the function of the object as I tried to articulate it two years ago" (Lacan, 2010b, p. 290). It is also in this seminar on desire that we can locate the inception of a new definition of the subject, a progressive re-write which will culminate in the gnomic formulation three years later that it is the signifier which represents the subject for another signifier. The big Other too is rewritten. Without explicitly referring to his admirably clear definition of this Other in *Seminar 3, The Psychoses* (1955–1956), he effectively demolishes the status accorded it in the earlier seminar where the Other "is that before which you make yourself recognised. But you can make yourself recognised by it only because it is recognized first [...] it is through recognizing it that you institute it [...] as an irreducible absolute [...]" (Lacan, 1993, p. 51). By the end of *Seminar 6* this necessary reciprocity has been bankrupted. On the 8th of April he clarifies that there is "no guarantee of any kind that this Other through what there is in his system can give me [...] what I gave him; his being and his essence as truth" (Lacan, 2010b, p. 206). So, this seminar is also a palimpsest by means of which through a relatively stable vocabulary, entirely new meanings and new facets of meaning come to be installed. And the remarkable thing about this re-write is that it is achieved without exiting the armature of Freudian doctrine.

A word about contexts – or at least about two of the contexts which might strike the reader. It could be said that literature is a constant reference in all of Lacan's work. However, the depth and nuance of this reference is very varied. Derrida has accused Lacan of illustrative and paradigmatic readings of literary texts (Derrida, 1967, p. 230). This critique is hard to refute, especially as Lacan himself embarks on *Hamlet* announcing that it "can help us to reinforce this sort of elaboration of the castration complex" (Lacan, 2010b, p. 162) and, in the redacted version of the seminar which appears in Shoshana Felman's *Literature and Psychoanalysis* (1977), he rather dismayingly declares his interest to be topological. "The story of Hamlet (and this is why I chose it) reveals a most vivid dramatic sense of this topology" (Felman, 1977, p. 11). What follows, however, is an impressively close textual reading which goes very much further than these reductionist intentions. Indeed, in terms of literariness, parts of the seminar, in particular sections 1 and 3, recall his earlier encounter with surrealism.

Perusing this seminar where for the first time the o-object begins to be profiled, it is hard not to recall André Breton in 1936, celebrating the most recent advance of surrealism as having produced a fundamental crisis of the object. Because of surrealism, for the very first time, Breton asserts, "it has been revealed that this object takes all the beauty that one sees in it from what it is not, and that furthermore in it alone is given us to recognise the marvellous precipitate of desire [...]" (Breton, 1988, p. 163). No direct link here but probably something more in line with adumbration, echo. Similarly, Lacan's new emphasis on gap, interval, the between, calls to mind that the only poem of his ever published was a romantic and rather incantatory piece entitled *Hiatus Irrationalis*. This was published in *Le Phare de Neuilly* in 1933 alongside contributions by Queneau and Asturias. So for Lacan, briefly a poet himself, Hiatus was an early literary concept. Third, the sombre dramatic vocabulary which makes its appearance in this seminar harks back in style to the second of the two articles which Lacan published in the surrealist journal *Minotaure*, also in 1933. This article about the horrific double murder committed by the Papin sisters is itself a superb piece of writing, arguably the finest example in all of Lacan's published work of his gift as a prose stylist: terse, tense and taut with tragic implications. Something of this dark power resurfaces in *Seminar 6* and again in the following year.

Just as the above literary echoes are faint, unremarked on and unlikely to have been deliberate, the subtle but perceptible shift in this seminar, from the opposition of being and having to an increased accent on being itself, is perhaps not a direct outcrop of the philosophical zeitgeist, dominated as it was by such publications as *Being and Time* (1927), *Being and Nothingness* (1992 [1943]) and indeed *Being and Having* (1949), a now forgotten work by the Catholic theologian Gabriel Marcel who seems close to stumbling onto Lacanian terrain when he poses the question whether having can be seen as a certain mode of being what one is not (Marcel, 1965 [1949]). And in terms of both literary and philosophical zeitgeist one would have to include the so-called Theatre of the Absurd exemplified by Beckett, where being is progressively stripped of all having.

Turning to the seminar itself it is easy to see that Lacan's journey through all of this is very much his own. So how to carve into such richness and to say what is happening when so much is happening? The seminar consists of four main sections: the dream of the dead father, the Ella Sharpe dream, *Hamlet* and lastly, summarising these three sections, Lacan indicates how they might usefully illuminate the everyday symptomatology of the psychoanalytic clinic. So, in three different configurations, Lacan presents a father, a son, death and the relation to desire.

I have chosen to focus on the first and, regretfully, to a lesser extent the third sections: the dream of the dead father and the theme of *Hamlet*. While these two sections echo each other thematically, they also each represent, in entirely different ways, unheralded points of entry into a more expanded exploration of Lacan's mantra "the unconscious is structured like a language" than the two rhetorical tropes metaphor and metonymy, already well-established in previous seminars. To take this mantra seriously would be to include in its ambit grammar and syntax. The linguist Emile Benveniste, who worked closely with Lacan in the 1950s, always insisted that what Freud had elucidated in *The Interpretation of Dreams* (1900) was the rhetoric and not the grammar of the unconscious. In the main, Lacan, influenced by Jakobson, tended to collapse this distinction.

Here, however, using for the most part only the resources of grammar, in the first section of this seminar Lacan takes the reader into the furthest reaches of the human condition marked as irremediably tragic. This is a towering achievement which cannot be seriously impugned by his pronouncement in his last spoken seminar that "in the structure of the unconscious it is necessary to eliminate grammar" (Lacan, 2013, p. 20).

Furthermore, to take this mantra seriously is also to include in its ambit, literature. Both the great twentieth century poet Paul Valery and the great literary critic Tsvetan Todorov are insistent here. For Valery, literature can be nothing other than a kind of extension to and application of certain properties of language, a view echoed by Todorov who sees literature as the first field of knowledge which can throw light on the properties of language itself.

So, in the opening section of *Seminar 6*, we encounter the tragedy subtending the subject of the unconscious in the interstices of grammatical usage, in the third we encounter this same subject in literature via the impasses of tragic form. In the first, the focus is directly on one of the formations of the unconscious, the dream, in the third on a work of art which, as Lacan suggests, is situated always in a transversal relation to the unconscious.

Seminar 6 begins with an extremely dense and difficult discussion of the relations between repression, representation and the primary process, but right from the start Lacan introduces his listeners to what will be the kernel, the pith of this year's teaching, the non-opposition of subject and object in the phantasy; a first move in the progressive leaching of status from the binary thinking which underpins the Symbolic order. In terms of the unconscious, subject and object cannot be set up as oppositional but only as correlative. The immediate effect of this is a shift from the solidity of locatable nouns into the more slippery territory of prepositions and adverbs. With respect to the grammar, rather than the rhetoric of the unconscious, a preliminary salvo had been fired the previous year when Lacan had linked the unconscious to the middle voice in the verb, a now obsolete voice which similarly unsettles the distinction between subject and object. The function of negation, brought into play again here, has of course been a constant reference in the seminars and added to this now are the pronominal problems posed for the subject of the unconscious insofar as it speaks.

Relying mainly on these three grammatical indications, the function of negation, the slippage of the personal pronoun and the collapse of the distinction between subject and object, Lacan introduces his listeners to the founding catastrophe which marks the inception of human subjectivity. The non-separability of subject and object undermines the very base line of grammatical structure but introduces the altogether specific intrication of subject and object which creates the fundamental fantasy, and is, in fact, a response to this founding catastrophe.

While Lacan returns to the topic of this catastrophe many times in the course of the seminar, there are two places, one at the beginning in November 1958 and one towards the end in May 1959, where he comes close to spelling out what one might call the existential emergency which triggers it. The first is at the point of the "*che vuoi?*", the absolute helplessness of the pre-subject *vis-à-vis* the demand/desire of the Other, the second, when this little pre-subject encounters not so much her own helplessness, but the helplessness, or at least the radical impotence of this big Other which does not have at its disposal the necessary signifier which would guarantee or authenticate this little pre-subject in her existence. The big Other at this point, Lacan says, can only respond in the name of a common tragedy since there *is* no possible signifier which can guarantee the authenticity of the sequence of signifiers. So Freud's *Hilflosigheit* in this seminar is situated not just on the side of the subject, but also and irremediably on the side of the big Other, and it is at this impasse, this panic point as Lacan calls it, that "there is produced on the part of the subject this something that he draws from elsewhere, that he brings in from the imaginary register something that we call o" (Lacan, 2010b, p. 264).

What might this object be? Throughout the seminar on desire, Lacan repeatedly reminds his listeners that this o-object has the closest possible relation with narcissistic passion, and indeed often vacillates in naming this essential support of the subject so that sometimes it is clearly o-object, and sometimes narcissistic eros, on occasion making one the core of the other. As Guy le Gaufey points out, it is not for nothing that these two notations o and o-object are so similar, the second bearing witness to its origins in the first (Le Gaufey, 2009, p. 27). In *Seminar 9, Identification* (1961–1962), one will be the mask of the other, in *Seminar 10, Anxiety* (1962–1963), the lining, and by 1962 he will be obliged to propose another form of imaginarisation adequate to a seriously complexified theorisation (Lacan, 2012).

Here, in this early elaboration, it remains soldered to narcissistic passion so the outline of Freud's description of a crisis averted by "narcissistic interest" is not breached. It has, however, become electric and urgent, since as Lacan goes on to say "the o-object is first of all defined as the support which the subject gives himself insofar as he is failing" (Lacan, 2010b, p. 256). There is a very palpable sense of brink here. One cannot but note the crucial, one might say, last-ditch juncture at which this o-object intervenes and the manner in which it serves as both the point of stoppage and its index. "Here every possibility of naming oneself comes to a stop" (Lacan, 2010b, p. 265). "But this stopping point is also the index, the index which is put forward which keeps him from being purely and simply cancelled out, losing consciousness of his existence" (ibid.). This, Lacan continues "is what constitutes the structure of what we call the phantasy" (ibid.).

Two of its grammatical features are visible in this formulation. First, a pronominal impasse; here the object is that which supports the subject in his very existence at the point where the "I" cannot say itself (Lacan, 2010b, p. 58). Second, speaking of how desire sustains itself by means of this fundamental fantasy, Lacan says it is "no longer just the function of the object [...] nor yet that of the subject... but the correlation which links the one to the other [...]" (Lacan, 2010b, p. 290).

So the subject of the unconscious is not to be found at either of the end terms, but is to be located in the interval, the between space, and this inextricable interdependency is what will maintain what Lacan calls the fragile equilibrium of one's desire. Fragile indeed, since the installation of the fantasy functions as "the slender footbridge thanks to which the subject does not feel himself directly overwhelmed by this abyss" (Lacan, 2010b, p. 80).

In the absence or the collapse of this fantasy which is clearly a bulwark, what might one expect to encounter? The pain of existence when desire is no longer there. There is nothing more intolerable, he goes on to say, than existence reduced to itself, existence sustained in the abolition of desire (Lacan, 2010b, p. 66). The dark and sombre resonance of Lacan's language here is arresting. And indeed, while he will offer us an algorithm for the fundamental fantasy, what he gives us in the opening lessons of this seminar is a powerful and poignant version of it in the dream of the dead father. As read by Freud this is an oedipal dream. Here it becomes a stark iconography, an austere etching of the pain of existence.

How does this come about? For Freud, the son's wish that the father's suffering might be cut short by death adumbrates and stirs into life the earlier now unconscious death wish of oedipal rivalry, so for Freud it is a near perfect example of repression functioning as omission, subtraction, more of its weight carried in the suppressed phrase "as he had wished" than in the preceding one "he did not know that he had died" (Lacan, 2010b, p. 166). Lacan's anamorphic feat is to preserve this oedipal frame while angling it to reveal the lineaments of the fundamental fantasy. For Lacan, in this phrase "he did not know that he had died" is hidden the dangerous proximity of the pain of existence carried and concealed by the three grammatical elements listed earlier: the slippage of the personal pronoun, the function of negation and the unsustainable loss of that which supports this subject in his existence. If the fundamental fantasy is itself a brink phenomenon Lacan situates the dream of the dead father on the knife edge of this brink.

In Lacan's reading, the son's rivalry had functioned effectively as a mask for the pain of existence, giving him a focus, a distracting dissatisfaction and an immediately engaging obstacle hiding the hopelessness of the human condition. But now, with the father's death Lacan suggests, "the son is from now on wrongly confronted with what the presence of the father protected him from up to then, namely with this something which is there, present in this pain of existing, the x, the signification of castration" (Lacan, 2010b, p. 67). So "the wish for the father to be castrated [...] is turned back onto the son since it is now his turn to be castrated [...] namely that must not be seen at any price" (Lacan, 2010b, p. 64). That this oedipal drama is an instantiation of something more fundamental is made quite explicit. In the same lesson he states: "here the wish is only the mask of what is most profound in the structure of desire as such" (Lacan, 2010b, p. 64). Overwhelming as the suffering of the dreamer may be, he is not altogether annihilated. In the precarious and senseless space of the other's not knowing, he, the dreamer, can maintain his existence, or as Lacan puts it, can maintain the veil which ensures that he continues to be a subject who speaks (Lacan, 2010b, p. 65).

For Lacan, the dream of the dead father encapsulates the all but unbearable pain of mourning. The switch of pronouns and the negation in the phrase "he did not know" (Lacan, 2010b, p. 63) are both a last-ditch attempt at not foundering entirely and an indication that this foundering has in fact occurred. The pain of existing, the impossibility of knowing, belong to the dreamer and necessitate some form of repudiation and, as Lacan puts it, "It is in the whole nature of the phantasy to transfer it onto the object" (Lacan, 2010b, p. 76). So this "he did not know" is an essentially subjective reference which goes to the foundation of the structure of the subject. Not only does he not know but he must not be told, since if he knew it he would be it. To demonstrate this, Lacan gestures to a dream of Trotsky in which Trotsky meets Lenin long after the death of the latter. Trotsky cannot let Lenin know that he has died and in the dream refers only to "the time when you were very ill" (Lacan, 2010b, p. 80). As if, Lacan remarks, a precise formulation of what was in question would by its very breath dissipate the shade before whom at this decisive moment of his existence Trotsky maintains himself.

Had this seminar taken place two years later, Lacan would have had a much more powerful dream at his disposal. In 1961, the literary critic Jean Pierre Richard published 202 newly discovered poetic fragments by one of France's greatest poets Stephane Mallarmé. These fragments, translated by Paul Auster, are collected under the title *A Tomb for Anatole* (1879, 2005) and like the dream of the dead father concern a father a son and death, except that this time it is a father trying to address the death of a beloved child. Mallarmé's son Anatole died in 1879 aged 8. The fragments, notes for a possible work, are, as Auster says, a kind of ur-text, the shards of a poem that simply could not be written. Very many of them describe a recurrent dream in which the beloved child returns because he does not know that he is dead. Several could be cited but one in particular captures the precipice visited each night by the distraught dreamer:

> What do you want, sweet
> Adored vision –
> Who often come
> Towards me and lean
> Over – as if

To listen to secret (of
My tears)
To know that you are
Dead
– what you do not know
– no I will not
Tell it
to you – for then you
would disappear –
and I would be alone
weeping,
[…]

(Auster, 2005,
pp. 149–150)

In my experience, this is a dream which does not recur in all mourning but only in those mournings which involve the loss of the o-object. While the formula for the fundamental fantasy is a writing of the subject as such, in lived experience its components are transferred onto the indispensable loves of ongoing life. Hence the death or disappearance of the one who occupies that indispensable place menaces the entire structure. What is supported by this object – the most important, most intimate part of oneself – is precisely what the subject cannot unveil even to herself; something Lacan says, which is at the edge of the greatest secret. Negation, the switch of pronouns and the vanishing of the "I" represent some of the grammatical sleights of hand available to the subject at this crisis point.

It is of course true that the conjunction of a negatory narrative and the impossibility of the "I" was one of Freud's earliest discoveries about the unconscious insofar as it speaks. In *Studies on Hysteria* (1895) he recognises that the memories encapsulating unconscious desire can only emerge as radically disowned. The subject will not approach this nexus with a widening sense of recognition, but will narrate and negate it in the same breath: "The deeper we go the more difficult it becomes for the emerging memories to be recognized, till near the nucleus we come upon memories which the patient disavows even in reproducing them" (Freud, 1895, p. 289). Here, in *Seminar 6*, a new existential weight tilts these insights towards a much starker vision freighted with the intensities of the imaginary and shot through with flashes of poetry. The pain of existence, intolerable concatenation, fundamental anguish, an evanescent pallid vanishing subject; these phrases are repeated almost as in poetry with a cumulative force which insists that, for every subject, Hamlet's question "to be or not to be" may well be answered in the affirmative but its answer is always marked by the same fragile equipoise as the question itself.

In this seminar, Lacan presents three guises under which the fundamental fantasy functions as a brink phenomenon interposed to protect the subject from an unsustainable knowing. In the dream of the dead father it is captured balanced on this brink. In the reading of the Ella Sharpe dream, we see it maintaining itself stably enough by underpinning an obsessional neurosis, and in the last section on *Hamlet* it collapses into its component parts only to be re-installed towards the end in a momentary flash.

And it is to *Hamlet* that we now turn. As early as *Seminar 2, The Ego in Freud's Theory* (1954–1955), we see the shadow of tragedy fall across Lacan's teaching when he quotes Oedipus, blind and crushed at Colonus: "Am I made man in the hour I cease to be?", highlighting the bleakness of this essential drama of destiny; the utter absence of charity, of fraternity, of anything whatsoever relating to human feeling (Lacan, 1988, p. 230). Also, already in *Seminar 2* for Lacan this ultimate suffering is captured in the phrase "*me phunai*", better not to be. Curiously, in both *Seminars 2 and 3, The Psychoses* (1955–1956), he correctly attributes this phrase to the chorus in *Oedipus at Colonus*. But, by the end of *Seminar 7* it will have become the final curse on existence of Oedipus himself and by *Seminar 8* will be designated as the true place of the subject as subject of the unconscious. Here, in *Seminar 6*, which marks his incursion into tragic form, the "*me phunai*" is defined, with less ferocity, as the pain of existence when desire is no longer there.

If, for Lacan, the subject comes into being on the cusp of tragic impossibility, it is not surprising that he should have turned to tragedy proper to illuminate and expand this theorisation. By the end of *Seminar 7* he will have found in it a modality which momentarily brings into focus something refractory to representation. Like the anamorphic cylindrical objects, popular in the seventeenth and eighteenth centuries, which, when twirled, flash an image not visible otherwise, tragedy can render perceptible a point in the coming into being of the subject that is on the very edges of representability: that inaugural threat to being which subtends the fundamental fantasy. This anamorphic recognition on Lacan's part is inspired, since there are two immediately discernible features common to both tragic form and the fundamental fantasy. In the first instance, both are to be located on the brink, poised between being and non-being. What Lacan asserts of Sophocles could with equal accuracy be applied to Shakespeare and Racine: "Sophocles presents us with man and questions him along the paths of his solitude; he situates the hero in a sphere where death encroaches on life where doubt is cast on all that is the place of being" (Lacan, 1992, p. 285). Second, when that which is unrepresentable is flashed forth in tragedy, the "I" disappears. Something has happened which is not amenable to first person narrative. At the end of the great tragedies the hero no longer speaks but is spoken about, is no longer "I" but "he". We even sometimes see something of this imminent vanishing, for example poignantly in *The Duchess of Malfi* (1623) when after the murder of her small children she disbelievingly murmurs "I am Duchess of Malfi still" (Webster, 1623, Act IV, scene II) and defiantly in *Antony and Cleopatra* when Antony, defeated and about to die roars "I am Antony yet".

What we see in the dream of the dead father is a subject poised on the edge of an impossible knowing. In *Hamlet* this edge has given way. Not only does the father know, but from the ghost scene on, Hamlet must founder under this impossible knowledge. As Lacan says of the ghost's revelation "something is lifted, a veil which weighs precisely on the articulation of the unconscious line" (Lacan, 2010b, p. 204). "What is laid bare is the irredeemable and unplumbable betrayal of love" (Lacan, 2010b, p. 205), a beyond of pact and of possibility identical to that evoked in *Seminar 7* for Oedipus and in *Seminar 8* for Sygne de Coufontaine. Speaking of *Hamlet*, Lacan's language is stark and uncompromising; "The betrayal is absolute, representing a radical cancelling out of anything resembling goodwill or fidelity. The truth of *Hamlet* is a truthless truth" (Lacan, 2010b, p. 206).

Where nothing holds any longer, the components of the fundamental fantasy, ordinarily indiscernible and indivisible, surge into visibility. As Lacan says, something vacillates in the phantasy allowing its components to appear (Lacan, 2010b, p. 14). While there are multifarious ways for this disaggregation to occur, what happens here is that the subject is dissolved while the object is debased and degraded. That which has been laid waste in Hamlet is his very life, the pith of his being which had been most vibrantly alive in his love for Ophelia. And it is in her presence that the degree to which he is unable to maintain himself as subject shows itself, initially in a bewildered loss of all bearings and then in a sustained attack on Ophelia herself as bud and blossom of life, carrier of future life in her young body. The close relation between the object which supports the subject in his being and narcissistic eros is very visible here. Hamlet's loss of bearings is conveyed in the complete disarray of his self-presentation when he comes before Ophelia:

> Lord Hamlet, with his doublet all unbraced
> No hat upon his head, his stockings fouled,
> Ungartered and down-gyved to his ankle.
> Pale as his shirt, his knees knocking each other.
> And with a look so piteous in purport
> As if he had been loosed out of Hell
> To speak of horrors [...]
> (Lacan, 2010b, p. 222).

Further on, Hamlet's targeting of his own life in the celebrated soliloquy: "To be or not to be [...]" (Lacan, 2010b, p. 304) switches with devastating swiftness into a pulverising assault on everything that Ophelia is: girlish, trusting, flowering in the beauty and promise of early youth. Kenneth Branagh's production very brilliantly uses mirrors to enact Hamlet's distortion of everything he had loved in Ophelia. In this great scene what is attacked is both Hamlet's own livingness and that of Ophelia as he squashes her beautiful face into horrifying unrecognisability against the mirror of his pained rage.

Given the sheer savagery of this laying waste, how could the fundamental fantasy re-install itself even momentarily? For Lacan, the graveyard scene is the decisive point in the play, the place where Hamlet takes the bit between his teeth, where something can be re-established which for a short moment will make a man of him. The moment, as Lacan says, where he can "lay hold again of his desire" (Lacan, 2010b, p. 198). But how is this done? Lacan's answer is simple: by way of mourning.

> It is in the measure that the object of desire has become an impossible object that it becomes once again for him object of his desire, noting that in the very structure of the foundation of desire there is always this note of impossibility.
>
> (Lacan, 2010b, p. 234)

None of this, however, is a thought, but rather a revelatory flash. In the instant that Laertes takes the dead Ophelia in his arms, Hamlet sees, and for the first and only time in the play, names himself: "it is I Hamlet the Dane" (Lacan, 2010b, p. 185). Momentarily, because it is not possible otherwise, as the o-object appears in a lightning bolt of recognition, the "I", which Lacan calls its analogue, can say itself.

Even the sections I have chosen in this seminar are too big and too wonderful to be travestied by summary. This is the first great seminar of the imaginary. Freudian in its terms of reference, it takes psychoanalysis onto the terrain of tragedy, a terrain commonly veiled even, Lacan says, by pessimism. Towards the end of the year he describes the work of the seminar as an attempt to define "this extreme point, this imaginary point in which the being of the subject resides with its greatest density" (Lacan, 2010b, p. 299). In the years that follow, he will go on with this attempt via daunting topological and mathematical pathways, forgoing the immediacy of literature. And yet, is there anywhere other than the arts which more powerfully bodies forth the role of the o-object to which this seminar introduces us and which is marvellously captured at the end of *Seminar 9*: while so much of life is there to make us miss it, "we know from our own experience that nothing has any veritable weight in the world except something which makes an allusion to this object" (Lacan, 2011, p. 308).

References

Auster, P. (2005). *A Tomb for Anatole*. (S. Mallarmé, Trans.). New York: New Directions. (Original work published 1879), pp. 149–150.

Breton, A., (1988). *Œuvres complètes*. Paris: Gallimard, éd. de La Pléiade. *Entretiens*, Paris: Gallimard, Collection Idées, p. 163.

Derrida, J. (1967). *L'Écriture et la différence*, Paris: Seuil.

Eagleton, T. (2003). *Sweet Violence*. Manchester: Blackwell.

Felman, S. (1977). *Literature and Psychoanalysis*. Baltimore: Johns Hopkins University Press, p. 11.

Freud, S. (1895). *Studies in Hysteria*. In J. Strachey (Ed. & Trans.), *The Standard Edition of the Complete Works of Sigmund Freud, Vol. II* (p. 273). London: Hogarth Press.

Freud, S. (1900). *The Interpretation of Dreams*. In J. Strachey (Ed. & Trans.), *The Standard Edition of the Complete Works of Sigmund Freud, Vol. IV*. London: Hogarth Press.

Lacan, J. (n.d. [1956–1957]). *The Seminar of Jacques Lacan, Book IV: Object Relations*. (C. Gallagher Trans.) Unpublished.

Lacan, J. (1988 [1954–1955]). *The Seminar of Jacques Lacan, Book II: The Ego in Freud's Theory and in the Technique of Psychoanalysis*. Cambridge: University of Cambridge Press.

Lacan, J. (1992 [1959–1960]). *The Seminar of Jacques Lacan, Book VII: The Ethics of Psychoanalysis*. London: Routledge.

Lacan, J. (1993 [1955–1956]). *The Seminar of Jacques Lacan, Book III: The Psychoses*. London: Routledge.

Lacan, J. (2008 [1960–1961]). *The Seminar of Jacques Lacan, Book VII: The Ethics of Psychoanalysis*. London: Routledge. p. 355.

Lacan, J. (2010a [1957–1958]). *The Seminar of Jacques Lacan, Book V: The Formations of the Unconscious*. (C. Gallagher Trans.) Unpublished.

Lacan, J. (2010b [1958–1959]). *The Seminar of Jacques Lacan, book VI. Desire and its Interpretation*. (C. Gallagher Trans.) Unpublished.

Lacan, J. (2010c [1960–1961]). *The Seminar of Jacques Lacan, Book VIII: Transference*. (C. Gallagher Trans.) Unpublished.

Lacan, J. (2011 [1961–1962]). *The Seminar of Jacques Lacan, Book IX: Identification*. (C. Gallagher Trans.) Unpublished.

Lacan, J. (2012 [1962–1963]). *The Seminar of Jacques Lacan, Book X: Anxiety*. (C. Gallagher Trans.) Unpublished.

Lacan, J. (2013 [1976–1977]). *The Seminar of Jacques Lacan, Book XXIV: L'insu que saitde l'une bevue s'aile a mourre*. Private Translation, Dan Collins. Unpublished.

Le Gaufey, G. (2009). *C'est a quel Sujet*. Paris: Epel

Marcel, G. (1965 [1949]). *Being and Having*. New York: Harper & Row.

Sartre, J.P. (1992 [1943]). *Being and Nothingness*. New York: Washington Square Press.

Webster, J. (1623 [1909]). *The Duchess of Malfi*. Vol. XLVII, Part 4. New York: The Harvard Classics.

Chapter 11

The phallus of the fifties

Those years of "tranquil possession"

"It is the fault of the pronouns" opines the speaker in the last volume of Beckett's great trilogy. Readers of Lacan face a different grammatical conundrum in the fate of the phallus as it moves from the status of noun to that of adjective over the course of the 25 seminars. As Guy le Gaufey has pointed out, in the first ten years of Lacan's teaching the phallus as noun appears more than 1,500 times. This drops to about 200 over the next ten years, and further subsides to not more than 40 in the final six years (Le Gaufey, 2009, p. 127). The initial surge is at its most insistent in the seminars under consideration in this book, Seminar IV *The Relation to the Object* and Seminar V *Formations of the Unconscious*. The teaching of these years represents the heyday of the phallus, held aloft and sustained on Lacan's part by some brilliant if questionable intellectual prosthetics.

Why would we look closely at seminars which stake out positions later modified and in some cases abandoned by Lacan? Surely the subsidence of the phallus as charted by Le Gaufey indicates that Lacan's own later insights will provide a more than adequate critique of these earlier stances. In this regard one could do worse than trace the slippage of the *Nom du père* along a path of uncertainty leading to the Beckettian position of *les non-dupes errent*. However a number of the major theoretical tenets established in Seminars IV and V continue to skew psychoanalytic thinking today, notably the extraordinary substitution of the multiple by the one with respect to the phallus and the Name of the Father. If as Alain Badiou says "the multiple is the law of being" (Badiou, 2001, p. 25), it could be argued that whereas a position of openness to the multiple is visible in Seminar I and is gradually re-established from Seminar VI onward, in Seminars IV and V, the proliferating medleys of imaginary formations are all subsumed under the term "imaginary phallus". In analogous fashion, the mesh of the Symbolic Order, the world of pact and law held together by the play of signifiers is gradually compressed into a totalitarian structure maintained in existence by a single signifier, the Name of the Father. This astonishing reductionism is brilliantly achieved and strongly insisted on by means of what Lacan in the seminar on identification calls the "Aristotelian" logic of patriarchy. This logic continues to prevail in psychoanalytic thinking.

In terms of general Lacanian scholarship it is always worth asking: how does Lacan build a given theory, and having built it when and how does he begin to undermine the edifice he has created? I would suggest that halfway through Seminar V, almost directly after the coping stone has been placed on the impressively theorized Oedipus complex, it is possible to discern faint tremors heralding a seismic shift in the underpinning of this enormous edifice. Not that Lacan wanted to altogether dismantle the edifice he had erected, but the lure of the Imaginary, visible in all his finest writing ever since his article in *Minotaure* on the Papin sisters starts to make itself felt with increasing magnetism.

Seminars IV and V represent the apogee of masculinism in Lacanian theory. Despite notable revisions regarding this bias he never quite succeeded in flying the nets of masculinist fantasy. That said, given that the world we live in is still imbued with masculinism, and given too that for many heterosexual men, the trajectory sketched out by Lacan rings absolutely true, Seminars IV and V remain important and relevant. It is not possible to remotely do justice to the sheer volume of text involved, so since an inadequate commentary is inevitable I will limit myself to three angles of approach: the manner in which the androcentric bias of the symbolic order, acknowledged in Seminar II, is tautologically justified as structural by way of this same bias, the vortical pressure on both the phallus and the Name of the Father to subsume multiplicity into totalitarian hegemony, and third, the manner in which the theory set forth in these seminars seems paradoxically to give rise to its own undoing. Surprisingly, in the wake of such a major statement of the primacy of the Symbolic, Lacan, more and more over the next few years, will veer towards the power and passion of the Imaginary.

An androcentric symbolic order

"Girls don't want to be the hero; they want to be had by the hero". In a recent film, *Their Finest*, set in the 1940s, a film director thus curbs the imaginative suggestions of a female scriptwriter, adding as a throwaway rider the terms of employment "Of course we won't be able to pay you as much as the chaps". Being and having. The film director is closer to Freud's sexual computation of these two essential verbs than to Lacan's, but the fall-out for women looks much the same. The obviousness of these statements to the speaker is what draws the attention today. In a similar manner the case Lacan makes in Seminars IV and V is impressive, and to a degree unassailable since both the symbolic order and the Oedipus complex which will be shown to underpin it are specified as androcentric, permitting him not only to reiterate but to expand Freud's phallocentrism.

A year or so before he embarked on the vast theorization of the Oedipus complex in the seminars under consideration Lacan unhesitatingly specified the symbolic order as androcentric and patriarchal. In Seminar II he makes it clear that it is only because of an androcentric bias that the penis takes on this imaginary value (Lacan, 1988b, p. 271), a situation which he posits in 1955 as "not without remedy". Lacan in these early years writes very persuasively of the power of this symbolic order. As he says in Seminar III it is "what yields us the entire world system [...] that which appears to be open to the neutrality of the world of human knowledge" as opposed to the Imaginary "which seems to be the very domain of the eroticization of the object" (Lacan, 1993, p. 177). The incommensurability of this symbolic system with the natural order is an observable fact. In the course of these years it is invoked in excess of 30 times as part of the prosthetics of the phallocentrism being established. It is unequivocally stated in Seminar III:

> It is in so far as the function of man and woman is symbolized, it is insofar as it is literally uprooted from the domain of the imaginary and situated in the domain of the symbolic, that any normal sexual position is realized. Genital realization is submitted to symbolization as an essential requirement that the man be virilized, that the woman truly accept her feminine function.
>
> (Lacan, 1993, p. 177)

He emphasizes its ineluctability. "It is in a human world organized by this symbolic order that the child appears, and this is what he must confront" (Seminar IV, lesson twenty-three, 26 June 1957, p. 472). Certain conditions exist in this world which as he says

> allow the subject to preserve a sufficient presence, not only in the real world but also in the symbolic world, that is to say so that he can tolerate himself in the real world organized as it is with its weft of the symbolic.
>
> (ibid., lesson twenty-one, 5 June 1957, p. 429)

These conditions pre-date the subject. "For as long as there have been signifiers that function, the psychic system of subjects has been organized by these signifiers" (ibid., lesson three, 5 December 1956, p. 47). In the 1950s, at the height of the post-World-War-II re-installation of patriarchy, it is perhaps understandable that Lacan would see 4,000 years of androcentrism as an immutable state of affairs. Furthermore if as he persuasively insists, the symbolic order is what literally gives us our world, it will be very difficult to think outside of this frame. Lucien Fèbvre's magisterial study of Rabelais in *The Problem of Unbelief in the 16th Century* is a vivid demonstration of this apparent impasse; an impasse created and maintained via a tautological torsion brought about by the parameters of the frame itself. The inevitable scotomizations and competing antagonisms involved are visible from outside the frame but of course much less so from within.

The symbolic order then is established as ineluctable and ineluctably andro-centric. "It is the particularities of the symbolic order as I have underlined in passing that give its prevalence for example to that element of the imaginary which is called the phallus" (Seminar IV, lesson twelve, 6 March 1957, p. 228). The consequence of this for women he says is that "one of the sexes is obliged to take the image of the other as the basis of its identification" (1993, p. 176). In fairness Lacan does not spell this out without fully recognizing the aporias to which it gives rise. Mapping it out for the first time in Seminar II he points to "the impasse into which the woman is pushed by her specific function in the symbolic order" (1988b, p. 262) acknowledging that there is "something insur-mountable, let us say unacceptable, in the fact of being placed in the position of an object (to be had by the hero) in the symbolic order" (ibid., p. 262). In Seminar IV, speaking of Freud's 1923 paper "Infantile Genital Organization" where Freud poses the primacy of phallic organization as a principle, Lacan, echoing Freud points out that making the possession or non-possession of the phallus into the principal differential element is actually founded on a mis-take, in particular, ignorance of the female sexual organ (Seminar IV, lesson six, 9 January 1957, p. 102). This exactly exemplifies the patriarchal framing of the symbolic order in question here.

How is difference to be computed? Is one looking at an apple and a non-apple or at an apple and a pear? If the task in hand is to count the apples, then what I see will correspond to the first distinction, if to categorize the fruits in front of me to the second. So two things can be equally present but only one "counts" as seen. A wonderful anecdote recounted by my American husband comes to mind. In 1818 in a town in Massachusetts the wives of the town burghers, incensed by something or other, called a women's meeting. To their consternation a black maid showed up asking the unanswerable question "Ain't I a woman?" Every day, babies in the womb with differing and very distinctive sexual organs are examined, but as recently as 2013 the "objective" findings of this examination were described in a psychoanalytic journal not as the presence of two different organs but in terms of presence and absence:

> Through nuchal translucency testing for example, the scientific machinery registers in advance the presence of the "wee-wee maker" in the fetus. There being or not "a wee-wee maker" thus discriminates the man from the woman on a certain evidence (there is or there is not).
>
> (Recalcati, 2013, p. 73)

This is a completely accurate instance of the workings of the symbolic order, seemingly so self-evident that its underpinning scotomization is not at all evi-dent. What extraordinary occlusion permits someone looking at a vulva, even the remarkably large vulva of an unborn baby girl to see not something but nothing, not presence but absence? The above is a perfect example of what patriarchy "sees" and this "seeing" is reflected with crystalline and repeated clarity in Freud's writings. One recalls, for example, his commentary on a dream where the phrase, "there's something missing", describes – I quote Freud, not his patient – "the principal feature of the female genitalia" (Freud, 1900a, p. 333). The blindness of the seeing eye to use Freud's own phrase (1895d, p. 117).

Lacan in fairness, repeats very regularly throughout Seminars IV and V that in the Real, with respect to female sexual organs there is nothing missing. But rather oddly for someone who less than a decade earlier in his article on "The Family Complexes" had emphasized the imago of the maternal womb as indelible (Lacan, 2010, p. 20) and its symbolization visible in burial practices as well as in dwelling houses and caverns (ibid., p. 22), now asserts that only the penis is amenable to symbolization because it can be seen, which thereby transforms it into the phallus: "Besides it isn't the penis, it's the phallus, that is to say something whose symbolic usage can be seen, because it is erected. There can be no possible symbolic usage for what is not seen, for what is hidden" (Lacan, 1988b, p. 272). A year later he takes this statement a little further, explaining that "where there is no symbolic material there is an obstacle, a defect in the way of bringing about the identification that is essential for the subject's sexuality to be realised" (Lacan, 1993, p. 176). Lacan's view here is that:

> this defect comes from the fact that on one point the symbolic lacks the material – for it does require material. The female sex is characterized by an absence, a hole which means that it happens to be less desirable than is the male sex for what he has that is provocative.

> [...]

> I should say that strictly speaking there is no symbolization of woman's sex as such because the imaginary only furnishes an absence where elsewhere there is a highly prevalent symbol.

> (ibid.)

Whose Imaginary? And what fuels this denegation? Towards the end of Seminar VI Lacan refers to "what is symbolically the most intolerable thing in our experience, namely the form which responds to it in the place of the female sexual organs" (Seminar VI, lesson twenty-three, 3 June 1959, p. 295). For whom is this intolerable? Hard not to line up this thinking with Freud's never borrowed/already returned pot! One is reminded too of Lacan's stellar reading of Freud's Irma dream in Seminar II where the horror evoked appears to be very much Lacan's and is not to be found in Freud's dry phraseology. Lacan describes Freud examining Irma's throat as the first break in the dream leading to:

> the apparition of the terrifying anxiety-provoking image, to this real Medusa's head, to the revelation of this something which is properly

speaking unnameable, the back of this throat, the complex unlocatable form which also makes it into the primitive object par excellence, the abyss of the female sexual organ from which all life emerges [...]

(1988b, p. 164)

The paradoxical result of this (possibly phobic) scotomization is that the female sexual organ is, Lacan says "never symbolically located as something which might have a meaning, It is always essentially problematic" (Seminar IV, lesson eight, 23 January, p. 158). The question which pervades the 1961–1962 seminar *Identification* "what counts?" is vividly exemplified here.

But while the phallus is indeed indubitably a "highly prevalent symbol" can Lacan really have thought that no equivalent female symbols existed? It is perhaps understandable that he might not have heard of *sheelagh na gigs*, the carvings of fertility goddesses with huge vulvas and deeply incised vaginas most commonly found in Ireland but also well disseminated throughout Western and Eastern Europe and certainly known to Mircea Eliade in France. More surprising is his apparent non-knowledge of the Paleolithic "Venus" carvings, the oldest of which dates from 35,000 years ago, figurines often deployed as apotropaic devices on gates, the vulva symbolized as the primordial gateway into life. Can he really not have known any of this?

Nonetheless while focussed on endorsing Freud's phallocentrism Lacan is unable to prevent himself from describing it as literally "stupefying". However, he opts for compliance: "well one must start with what is stupefying" (Seminar IV, lesson eleven, 27 February 1957, p. 219). The result is that like Freud, he can only see the woman as existing for the other, in effect the masculine partner. Colette Soler points out that *all* of the formulations Lacan provided to specify the place of woman make her a partner of the masculine subject: 1. being the phallus, that is the representative of what man is missing; 2. being the object that serves as cause of his desire; and 3. being the symptom on which his jouissance is fixated (Soler, 2002, p. 102). As Soler adds "the result is that everything that can be said about women is said from the point of view of the Other, their own being remaining [...] foreclosed from discourse" (ibid., p. 102).

So the necessity for an androcentric symbolic order will be examined through the prism of androcentrism itself. When Lacan provides a compelling justification for patriarchy he is simply re-stating its own premisses.

From the multiple to the one

While the shortfall occasioned by this androcentric framing is the focus here it is important to recognize that notwithstanding their masculinism many of the theoretical elaborations to which this gives rise are so rich, so complex, so insightful, and so brilliant that they have tended to carry the day and have made it difficult to separate out some of their questionable underpinnings. In particular his starting point in Seminar IV, the concept of the imaginary phallus, represents a tremendous widening and deepening of the existential drama undergone in the Freudian Oedipus. This concept, unknown to Freud, fits like a glove into two major tenets of Freud's phallocentrism, *penisneid* and fetishism, and widens out for Lacan into enormously evocative questions about desire: how shocking is it to realize that the Other on whom I depend is herself lacking? What does the other see in me? Can I be what the other desires? Or might it be something other than me? And the most momentous question of all: how is the transition to be effected from the impossible exigencies of the Imaginary to the relative stability of a symbolically validated identity which bears "the mark which modifies desire"? (Seminar V, lesson seventeen, 26 March 1958, p. 225). In effect this last question will be answered via an interplay of penis, phallus, and Name of the Father largely endorsed by and therefore presumably commensurate with male experience. The imaginary phallus also very impressively steps into the breach over and over with respect to all of these questions. Perhaps too impressively, obscuring the fact that some of them are unanswerable or would best be answered with an X. Unlike certain Lacanian algorithms such as o-object, barred S, etc., the word phallus enters our vocabulary freighted with centuries of semantic ballast which cannot but render questionable its all-encompassing range of reference. When Lacan a few years later justifies the "algebraic equation" that is the o-object he describes it as "something very straightforward that's designed to make something very complicated manageable" (Lacan, 2014, p. 65). The semantic history of the phallus renders it unsuitable for this task. As he himself says in *Encore*, language "brings with it considerable inertia compared to mathemes" (Lacan, 1975, p. 110). So the polyvalence accorded to the imaginary phallus in these seminars means that it colonizes territories far outside its proper range of reference.

One standard example: female power, undoubtedly a force in human affairs is "phallic", a distortion which continues in psychoanalytic writing. Anything a woman could possibly want, a life, a career, a child will devolve from a single avatar, the phallus. Anything she might want to be, will similarly be unimaginable outside of this monolithic silhouette.

Initially, in Seminar IV, the phallus appears as something that disrupts the mother/child dyad, but as stated above, it rapidly becomes the single answer to a series of crucial and complex questions. The phallus is insistently evoked each time these reiterated questions surface. Far less frequently Lacan recognizes simply that "what is loved in a being is beyond what he is" (Seminar IV, lesson eight, 23 January 1957, p. 158). The baby in fact occupies a place in the mother's desire and unconscious fantasy which will forever be inaccessible to both of them. Similarly for every subject his/her "lived incompleteness" will attach itself to specific signifiers not always reducible to a universal avatar (Seminar IV, lesson ten, 6 February 1957, p. 201). Lacan very effectively fuses Freud's primordially lost object with the imaginary phallus in these seminars. One year later he will develop this strand of his thinking with great power and poignancy via his introduction of the o-object. Guy le Gaufey has pointed to the similarity in Lacan's writing of the notations o and o–object as evidence that the second had its origins in the first (Le Gaufey, 2009, p. 27). In Seminar V something of the same rapprochement is visible with respect to the phallus when in lesson eight he specifies the relation of the ego to the specular image as "more than" the homologue of what he describes as "this phallus as fundamental function to which the subject imaginarily identifies himself" (Lesson eight, 8 January 1958, p. 112), specifying "it is in a way in a mirror that the subject identifies himself with what is the object of desire of the mother, and this is [...] the primitive phallic phase" (Lesson ten, 22 January 1958, p. 137). Despite the ever-widening claims for the circumference of the phallus, it nonetheless comes as somewhat of a surprise to the unwary reader when in lesson thirteen of Seminar V it becomes the single signifier upholding the whole world of meaning: "The signifier of the signified is in general the phallus" (12 February 1958, p. 173), a leap into the ludicrous repeated some months later in his Munich paper "The Signification of the Phallus" where it is "the signifier intended to designate as a whole the effects of the signified" (Lacan, 2006, p. 285).

While Lacan himself certainly went on to think somewhat differently, the effects of this leap are still visible in psychoanalytic writing which on this topic sometimes looks as if authored by Wallace Stevens':

> lunatic of one idea
> in a world of ideas, who would have all the people
>   live work suffer and die in that idea
> in a world of ideas.
> (Stevens, 2006, p. 285)

And indeed its effects have been felt beyond psychoanalysis via a perhaps now outmoded semiotic shift whereby "the phallus" absorbed into itself a whole range of meanings, hitherto moored to entirely different concepts. As Marina Warner pointed out in 1985, prior to Lacan's setting up of the phallus as the organizing principle which maintains the Symbolic order itself in existence, binary thinking, with its simple and complex processes of discrimination was presumed to be a property of thought itself.

> The phallus today has absorbed into itself these meanings, but only today. Thought processes themselves, especially during the Aristotelian Christian centuries, were considered to achieve fine discriminations between one thing and another; Aquinas' *Summa*, constructed in question and answer form, represents a perfect model of a binary mode [...]
> (Warner, 1985, p. 160)

Today – and in some psychoanalytic circles unquestioningly – the phallus has been gifted with this ability to uphold binarism. Its function is that of ordering, selecting, separating and unifying. (A naïve thinker might come up with a quite different set of "phallic" adjectives – thrusting, surging, insisting, even perhaps, drooping, but no; these do not figure in the usual descriptions of "the phallic function".) As well as the above, a recent superficial trawl through psychoanalytic literature provided the following results. The universalizing and totalizing drive of Western epistemology is now characterized as phallic, as is the circuit of production and consumption. It functions as the bar between signifier and signified. It is of course *the* signifier of lack, rather than one of several possible and plausible such signifiers. It functions as a synonym for the verb "sexualized" ("sexualized that is phallicised" – Verhaeghe, 2002, p. 114). It is named as S1, the master signifier. The statement that the conditions of desire are unconscious for each of us can apparently be much more effectively conveyed by saying that the phallus always functions as veiled. Bizarrely given the claims Lacan makes for it in these seminars as that which grounds all meaning, it also manages to be the sole signifier whose very meaning is its failure to signify – that which ruins the very possibility of affirmation or negation (Copjec, 1995, p. 215).

Although we laughed at it 30 years ago, the barb circulating in our training group about the Symbolic order being peopled by a solitary regal inhabitant, the phallus, still commands a degree of recognition.

How did this happen? And when? And what is the relation between the phallus and the other signifier which fulfils this all-encompassing function with respect to the symbolic order, the Name of the Father? At the beginning of Lacan's teaching, in Seminar I the symbolic order is a mesh. The pact which links subjects is founded on laws and contracts (Lacan, 1988a, p. 230) and is extraordinarily intricate, marked as it is by "the property of criss-crossing":

> every easily isolable linguistic symbol is not only at one with the totality but is cut across and constituted by a series of overflowings, of oppositional overdeterminations which place it at one and the same time in several registers.

> (ibid., pp. 53–54)

The transference which maintains the enigmatic authority of this mesh-like structure is ordinarily not locatable. History demonstrates that the social fabric alters its shape but does not easily tear apart. It appears to be held together by a necessary though unsubstantiated belief in meaning as such as opposed to its absence. Lévi-Strauss called this the zero institution, something devoid of any positive determinative function (Lévi-Strauss, 1963, pp. 131–163). Žižek, commenting on this zero institution sees its only function as the purely negative one of signalling "the presence and actuality of social institution as such, in opposition to its absence, that is in opposition to social chaos" (Žižek, 2002, p. 62).

While Lacan, throughout Seminars II, III, and IV continues to use the phrase "the play of signifiers" in describing the symbolic order, the number of signifiers involved begins to shrink from Seminar III onward.

The assertion that there exist "basic signifiers without which the order of human meaning would be unable to establish itself and that all sorts of cultural myths embody these signifiers" (1993, p. 200) becomes soldered to the Oedipus complex in a manner which is both a tremendous tribute to Freud and a tremendous re-centring of the relevance of psychoanalysis to modernity. These primordial signifiers, the mesh that sustains the symbolic order, are, in Lacan's view, very few in number: "the significant points of purchase that uphold the little world of the solitary little men in the modern crowd, are very few in number" (ibid., p. 203). In fact at this point it is no longer the metaphor of the intricate criss-crossing of a mesh-like structure that is in question but the rather homelier metaphor of a three-legged stool. "Not every stool has four legs. There are some that have only three. Here though there is no question of their lacking any, otherwise things go very badly indeed" (ibid.). But a degree of plurality is still what is in question: "as the signifier is never solitary, the lack of one signifier necessarily brings the subject to the point of calling the set of signifiers into question" (ibid., p. 203). What needs to be established is a signifying element which is irreducible to any type of imaginary conditioning, he says (Lacan, 1993, p. 316). And while the Name of the Father as he theorizes it will work well here, Lacan at this time eschews the encroaching exclusivity of the next two years: "I'm not saying that the Name of the Father is the only one of which we can say this" (ibid.).

Two years later, returning to the topic of psychosis in Seminar V it has indeed become the one and only signifier to fulfil this role. In lesson eight, commenting on a presentation by Gisela Pankow, a distinguished clinician in the field of the psychoses, Lacan propounds the necessity for "a word which will stabilize the whole signifying system, which will ground signification itself" (Lesson eight, 8 January 1958, p. 102) and proposes one word only for this task. "There is something that authorises the text of the law [...] namely the name of the father, that gives support to the law, that grounds the law" (ibid., p. 103). This idea gathers momentum in the early months of 1958, so five weeks after the above statement it is expressed in even stronger terms: "in a way within the signifying system, the Name of the Father has the function of the whole signifying system, the one who signifies, who authorises the signifying system to exist, who establishes its law" (Seminar V, lesson thirteen, 12 February 1958, p. 173). The not always clearly marked interplay between phallus and Name of the Father had been specified as metaphorical a little earlier. The desired outcome of the Oedipus complex "this relation to the power of the law [...] corresponds to, metaphorically echoes, the relation to the phantastical object which is the phallus [...]" (Lesson eleven, 29 January 1958, p. 152). But Lacan is not entirely at ease with how this transmutation comes about. In lesson ten he tries to articulate step by step "the thing that in it is not altogether clear, nor altogether clearly symbolised [...] this 'genesis' which ensures that the position of the father in the symbol is fundamental for the position of the phallus in the imaginary plane" (Lesson ten, 6 February 1958, p. 131). This doubt persists and

will surface again in the seminar on identification. Here in 1958 the ground-
work for the reduction to this one metaphor is laid by relegating the mother to
the Imaginary ("the imaginary pure and simple, namely the mother") (Lesson
twelve, 5 February 1958, p. 163) and therefore in need of subsumption by a
superior symbolic power. So what of the penis then? Not to be tucked away
in the folds of metaphor it would seem. Entry into the symbolic order cannot
happen "without the male sexual organ playing a role of the first importance"
(Seminar V, lesson eleven, 29 January 1958, p. 141). It and not the phallus or
the Name of the Father, is the pivot, although referencing this statement five
minutes later, this pivot is now the phallus (ibid., p. 142). This non-separability
is evident throughout these seminars. The Name of the Father is also inextric-
ably linked to the penis since it corresponds to the "title deeds" ensuring that
"in the most successful cases" the subject can assume "in all tranquillity [...] the
fact of having a penis" (ibid., p. 147). So it would seem that what we have here
is a kind of three in one, with all psychic reality converging on one metaphoric
transmutation.

The whole thrust of Seminar V up to a certain point has been this phenom-
enally comprehensive installation of the paternal metaphor as the lynchpin of a
world where sexuality is humanized and desire has a liveable space in which to
function. However, it is only in totalitarian regimes that one signifier can take
on this task by basing itself on a founding exclusion, and invariably this gesture provokes protest. Furthermore metaphor tends to search out multiplicities.
It is closer to the *mi-dit* of the later Lacan than to the implausible tyranny of
that "which authorises the signifying system to exist" and it is to Lacan's credit
that the successful trajectory traced under the auspices of this solitary signifier
cannot but appear ridiculous.

Tranquillity disrupted

Anyone engaging with the enormous corpus of Lacan's work will recognize
the aptness of the Moebius strip as metaphor for the experience of reading.
Transitions occur and the same vocabulary is imbued with new meaning
brought about by serpentine and not easily discernible moves from one surface
to another. Lacan himself does not facilitate the wish to create lines of demar-
cation, often blurring innovative edges by retrospective gestures of inclusion.
So we are fortunate in being able to recognize an entirely new strand in Lacan's
thinking making its first appearance in Seminar V. Having very convincingly
outlined the trajectory of the successful Oedipus with the installation of the
paternal metaphor Lacan cannot but see that the emerging subject, with the
title deeds to the penis stuffed tranquilly in his pocket is, if not a bit of a prick,
at least overly cocksure: "insofar as he is virile a man is always more or less his
own metaphor. This is even what attaches to the term virility a certain shadow
of ridicule" (Seminar V, lesson ten, 22 January 1958, p. 140). So if a real man is
a prick, what would a real woman be after this alienating process whereby she

has been "obliged to take the image of the other sex as the basis of her identification" (Lacan, 1993, p. 176)? Astray in the head says Lacan: "real women
always have something a bit astray [*égarée*] about them" (Seminar V, lesson ten,
22 January 1959, p. 140). Well! These observations which might seem to shaft
the impressive theoretical edifice he has just erected do not in fact signal any
overt change of direction in the general thrust of Seminar V. They are nonetheless worth noting. But the attentive reader will also register the appearance for
the first time in lesson thirteen of an altogether new vocabulary, a vocabulary
edging towards poetry and that will infuse that great seminar of the Imaginary,
Seminar VI, one year later.

The *Moebian* shift from one surface to another is remarkable. By the middle of
Seminar V the Oedipus complex had subsumed the exigencies of the Imaginary
from the domain of the impossible into that of the feasible. A year later Lacan
will reverse this orientation and open up an altogether new dimension to psychoanalytic theory. This dimension is tragedy. It will be explored and made
explicit over the next two years to the point that the final section of Seminar
VII will bear the title *The Tragic Dimension of Psychoanalytic Experience*. The more
sombre dramatic vocabulary in which Lacan will explicate this theme is heard
first in lesson thirteen of Seminar V, and – not surprisingly – in the context of
phantasy. In Seminar IV Lacan had just once referred to "that passage through
annihilation we call the Oedipus complex" (Seminar IV, lesson twenty-one, 5
June 1957, p. 429). Here for the first time the phrase "the pain of being" – a
pivotal concept in Seminar VI – appears: "this pain of being is something really
fundamental to him as being linked to the very existence of the living being"
(Seminar V, lesson thirteen, 12 February 1958, p. 178). Annihilation is spelt
out similarly to Seminar VI as something that "reduces to nothing the subject
as desiring", tending to abolish him (ibid., p. 171) and the phrase "*me phunai*"
"better not to be", taken from Sophocles' *Oedipus at Colonus*, attributed correctly in earlier seminars to the chorus now for the first time is (wrongly)
cited as the final curse on existence of Oedipus himself, a misquote which
will be hugely expanded on in Seminars VI, VII, and VIII. Also in this lesson,
the St. Augustine story which had featured in Lacan's work since the 1940s
reappears with a new tragic resonance. From the seminar on desire to that on
Anxiety it will be invoked as the specimen story for the founding catastrophe
which marks the birth of the Imaginary. Furthermore still in the remarkable
lesson, which is lesson thirteen, after this lengthy and brilliant exposition of a
process of subjectification installed as resting on the phallus and the Name of
the Father, Lacan re-states it in much less constricted terms:

> human beings are as such all under the rod, that is to be a human being who
> has entered into the world of desire, it is well and truly in the first place to
> suffer from this something which exists beyond – that we should call it the
> father has no longer any importance here, it does not matter, it is the law.
> (Seminar V, lesson thirteen, 12 February 1958, pp. 175–176)

And four weeks after the appearance of this new direction, in lesson seventeen a hitherto unheard of notation is written on the board. The big Other is barred, marked as failing, a notation of enormous import, to be developed at length over the following years.

In Seminar VI he will call Ophelia the bud and blossom of life, alternatively referring to her as the phallus and "at the place of the o-object". A year later Antigone rivets onlookers with her *éclat*. It is probably idle to wonder if Lacan was at all close at that time to recognizing that there are avatars other than the phallus, but including the latter, for the surge of life and its brief flowering. One thinks of Proust's "*jeunes filles en fleur*", but the adolescent boy or the child as well as countless other images, can also occupy this place.

The tranquil certainties of Seminar V will be left far behind as Lacan turns his attention to the "subjective elision" attendant on the coming into being of the subject.

While it is fair to say that in the following years he in no way modifies his phallocentric stance to pursue the power and pathos that subtend the dramas of the Imaginary, his new focus on the verb "to be" begins to undercut the masculinist opposition of the verbs "to be" and "to have". What will be in question in Seminar VI is "a subjective assumption inflected between being and having" (Seminar VI, lesson twelve, 11 February 1959, p. 150).

But the phallus of the 1950s cast a long shadow, making it necessary for girls who wanted to *be* the hero rather than be *had* by him to look outside of psychoanalytic theory for the necessary *derring-do*.

References

Badiou, A. (2001). *Ethics: An Essay of Understanding Evil.* London: Verso.

Copjec, J. (1995). *Read my Desire.* London and Cambridge: MIT Press.

Freud, S. (1900a). *The Interpretation of Dreams.* S.E., 4–5. London: Hogarth Press.

Freud, S. (1895d). *Studies on Hysteria.* S.E., 2. London: Hogarth Press.

Lacan, J. (1956–1957). *The Seminar of Jacques Lacan Book IV The Relation to the Object.* Unpublished translation, A.V. Roche

Lacan, J. (1957–1958). *The Seminar of Jacques Lacan Book V The Formations of the Unconscious.* C. Gallagher (Trans.). Available at: http://www.lacaninireland.com/web/wp-content/uploads/2010/.

Lacan, J. (1958–1959). *The Seminar of Jacques Lacan Book VI Desire and its Interpretation.* Unpublished. C. Gallagher (Trans.). Available at: http://www.lacaninireland.com/web/wp-content/uploads/2010/06/Book-06-Desire-and-its-interpretation.pdf.

Lacan, J. (1975). *Encore: The Seminar of Jacques Lacan XX. On Feminine Sexuality, The Limits of Love and Knowledge, 1972–1973.* B. Fink (Trans.). New York & London: W.W. Norton.

Lacan, J. (1988a). *Freud's Papers on Technique. The Seminar of Jacques Lacan, Book I (1953–1954).* Cambridge: Cambridge University Press.

Lacan, J. (1988b). *The Ego in Freud's Theory and in the Technique of Analysis.* Cambridge: Cambridge University Press.

Lacan, J. (1993). *The Seminar of Jacques Lacan Book III The Psychoses* (1955–1956). London: Routledge.

Lacan, J. (2006). The Signification of the Phallus. In: *Écrits. The First Complete Edition in English*. J.-A. Miller (Ed.), B. Fink (Trans.). New York and London: W.W. Norton & Co (pp. 575–584).

Lacan, J. (2010). *The Seminar of Jacques Lacan. Book X. Anxiety*. J.-A. Miller (Ed.), A. Johnson (Trans.). Cambridge: Polity Press.

Le Gaufey, G. (2009). *C'est a quel sujet?* Paris: Epel.

Lévi-Strauss, C. (1963). *Cultural Anthropology*. New York: Basic Books.

Recalcati, M. (2013). Love and Feminine Jouissance. In: *Lacunae 2*: 2, 2013.

Soler, C. (2002). What does the Unconscious Know About Women? In: *Reading Seminar 20* (pp. 99–108). S. Barnard and B. Fink (Eds.). Albany: State University of New York Press.

Stevens, W. (2006). *Collected Poems*. London: Faber & Faber.

Verhaeghe, P. (2002). Lacan's Answer to the Classical Mind/Body Deadlock, In: *Reading Seminar XX* (pp. 109–140). Barnard S. and B. Fink (Eds.) Albany: State University of New York Press.

Warner, M. (1985). *Monuments and Maidens*. London: Picador.

Žižek, S. (2002). The Real of Sexual Difference. In: *Reading Seminar XX* (pp. 57–75). Barnard, S. and B. Fink (Eds.). Albany: State University of New York Press.

Badiou, A. (2001). *Ethics: An Essay of Understanding Evil*. London: Verso.

Copjec, J. (1995). *Read my Desire*. London and Cambridge: MIT Press.

Freud, S. (1900a). *The Interpretation of Dreams. S.E.*, 4–5. London: Hogarth Press.

Freud, S. (1895d). *Studies on Hysteria. S.E.*, 2. London: Hogarth Press.

Lacan, J. (1956–1957). *The Seminar of Jacques Lacan Book IV The Relation to the Object*. Unpublished translation, A.V. Roche

Lacan, J. (1957–1958). *The Seminar of Jacques Lacan Book V The Formations of the Unconscious*. C. Gallagher (Trans.). Available at: http://www.lacaninireland.com/web/wp-

Lacan, J. (1958–1959). *The Seminar of Jacques Lacan Book VI Desire and its Interpretation*. Unpublished. C. Gallagher (Trans.). Available at: http://www.lacaninireland.com/web/wp-content/uploads/2010/06/Book-06-Desire-and-its-interpretation.pdf.

Lacan, J. (1975). *Encore: The Seminar of Jacques Lacan XX. On Feminine Sexuality, The Limits of Love and Knowledge, 1972–1973*. B. Fink (Trans.). New York & London: W.W. Norton.

Lacan, J. (1988a). *Freud's Papers on Technique. The Seminar of Jacques Lacan, Book I (1953–1954)*. Cambridge: Cambridge University Press.

Lacan, J. (1988b). *The Ego in Freud's Theory and in the Technique of Analysis*. Cambridge: Cambridge University Press.

Lacan, J. (1993). *The Seminar of Jacques Lacan Book III The Psychoses* (1955–1956). London: Routledge.

Lacan, J. (2006). The Signification of the Phallus. In: *Écrits. The First Complete Edition in English*. J.-A. Miller (Ed.), B. Fink (Trans.). New York and London: W.W. Norton & Co (pp. 575–584).

Lacan, J. (2010). *The Seminar of Jacques Lacan. Book X. Anxiety*. J.-A. Miller (Ed.), A. Johnson (Trans.). Cambridge: Polity Press.

Le Gaufey, G. (2009). *C'est a quel sujet?* Paris: Epel.

Lévi-Strauss , C. (1963). *Cultural Anthropology*. New York: Basic Books.

Recalcati, M. (2013). Love and Feminine Jouissance. In: *Lacunae 2*: 2, 2013.

Soler, C. (2002). What does the Unconscious Know About Women? In: *Reading Seminar* 20 (pp. 99–108). S. Barnard and B. Fink (Eds.). Albany: State University of New York Press.

Stevens, W. (2006). *Collected Poems*. London: Faber & Faber.

Verhaeghe, P. (2002). Lacan's Answer to the Classical Mind/Body Deadlock, In: *Reading Seminar XX* (pp. 109–140). Barnard S. and B. Fink (Eds.) Albany: State University of New York Press.

Warner, M. (1985). *Monuments and Maidens*. London: Picador.

Žižek, S. (2002). The Real of Sexual Difference. In: *Reading Seminar* XX (pp. 57–75). Barnard, S. and B. Fink (Eds.). Albany: State University of New York Press.

Index

For Product Safety Concerns and Information please contact our EU
representative GPSR@taylorandfrancis.com
Taylor & Francis Verlag GmbH, Kaufingerstraße 24, 80331 München, Germany

* 9 7 8 0 3 6 7 3 5 3 4 4 5 *